THE GREAT ONES
& OTHER WRITINGS

Eddie Waring

THE GREAT ONES
& Other Writings

Scratching Shed Publishing Ltd

Rugby League Classics

This edition published by Scratching Shed Publishing Ltd, 2010
Registered in England & Wales No. 6588772.
Registered office:
47 Street Lane, Leeds, West Yorkshire. LS8 1AP

www.scratchingshedpublishing.co.uk

Introduction © Harry Edgar 2010
Afterword © Tony Waring 2010
The Great Ones © Eddie Waring
England To Australia and New Zealand © Eddie Waring
Assorted journalism - all © Eddie Waring

The Great Ones was originally published by Pelham Books Ltd in 1969
England To Australia And New Zealand
was originally published by County Press, Leeds, 1947

A catalogue record for this book is available from the British Library.

ISBN 978-0956478726

Typeset in Warnock Pro Semi Bold and Palatino

Printed and bound in the United Kingdom by
L.P.P.S.Ltd, Wellingborough, Northants, NN8 3PJ

Rugby League Classics

The Great Ones & Other Writings is the fifth in a series of historically significant Rugby League Classics, all of them rescued, re-branded and re-issued in paperback, often after having been long out-of-print.

Each Rugby League Classic comes complete with at least one original manuscript intact and contains a wealth of new and updated material, including an introductory overview by a relevant writer, evocative photographs, appendices and the modern-day recollections of those closest to the book's primary subject, i.e. family members, former team-mates and other contemporary figures.

In order to stay as true to the spirit of the original text as possible, all editing has purposely been kept to a minimum. Readers should be aware, therefore, that although factual inaccuracies by the original writer - should they occur - may be referred to and corrected in the accompanying introduction, in the main text they will be allowed to stand. In the interests of readability, however, paragraph breaks have been added where necessary, and any errors in spelling and grammar (which may well have frustrated the author at the time) are now amended.

Acknowledgements

The publishers are grateful for the kind permission of Tony Waring, Eddie's son, who not only allowed us to re-publish *The Great Ones* and a number of his father's other writings, he contributed an afterword to the project too.

Thanks also to our own Ros Caplan for transcribing the original manuscripts, Eddie's nephew Harry Waring for access to the very rare *England to Australia and New Zealand* booklet, and Harry Edgar for his fine introduction to this book and support for the Scratching Shed ethos throughout.

Most of all, however, our thanks must go to the one and only Eddie Waring. Truly, there will never be another.

Contents

Contents continued

INTRODUCTION

by Harry Edgar
Publisher-Editor of *Rugby League Journal*
and founder of the former *Open Rugby* magazine

Eddie Waring was recognised as the voice of rugby league in Britain for over a quarter of a century. As the BBC's television commentator he was a broadcaster so distinctive that he eventually became a caricature of himself and was, without question, far more famous than any other individual in the game, including all its star players. Remarkably, to many people he still is, which is a pretty incredible measure of the impact he made, since his last broadcast commentary was way back in 1981.

But there was much more to Eddie's career than being the man behind the BBC microphone, or even the happy-go-lucky character appearing on some of the nation's favourite comedy and light entertainment programmes in the 1970s. As a journalist, author, team-manager, publicist and all-round promoter of the game he loved, Eddie was undoubtedly a man ahead of his time. And those of us who are aware of the enormous contribution he made to rugby league and were inspired by his pioneering spirit, have long believed that his real talents should be recognised.

For Eddie, working life began as a typewriter salesman in his home town of Dewsbury in the West Riding of Yorkshire. He obviously learned to use the keys himself very quickly and productively as, within a few years, he had become the nation's best known and most widely read reporter on his favourite sport, rugby league. But even before he began to establish his reputation as a writer, the young Waring had shown his charisma, footballing knowledge and flair for publicity by becoming a highly successful team manager.

First, as a teenager in Dewsbury, Eddie set up a youth team which he called 'The Black Knights', some sixty years before such nicknames became *de riguer* in rugby league. Most lads of his age just wanted to play the game, but Eddie took responsibility and centre stage as coach and manager of the team. By the time he was 26 years of age he had become the youngest secretary-manager in the professional game when he succeeded Harry Fortesque at the helm of the Dewsbury club in 1936. He went on to bring enormous success to his home town club during the eight years he was their manager. Initially, the young Eddie faced an enormous task but he set up new fund-raising schemes and set about signing new players. Just as things were starting to look brighter for Dewsbury, the Second World War was declared in 1939, but in a spectacular 'Waring scoop' Eddie brought the New Zealand touring team to Crown Flatt to play the only professional game to take place in the UK that day. Carrying gas masks and joining in spontaneous community singing, the crowd of over 6,000 saw Dewsbury lose to the Kiwis 22-10. But Eddie Waring's efforts in arranging the match - thereby helping the New Zealanders to raise some much needed funds as the outbreak of war forced them to abandon their tour after just one scheduled fixture - were deeply appreciated by people in the faraway land of the long white cloud.

Eddie was to play a major role in maintaining rugby league activity during the war, which did much to keep spirits up in towns across the north of England. The introduction of war-time football saw clubs allowed to field guest players and, thanks to Eddie Waring's enterprise, Dewsbury took more advantage of this than any of their rivals with over thirty-five guest internationals appearing in their red, amber and black hoops, among them the legendary Jim Sullivan. Eddie's team appeared in three successive Championship Finals and won the Challenge Cup in the 1942-43 season.

The success of the Dewsbury club, both on the field of play and financially, in the eight years Eddie had been at the helm prompted Leeds to recruit him to become their manager. Already, the Waring name was being sprinkled with stardust, but he didn't stay long at Headingley as a much bigger world was calling and Eddie had a vision for rugby league - and his own role in it - far wider than that of being involved with one individual club, even if it was one the richest and most glamorous in the game.

He paid his own fare to accompany the 1946 British Lions touring team as they sailed on the aircraft carrier *HMS Indomitable* to Australia, having arranged to supply several English newspapers as a freelance reporter. What turned out to be an epic adventure for captain Gus Risman and his team who carved their niche in rugby league history forever as 'The Indomitables', truly evolved into a voyage of discovery for Eddie Waring. The generous optimism and colourful language of the Australians, the wide open spaces and huge crowds at the Sydney Cricket Ground, the way the rugby league game was promoted with such flair and brashness by rival newspapers and commercial radio stations in a vibrant city like Sydney, all made a massive impression on Eddie.

That first visit to Australia proved to be a huge factor in influencing the colourful career that followed for Eddie Waring. Not only did it establish him as one of rugby league's highest profile newspaper reporters with the *Sunday Pictorial*, it also gave him the opportunity to show his wider talents as a writer with the subsequent publication of his book *England to Australia and New Zealand* - reprinted here in full - in which Eddie penned a remarkably vivid travelogue of what must have been an incredible adventure for a young man from Dewsbury travelling around the world with the 1946 touring team. In it he vowed, in his own words, to take rugby league 'out of the wilderness', which was a reference to the fact that no books on the mighty deeds of Britain's rugby league footballers had ever been published before, and Eddie believed it was high time there was. I don't know if Eddie had any ambitions to be a travel writer at the time, but that little booklet must have made a huge impact on many wide-eyed young rugby league fans back home in the north of England, whose own experience of travel would have rarely taken them much further than Blackpool or Bridlington.

Yet that was just the start of Eddie Waring's inspirational pioneering of wider horizons to future generations, because whilst in Australia he made his own cine films of the tourists in action and came home with the germ of an idea to let fans in England see them at shows staged around the country. The very first of those was at a Working Mens' Club in Hunslet and Eddie, along with his elder brother Harry and young nephew of the same name, travelled by bus from Dewsbury to Leeds and then walked to Hunslet south over the Leeds bridge, carrying his heavy leather suitcase which had accompanied him to Australia and back, and was packed with films, programmes and rugby shirts from the tour.

That was in early 1947 and the start of what became a Rugby League institution. The *Eddie Waring Show* continued for over 30 years, right up to the late 'seventies, and raised many hundreds of thousands of pounds for players' benefits and testimonials as well as helping the amateur game across the country. Eddie's shows brought so much pleasure to rugby league followers and were much sought after as a guaranteed big fund-raiser, and throughout those three decades Eddie never took a penny in expenses.

It was at one of these shows that I first met Eddie when he came to my home town, Whitehaven, in early 1963. It was during the notorious winter 'freeze' of that year and I was one of the kids who got up onto the stage to join Eddie for the quiz. He gave us all a prize of a programme from the 1962 Lions tour, none of us had ever seen a programme from Australia before, so Eddie really was opening up a whole new world for youngsters like me. Eddie also dressed us in international jerseys during the quiz and I remember being given Mel Cooke's New Zealand number thirteen shirt to wear. The films he showed that night were from the 1962 tour, which featured our local hero Dick Huddart tearing through the Australian defences. In those days, of course, we did not get any television coverage from the tours so when Eddie brought his show to town it was the first time anybody in the UK was actually able to see any film of the rugby league Tests in Australia, and I can remember vividly all the audience that night in Whitehaven College getting up on their feet and cheering every time Huddart made one of his searing breaks, just as if they were watching it live from the terraces.

By this time, Eddie's reputation as the highest profile

name in rugby league had already been cemented. His columns in the *Sunday Pictorial* (which later evolved into the *Sunday Mirror*) were eagerly awaited every week, and he had become 'Mr. Rugby League' as the BBC's exclusive television commentator at a time when the game was watched by audiences of several million people regularly on Saturday afternoon *Grandstand* and even more millions on the midweek programme *Sportsview*. At the same time he had ventured into publishing with the launch of his *Eddie Waring Annual* in 1959 and throughout the first half of the 'sixties these action-packed little books (whose biggest selling point always appeared to be having Eddie's smiling face and name in block headlines on the front cover) were essential reading for every rugby league fan. They became symbolic of the launch of each new season every bit as much as the re-assuring smell of linament and newly mown grass on a balmy late-August evening.

One of Eddie's boldest claims to fame during the 1960s was that he was the only man to have seen every British touring side in Australia since World War Two. That journey on the aircraft carrier *HMS Indomitable* in 1946 was the first of eight adventures down-under as he covered every Lions tour up to the triumphant 1970 visit, plus the 1957 World Cup in Australia. The experience he built up during that time made Eddie a very valuable member of every touring party and many Great Britain managers came to rely on him, particularly when it came to organising social events for their players as well as arranging publicity. The Australians would often comment that whenever they needed to sort out anything with the touring teams they would bypass the managers and go straight to Eddie Waring, because he was the man who could really get things done (and they weren't joking!). This enabled Eddie to become very popular with the players, who trusted him and looked upon him as a friend who always had their best interests at heart. His closeness to the players did arouse quite a lot of jealously among some of Eddie's rival reporters, most notably during the controversial 1958 Lions tour on which he became a close ally of team manager Tom Mitchell, who found himself at loggerheads with his co-manager Bennett Manson and the team coach Jim Brough. The British captain Alan Prescott and his players welcomed Eddie into their inner sanctum whilst, at the same time, signing a memo requesting that one of his major Sunday newspaper rivals should not be allowed even to stay at the same hotel.

The competition between Eddie Waring at the *Sunday Pictorial* and rival popular Sunday newspapers to get the latest scoops on rugby league was very intense, but such was Eddie's influence in the game that he often not only wrote the big stories, he also helped create them. On many occasions he acted as a forerunner of the players' agents so prevalent in sport today and arranged for numerous Australian players to join English clubs, using the contacts he had made on his first visit down-under in 1946. And he was very closely involved in several 'cloak and dagger' negotiations attempting to pull off star signings for clubs so that he could reveal them exclusively in his Sunday column. One of the biggest Eddie was proud to recall was signing the future Lions captain Dickie Williams for Leeds whilst travelling with the Welshman in a railway carriage. But he was not so lucky in negotiating on Hunslet's behalf to get the signature of the one and only Billy Boston, as Billy chose to sign for Wigan instead and Eddie missed out on his exclusive.

Eddie got his biggest scoop for the *Sunday Pictorial* in July, 1953 when, after weeks of clandestine negotiations, he was able to reveal in banner backpage headlines that the world's fastest sprinter, McDonald Bailey, had signed to play rugby league for Leigh. It was a story described as the 'sport sensation of the year' and McDonald Bailey actually signed the forms at a secret rendezvous in the *Sunday Pictorial* office, so desperate was Eddie to ensure nobody else got a sniff of the massive story he was about to break.

All this illustrates just how high profile Eddie Waring already was as a writer before he shot to wider national fame as a television commentator. Eddie always claimed it was a chance meeting with the movie star comedian Bob Hope in Hollywood in 1950 (as Eddie was en route home from covering his second Lions tour) that convinced him to get into television, and it proved to be wonderful advice from Bob. But Eddie never abandoned his first love of tinkling the typewriter keys and, despite his growing fame, he never forgot his roots as a rugby league enthusiast from Dewsbury. For several years, he continued to write a regular column for the game's first specialist magazine *Rugby League Review*, published by Stanley Chadwick of Huddersfield. It was a strictly low budget operation as Chadwick continually battled against financial problems and Eddie was his biggest name contributor by far - but the sheer passion of both men in their campaigning on behalf of the game shone through in every issue.

Eddie and Stanley were unlikely bedfellows, but there was obviously a great mutual respect between them and recognition of each other's talents and qualities. No doubt Eddie, since he was a boy, had loved the idea of being involved in a specialist rugby league magazine in which he could express his opinions for the betterment of the game unhindered, and Stanley Chadwick gladly provided him with that opportunity. Admirably, Eddie stayed loyal to Chadwick despite the fact that Stanley quickly became something of a renegade by upsetting the Rugby Football League's secretary Bill Fallowfield, with the result that

Introduction

Rugby League Review got little or no co-operation from League headquarters and, eventually, Fallowfield arranged for a rival magazine to be given 'official status' by the RFL.

That didn't worry Eddie Waring, who was far too self confident in his own knowledge of the game to worry about petty officialdom, and I have to admit that my own personal favourites of all Eddie's writing throughout his long career remain the columns he wrote for Stanley Chadwick's *Rugby League Review*, a few of which are reproduced at the rear of this edition. Always accompanied by a photo of Eddie, at first wearing a raincoat and trilby clutching a radio microphone and later sitting at his typewriter, it was campaigning journalism at its very best and proved to be an inspiration to me when I was publishing *Open Rugby* magazine many years later.

Eddie was always very supportive of anybody who wanted to do something for the game. I discovered this myself the second time I attended one of his shows and ended up being on the stage again, but this time as a member of the panel taking questions from the audience. It was eight years on from the first one in 1963 and, by this time, although still at school, my own writing career had begun as I was compiling the Whitehaven club programme and had produced several early fanzines. I was sitting in the audience at the Whitehaven Civic Hall waiting for the show to start, having paid my entrance money just like everyone else, when somebody grabbed me and said: 'They want you on the panel, they're a man short.' I think it was Keith Jarrett, the Welsh star who played for Barrow, who was the celebrity panellist who hadn't shown up, so I got pushed into it. The other people on the stage were very well known rugby league figures, including the legendary Gus Risman, Jim Brough, Sol Roper and the Irishman Ken Goodall, so you can imagine how out of place I felt as a young kid.

I had to go backstage to be introduced to Eddie Waring in his dressing room before the show started. He asked me about Whitehaven and memorised the details I gave him word for word. He was very professional. Eddie thanked me for stepping in at the last minute and could see I was nervous, so he was very kind in the way he told me not to worry and that he would look after me. In the years that followed I bumped into Eddie numerous times and, always, he would remember me as 'the lad who told me all about Whitehaven'.

I am sure I was only one of thousands of young rugby league fans to be inspired by Eddie. It wasn't just the eager dash to get the *Pictorial* every Sunday, or to devour his annual when it appeared at the start of the season, for me it was also the wide vision he presented for the game's potential, never more than when he helped to present an American television programme in 1965 promoting the game's virtues by showing the exciting Wembley final between Hunslet and Wigan. It was no surprise that Eddie was a most enthusiastic supporter of the Southern Amateur Rugby League, the Universities and BARLA; he even promoted a national sevens competition for Methodist Youth Clubs which was to culminate with a final staged in the Royal Albert Hall. And he was the key figure in launching a European Club Championship match between British and French champions and attracting some of the first sponsors to rugby league in the 1960s.

He may have become a major television personality, but Eddie always loved writing about the game and its players, many of them his boyhood heroes and others from a later generation he had come to know as friends. The *Eddie Waring Book of Rugby League* was his first major title to be published in hardback when it appeared in 1966 (less than twenty years after his first literary effort chronicling his first tour with The Indomitables, but in what had become a vastly different world.) Eddie introduced that 1966 book by writing: 'I have had many invitations to write a book about Rugby League football, but have never felt that the time was really right until the game had reached a time span of three score years and ten. Well, that time was reached in August 1965, so here's the book.'

That obviously whetted his appetite to write more about the famous players he admired so much and three years later, in 1969, his book *Rugby League - The Great Ones* was published, the primary subject of this latest Rugby League Classic. *The Great Ones* showcased once again Eddie's talent as a descriptive writer with a vast knowledge of the game and its history which he had first revealed as that young tourist back in 1946.

The natural showman in Eddie meant he loved to give the game's personalities nicknames to help promote them as characters to his television audience. He was given a few himself, from 'Uncle Eddie' to 'The Talking Trilby'. But most of all, he was quite simply 'Mr Rugby League', and the legacy of his vast contribution to the game should never be forgotten by all who care about it.

Harry Edgar

Eddie Waring

Author, columnist, broadcaster. Rugby League writer. Former manager. Only man to have seen all post war Test matches between Great Britain and Australia.

Toured six time to Australia, all post war tours. 1946-1966.

Television commentator with BBC.

Regular commentator on Rugby League since 1956, including all Cup Finals.

Six round the world trips, broadcast in many countries. Did commentary for first Rugby League colour film shown in the USA and Canada.

Original jacket biography (1969)

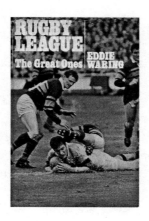

Original jacket notes (1969)

It's as North as Hot Pot and Yorkshire Pudding ... It's as tough as teak... It's Rugby League - a man's game if ever there was one.

Somebody once said of Rugby Union 'a game for ruffians played by gentlemen'. And as Rugby, the Webb-Ellis variety, developed from Soccer, so Rugby League branched out from the Twickenham type of game. Gentlemen have played Rugby League. Gentlemen still do. But the hard core of Rugby League players, with their cauliflower ears, their broken noses, their busted and bruised bones, would far rather be called, to use a three letter word, MEN. There is nothing gentle about Rugby League! It's a down-to-earth game played by down-to-earth people. Good people. Solid People. To use that three-lettered word again, MEN.

From the pits, from factory floors, Rugby League players emerge each Saturday afternoon to provide entertainment and excitement to a critical public. To the men - and women - of the North, Rugby League is more than a game. It's a way of life.

Out of this environment has come a multitude of characters. Rugby League characters. Their stories, their anecdotes, are indicative not only of the game they play.

21

The Great Ones

They help to explain why men risk neck and limb for a game of football.

It takes thirteen players to form a Rugby League side. The story the author tells is of thirteen of the great names of a great game. They are names that have become household names. And perhaps the greatest bouquet of all, public household names! They are symptomatic of the type of man who works six days a week and on the seventh becomes a sporting hero. They are men with guts and immeasurable courage. Men of character. Men who play Rugby League. The author calls them the Plucky Thirteen.

The game of Rugby League football is now a national game, followed by millions, through the medium of television, from Land's End to John O'Groats.

1

Harold Wagstaff & Billy Batten

It's an established fact that there are more acres in Yorkshire than words in the Bible. I guess it must have been a Yorkshireman who took the trouble to count them all.

I do know it was a couple of Yorkshiremen who took the trouble to help write them! For John Wycliffe and Miles Coverdale, Yorkshiremen good and true, were responsible for the English translation of the good book.

The county of broad acres is quite a place. Split into three Ridings - a word meaning a third - it occupies one-eighth of the land surface of England. There's the North Riding, the East Riding and the West Riding. It is in the West Riding where it all started. The wonderful game of Rugby League. A game conceived by men for men. A game born in a hotel just round the corner from Huddersfield railway station.

It was here in 1895 that representatives of the 22 breakaway Rugby Union clubs held their fateful meeting at the George Hotel and decided to form the Northern Union - or Rugby League as we know it today.

The Great Ones

At Rugby school there's a proud plaque to record the fact that the game of Rugby Union football started there. I recently looked around the George Hotel in Huddersfield to find some similar record of Rugby League's foundation.

Not even a sign to say: 'Rugby League started here.' People attached to the professional code are inclined to hide their lights and beginnings.

Plaques or no plaques, sport - both cricket and Rugby League - has made the name of Huddersfield known far and wide.

Ask any old Huddersfield followers for the name of the two most famous cricketers in the world and I'll guess they will say 'George Herbert' and 'Wilfred'. Should you be so uneducated in sporting knowledge to reply 'Who?' the answer, with a withering look, would be 'George Herbert Hirst and Wilfred Rhodes.'

Both of these world renowned cricketers came from one of the villages surrounding Huddersfield. A very small one called Kirkheaton, a civil parish with a population of 2,545. It is known locally as 'Yetton' but the deeds of its two famous sons are remarkable.

George Hirst scored 32,232 runs for Yorkshire and took 2,569 wickets. For England in 24 Tests, he scored 792 runs, took 59 wickets and 16 catches. Wilfred Rhodes scored 31,156 runs for the White Rose county with 3,608 wickets. And for England Wilfred in 58 Tests, scored 2,325 runs and had 127 victims and took 58 catches. A remarkable pair.

In another village called Underbank, near Holmfirth, not far from where the BBC have their tall Holme Moss television mast perched on top of the bleak Pennines, there was another star born. Wagstaff was the name. Harold Wagstaff. Better known to the Rugby League world as 'Ahr Waggy'.

Waggy was born four years before the Rugby League

24

came into being, or if you prefer he joined Huddersfield in the Rugby League 11 years after the big breakaway. The remarkable thing about Harold Wagstaff to me is the legend which has been built around and about him. I have never yet been to Australia without someone mentioning his name. I suppose the age in which he played Rugby League may be forgotten but the name Wagstaff still means much.

Five gold sovereigns were given to young Harold Wagstaff when he signed for Huddersfield from the junior club of Underbank.

Huddersfield's most noted rivals were Halifax and they had been looking at the form of this youngster. The Halifax scout said 'sign him' but the Halifax committee said they wanted 'men not boys'.

Wagstaff was a boy, aged fifteen in fact, when he played his first team game of Rugby League at the Barley Mow, Bramley, on the 10th November, 1906. It would not have been possible to sign him in these days until he reached sixteen years of age.

There was so much doubt and speculation about his real age that the Huddersfield club printed a copy of his birth certificate in the club programme. What a boy prodigy he must have been, for at the age of seventeen he started an international career which was to last from January, 1909, to January, 1922.

Harold Wagstaff wore the claret and gold jersey in 474 games for Huddersfield. He captained England as the international team was then known, in Australia on the 1914 and 1920 tours. He became captain of Huddersfield in the 1911/12 season and led his team to many famous victories. He was a one-club man - how rare in these days I suppose - and in his wonderful seventeen seasons he scored 195 tries and kicked 14 goals.

'Waggy' as his try-scoring figures show was not a

sensational individual points getter. He was a creator in all he did and the Huddersfield club's record of 1,269 points in 47 matches in the 1914/15 season owed much the creations of Harold Wagstaff.

Although Wagstaff finished his international career in 1922 he continued to play for Huddersfield for another three years. After a year as player-coach he retired after a game against Oldham in March 1925. In 1920 he had a benefit which brought him over £1,000 - real money in those times.

It is a remarkable thing that few great footballers make good coaches. Wagstaff, like many others, was not successful as a coach. He took over the spells at Halifax, Rochdale, and the now defunct club Broughton Rangers. He was unable to give the players he coached his natural playing ability. Like many other ex-Rugby League players, he took over a public house.

In the 1939 Cup Final between Halifax and Salford at Wembley I sat next to Harold Wagstaff and his quiet comments about the match indicated the thinking man he was. He died two months later in July 1939.

'Waggy' was the player who introduced what was often described as 'scientific obstruction'. He drilled his crack team which won all four cups in 1914. Only Hunslet and Swinton, along with Huddersfield, have ever done this. The four cups being the League Championship, The Challenge Cup, The County Cup and the County League Cup.

In this period of success Huddersfield had many great players like Welshman Johnny Rogers, and a great Cumbrian forward Douglas Clark, also a wrestling champion. The Huddersfield goal kicking star was Ben Gronow from Bridgend, South Wales. Gronow had played for Wales in the first ever Rugby Union International match at Twickenham and had been the first to kick off on this sacred turf.

Harold Wagstaff & Billy Batten

Wagstaff's Test appearance varies according to which statistician you follow. The international match in 1909 has been described as a Test match in some books, but the Rugby League called it a Northern Union side against Australia and give 1911 as the start of Wagstaff's Test career. There is no doubt his career ended in 1922 when he returned to the Test scene after disappointments in the 1920 series in Australia when England lost the Ashes.

It was a damp, dark muddy day at Salford in January 1922 but a bright, bright day for 'Waggy' when he led his team to victory and the Ashes win. Wagstaff was carried off shoulder high and some reports say his jersey was torn by admirers who knew this was the last to be seen of Harold in the international jersey.

Harold Wagstaff's greatest personal triumph was in Sydney in 1914. A game which became known and accepted even in the official Rugby League guide as 'Rorke's Drift'. This name was given to the match by an Australian in memory of the great fighting stand taken by a small group of English soldiers in the Zulu war of 1879.

The 1914 third Test had been preceded by a row between the two countries' officials over the match date, for only twelve days were allowed to play three Test matches. The English manager objected, but on instructions from England was ordered to play the match. A telegram from England said 'England expects every man to do his duty'.

Wagstaff had a crippled side and included players on the Sydney ground who were not really fit to play, particularly as the match was an Ashes decider.

England took the field with a determination never seen before, or probably since, on a question of right versus wrong as one English manager later described it.

'Dame Luck' was not on the side of the team in the 'right' not so far as injuries were concerned, for before the match was over it was a case of ten men against thirteen. The ten men being the wearers of the red, white and blue jersey. The first man to leave with a leg injury was Frank Williams of Halifax. Yet at half-time England led by 9 point to 3 points.

Douglas Clark broke his arm and twice asked to return to play with it strapped up. The tough Cumbrian, a wrestling champion cried when he could not return and when Billy Hall, a centre from Oldham, left the field England had ten men and half an hour to go.

Harold Wagstaff said, 'Never have I had nine such men on a field with me as I had that day.' England packed three forwards and won the scrums, and went on to win by 14 points to 6 points. 'The greatest display of football courage ever seen,' wrote one Australian journalist.

W.A. Davies of Leeds played only one Test for England yet one he was proud of, for he scored a try in this memorable Test. Albert 'Chick' Johnson (Widnes) scored the other try and fullback A.E.Wood of Oldham kicked four goals.

Wagstaff's footballing days were not confined to Rugby League. During the First World War period he played with a famous service side called the Grove Park ASC at Rugby Union. When I have spoken of Wagstaff on television I have often had letters from people who remember him with this team.

The Huddersfield side of that era, when they won the four cups, all had a lot of talent. In the final of the Challenge Cup they played Major Holland; Rosenfeld, Gleeson, Wagstaff, Moorhouse; Grey and Davies; Higson, Lee, Clark, Gronow, Longstaff and Chilcott.

Even the War could not stop the brilliance of Wagstaff and his merry men, for in the first post-war Cup Final in 1920 Huddersfield were back again with Rogers and Habron at half-back, Pogson and Todd on the wings, but the centre strength of Wagstaff and Gleeson was still evident when Huddersfield beat Wigan at Headingley.

This was Wagstaff's last Challenge Cup Final, but not his last triumph as I have written, for his 1922 Test success at The Willows, Salford, followed, to end his international career. Wagstaff returned to his birthplace in the summer of 1939. Holmfirth cemetery was his last resting place, carried by eight of his former team colleagues.

Harold Wagstaff was only forty-eight years of age when he died. Truly one of the 'greats': a leader of men as well as being a great footballer.

It would not be possible to write about centre-threequarters without writing about William (Billy) Batten. Like Wagstaff, Batten came from a village in the West Riding, a mining village - Kinsley, near Fitzwilliam.

Billy Batten was possibly the most colourful character in League football during the era before and after the First World War. He played for Hunslet before being transferred to Hull in April 1913. During his Hunslet days he toured with England on their first tour in 1910, under the captaincy of Jim Lomas, and was a try scorer when England played on the Sydney show ground, a game which was won by 27 points to 20 points.

Batten's transfer to Humberside was sensational with the fee amounting to a record £600. The big fee brought critical comments from supporters, but these comments were quickly silenced when twenty-three-year-old Batten added £500 more to each of the games he played in before the season ended.

Big, black-haired, beetle-browned Batten was a tremendous centre who hurled over opponents. When he played in New Zealand he was opposed by a Maori centre, Opai Asher. Both were 'jumpers' and in one match they jumped at each other. Batten continued his way, Asher didn't, I was told by one impressed New Zealand man.

Batten's entry into Hull football brought immediate success, something which the club had never had. Prior to his arrival at the Boulevard, Hull had never won a major Rugby League trophy. Before he left they had won all of them.

The first, the R.L. Cup, in Batten's full season of 1913/14, was a most impressive one. So was their side which beat Wakefield: Ned Rogers; Alf Francis, Bert Gilbert, Billy Batten, Jack Harrison; Jimmy Devereux and W. Anderson; W. Holder, T. Heriridge, R. Taylor, J. Hammill, A. Grice and Steve Darmody.

An interesting feature of that side was the fact that the captain, Herbert Gilbert, was the first Australian to have his name put on the Challenge Cup. In addition Jack Harrison who later became Lt Jack Harrison, was awarded the Victoria and the Military Cross for bravery in France. Harrison, a Hull schoolmaster, was killed in action.

Batten's personality stamped itself for ever on the football scene of Hull. He was paid £14 a week and a special bonus, but he put thousands on to the gates at the Boulevard. When Batten was certain to play, a sticker saying 'Batten certain to play' was put over the match posters around Hull and it brought in the spectators.

Battens' theory on Rugby was 'the shortest way to the line is the best and quickest'. Players who knew him in his halcyon days have told me he was a fearsome sight in full flight and very hard to tackle.

His own tackling was a 'killer'. He would put his 14-stone of bone and muscle into a tackle and shattered his opponents. Some of his tough tackling had reactions on his health before he died.

Batten's wage of £14 was big money in those days.

During the depression years Batten was known to buy food and give money to the villagers around his native Kinsley districts.

It would be appropriate in the Batten story to mention the name of Bob Taylor, a member of the Salvation Army but as tough a forward, I am told, as could be.

Bob was a try-scoring forward who played for England, and his club record of 177 tries in 317 games is quite remarkable for a forward. In the season 1926/27 Taylor scored 36 tries, including two tries against New Zealand on a fateful New Zealand tour to this country.

Batten and Wagstaff were possibly the greatest centre pair ever to play for any country in any code of Rugby. They did not have many Test matches together, but for Yorkshire and representative games they were unique. Wagstaff, with his polish and creations; Batten with his power and personality.

Batten played his last Test match, curiously at Hull in 1921 when England lost the second Test by 16 points to 2. One report of the last appearance writes about 'Batten's terrific tackling of Blinkhorn the Australian winger'.

Billy continued to play for Hull until 1924 when he was transferred to Wakefield Trinity.

He was given a benefit of £1,079 in 1920 which was a record figure and no doubt record value compared with the £2,000 plus which Alex Murphy received from St Helens in 1967. A fine figure of a man, a remarkable footballer and a real personality.

Billy Batten's son Eric, who jumped over opponents like his father did until it was outlawed, had a good career for Hunslet, Wakefield, Bradford and Great Britain, playing Test football. A grandson of Billy, Ray Batten, started his career well with a Cup winners' medal for Leeds in 1968. The name of Batten lives on.

2

Gus Risman & Bev

The gaslight hissed above his desk as the games master picked up his pencil. He was about to tackle the most difficult job of the week. Fifteen names had to be placed on the blank sheet of paper before him.

Finding fifteen players for the school rugby team was not the trouble. Not at Barry County school in the heart of the rugby hot-bed of South Wales. The difficulty was who to leave out.

One name he couldn't ignore was Augustus John Ferdinand Risman. In typical schoolmaster's scrawl it was the first to appear on that team sheet every week.

That games master knew his business. Risman was to become one of the all-time great Rugby League players.

The amazing Risman story started back in 1929 - the year that the Rugby League Council inspired by its secretary John Wilson decided to take the Challenge Cup Final to Wembley.

'Gus' Risman, as he is internationally known, born in Tiger Bay, Cardiff, was at school in South Wales. He played

Rugby Union with Barry County school and Cardiff Scottish Rugby Union Football Club. That must have been some club with a name like that in South Wales.

Years earlier around 1906 Leeds Rugby League club had been to Wales and signed a good full-back, Frank 'Bucket' Young. He was given the 'Bucket' tag for his amazing ability to catch a football from any height or direction. Frank Young had represented England as the international side was then called, in a Test match against the Australians in 1909.

Like most Welshmen who 'went North', he returned to Wales after his playing career at Headingley and became a scout for Leeds.

Unknown to the seventeen-year-old Gus Risman, Frank Young spent a lot of time watching him play Rugby Union. He was so impressed with Risman, who was playing in Young's old position at full-back, that he suggested to Leeds they should give this boy trials. To Mr Young's dismay, Leeds didn't want to know about Risman.

What a grave error of judgement that turned out to be. Just before Christmas 1929 Frank Young tipped Salford about the prowess of Gus Risman. Lance Todd, the Salford manager, suggested four trials in which Risman played under an assumed name.

While Risman was up in the Coronation Street country of Salford having his trials, officials of Tottenham were seeking Risman to offer him trials with Spurs.

Risman's soccer ability was sufficient to play in Welsh schoolboys' International final trial. Soccer or Rugby provided Risman with much thinking about his future. He played alternative weeks in the two codes.

Salford, the Rugby League club who had a penchant for Welsh players, saw the possibilities of Risman and at the age of seventeen years ten months A.J.F. Risman signed for them as a professional.

The Great Ones

When Gus signed on that cold January day he was given £25 down for his signature. He was given £1 a week, payable every week for fifty-two weeks, and a further £25 when the year was completed. Just £102 in all for one of the greatest ever footballers to play the professional code of Rugby!

If you have any doubt of this, look at his record. He played for Great Britain on three tours to Australia in 1932, 1936 and 1946. But for the war he would surely have been on at least one more tour. He captained Great Britain in a Test on the Sydney cricket ground in 1936 and was tour captain in 1946. He played from the age of eighteen years to forty-three years of age with every honour in the game coming to him. And all for an initial cost of £102!

Many fans have argued which was the best position for Gus Risman. He had moved about the back positions from full-back to centre and stand off. And believe it or not, he scored a great try for England from the scrum-half position. This was the try he is willing to talk about.

He was playing on the Sydney cricket ground against New South Wales. His own story of that try: 'I picked up a ball from a scrum at the half-way line, ran round the blind side and continued a diagonal run to the corner flag. I touched down without a finger being laid on me, to a single stentorian shout from the famous Sydney hill 'You Pommie B ...' '

Not the first or the last time an Englishman has been so called from the Sydney Hill, but the try is one of the few which 'Rissy', as his tour mates called him, could describe.

During his long career, which started with Salford in 1929 and finished with Batley in 1954, Gus scored 232 tries kicked 1,679 goals to make a total of 4,054 points. In addition to the two clubs mentioned, Gus also played full-time for Workington Town and guested for Dewsbury, Leeds and Bradford.

I think his happiest moments in Rugby League were in Cumberland playing for Workington. On the way back from Australia and New Zealand in 1946 I talked with Risman about his future.

We were on the New Zealand ship *Rangitiki* coming home via the Panama canal and there were many hours to talk rugby. Gus was ready to leave Salford and had his eyes on taking over the Workington club as player-manager.

It was a brave step to take but a successful one which ended in disappointment after many glorious years and stardom for Workington. Gus admits his greatest moment of elation throughout his football career was at Workington. It was in the merry month of May, 1951.

The scene; Maine Road, Manchester, home of Manchester City. The occasion: The Rugby League Championship final between Workington Town and Warrington. Workington were still only babes so far as Rugby League was concerned. They had scouted and signed well under the guidance of Gus Risman. They had produced some good locals and brought Australian Rugby Union players in John Mudge and Tony Paskins.

They had created a happy family up in Cumberland, with Risman having great help from his wife Ethel. Cumberland fans supported the club with a fanatical fervour and they came to Manchester in their thousands.

There is a moment in every match where there is a turning point to success or failure. On this match Risman told me: 'Halfway through the second half of this game I realised, barring accidents, we had the Cup won. At that particular moment I have never experienced any greater feeling of elation at any period of my football career.'

Workington had no bad luck, in fact possibly a little good luck; in any case they went on to win their first major trophy by 21 points to 11. Cumberland Rugby League had arrived.

The Great Ones

It was their most joyous night as they sang 'John Peel' all the way back to the villages and towns which produced Rugby footballers long before Workington or Whitehaven joined the Northern Rugby League.

Twelve months later in 1952 there was possibly a greater achievement for Workington Town. Captained by Risman, playing in his favourite position at full-back, Workington met and defeated Featherstone Rovers at Wembley to take the Challenge Cup back to Cumberland.

Three years later Workington were back at Wembley - but without Risman. And they lost. The glorious years for Risman and Workington had ended on a sad note.

The Town club had signed another full-back, Stan Thompson from Yorkshire. Gus was not happy about the signing and in no time at all he had left the club. He sold his sports shop and left both the county and town of Cockermouth he had learned to love so much.

In the light of the cold dawn Gus knows he made a mistake in leaving Cumberland, where he was the crowned king of the county. He had done a tremendous job for Rugby League in this area and made hundreds of friends during his eight years there.

There has been much speculation how many tours to Australia he might have made had it not been for the Second World War. Sergeant Risman became Lt Risman, and when he could he played rugby mainly for Dewsbury.

He also played Soccer during the war alongside such stalwarts as Matt Busby and Stan Cullis. Even more he played on many Rugby Union grounds which could not have happened in peace-time. What a pity!

He played at Swansea, Cardiff Arms Park, Murrayfield, Belfast and many other Rugby Union grounds for the Welsh International Services and Army Representative sides. He played for the British Army Rugby Union side against the

French Services when the Germans were being kicked out of Paris.

His best goal in his own opinion was kicked on a Rugby Union ground at the holy of all holy grounds, Murrayfield, Scotland. And he got the 'bird' before he even attempted the kick. He was playing for the Scottish command against the R.A.F. His side was given a penalty on the half-way line. As he began to dig the hole to place the ball in there were cries of derision from the stand.

He was not sure whether the crowd was concerned with spoiling the sacred turf or thinking he was wasting time taking such a long shot. But he had the greatest satisfaction when the ball went soaring high over the cross bar to stun an unbelieving crowd.

Many matches were played in wartime with a mixture of Rugby Union and Rugby League players for charities. I still possess a programme of a match played in February 1942 for the British Red Cross at the St Helens ground Swansea. The two selected teams were English Services: P.O.Rankin (RAF and Australia), 2nd Lt E.J.Williams (Army and Cambridge), Sgt. S. Brogden (Army Leeds and England Rugby League), Lt F. Edwards (Army , Gloucester and England), Lt G. A. Holliss (Royal Navy and Oxford University), Group Captain G. A. Walker (RAF Blackheath and England) and Captain J. Ellis (Army, Wakefield and England): forwards Capt. R.E. Prescott (Army, Harlequins and England. capt.), Sq Ldr C.G. Gilthorpe (RAF, Coventry and England), Cpl R.F. Longland (RAF, Northampton and England), Capt. T.F. Huskisson (Army, OMT and England), Cpl J. Mycock (RAF and Harlequins), Pay Lt J. K. Watkin (Royal Navy, Utd. Services and England) P.O.O.W. Wright (RNZAF) ... Welsh Services: Sapr Howard Davies (Army, Swansea and Wales); Cpl Sid Williams (Army, Aberavon and Salford), Driver T. Sullivan (Army, and Swansea), Sgt. A.J.Risman (Army and Salford) cpt., Cpl Alan Edwards (RAF Salford and Wales), Sgt. Haydn Tanner (Army, Swansea and Wales) and Sgt W.T. Davies (RAF Swansea and Bradford Northern). Forwards: Sgt. W.H. Travers (Army, Newport and Wales), vice captain, Capt W.E.N. Davies (Army, Cardiff and Wales), Marine H. Payne (Royal Navy, Swansea and Wales), Sgt. R.E.Price (RAF and Wales), L.Cpl L. Thomas (Army and Llanelly), Cpl L. Manfield (RAF, Cardiff and Wales), L.Cpl Gwyn Williams (Army, Cardiff and Wigan), Sgt. T. Foster (Army and Bradford Northern).

There was a Wales v England match at St Helens, Swansea on the 25th November 1944 for wartime charities. England had L.Cpl Ernest Ward of Bradford Northern and Great Britain fame as the sole Rugby League representative in the white jersey but Wales had Lt A. J. Risman at stand-off partnering Lt H. Tanner, while in the threequarters Cpl Sid Williams of Salford was on the wing partnered by P.O. B.L. Williams of Cardiff and on the left flank F.O.J. Idwal Davies (Leeds Rugby League Football Club) was centre to Cpl J.L. Knowles of Swansea and the RAF.

In the eight forwards for Wales, Rugby League players had a prominent part. Six of them were Rugby League players. Sgt. I Owen (Leeds and Aberavon), Sgt. E. Watkins (Wigan and Cardiff) both RAF, S.S.I. Trevor Foster (Cardiff and Bradford), Cpl Doug Phillips (Swansea and Belle Vue Rangers), B.S.M. H. Thomas (Salford and Neath) and L/Bdr E. Evans (Llanelly and Salford). These were the days when Rugby Union players and League players could play with each other without fear of trouble. The wartime troubles brought the codes together. But after the war the restrictions were reimposed in all respects.

While I can see the Union point of view in their attitude I am at a loss to understand why young men who have played Rugby League at University or with work teams should be banned from Rugby Union if they played over the age of eighteen years.

Out of uniform and back into civilian life where Gus Risman had been a cinema manager in Salford, the life of the Risman family changed when he joined Workington Town and took up residence in Cockermouth.

His enjoyment in this part of the Wordsworth country was sufficient to take him back again in 1968 when he left his bleak Pennine Hotel at Scammondon to live in Cockermouth once again. Was he searching again for his lost glories? Certainly he had many pleasant memories to restart in Cumberland.

It was here where young Augustus Beverley Walter Risman enjoyed his formative years. Obviously 'Bev' had to live under the shadow of his illustrious father, and like Sir Len Hutton and his sons, so 'Gus' Risman's two sons 'Bev' and John were often compared with their father. There was no case of 'Like father like son' in the case of the Rismans.

Bev, much shorter than Gus, had not the same flair on the field. Although Gus was no speed merchant he was faster than Bev - or probably he looked faster. But the classy style of young Risman asserted itself in an emphatic way both at Manchester University, where he obtained a B.Sc. honours degree, and at Loughborough Training College, where he obtained a P.E. diploma.

Bev, like many other sons of famous Rugby League fathers, played Union. The position he preferred was stand-off, and in 1959 he achieved his ambition by touring New Zealand with the British Lions.

He had a most successful tour and a wonderful try he scored in the fourth Test at Eden Park, Auckland, is still talked about in Rugby Union circles.

With his family background it was pretty obvious that

The Great Ones

Bev Risman would eventually take the professional ticket. He did in season 1960/61 and the club he chose was Leigh, the club who had caused a sensation some years before when they signed as a professional Rugby League player the crack sprinter McDonald Bailey.

There was a difference between the signing fee which Risman senior was given when he joined Salford some thirty years earlier and the amount Risman junior got. A difference of £6,000. Bev Risman was a stand-off and that was the position in which he wanted to play.

His signing at Hilton Park was a blow to the English Rugby Union, but it was inevitable. It was just as inevitable, I felt, although Bev will not agree, that he was not fast enough to make the grade in Rugby League as a stand-off.

His years at Leigh were not as fruitful as he had hoped. He still felt stand-off was his best position but the Leigh club wanted to move him. Time was running out for Bev Risman, who was missing the honours he wanted.

As his future was in some doubt as far as his footballing career was concerned he was included at stand-off for Leigh in a match against Leeds which was televised. Leeds had always had an interest in him - but as a full-back. Risman played well in this match against Leeds and eventually he was sold to the Headingley club and with one wave of the wand Risman was soon to repeat some of the successes of his father's.

He agreed to play at full-back for a time. But the more he played in the full-back position the more he liked it. His first international match was against France at Paris in February 1968, when he scored sixteen points and showed his undoubted leadership and ability.

Within three months - at the age of thirty years - he was flying to Australia as captain of the 1968 World Championship team. He had had a long wait, but it was worth it. Unfortunately, there was no Cinderella and Prince Charming ending to this passage, for Great Britain did not win the World Championship.

Yet 1968 was a year of happy memories for the younger Risman.

He was the leading goal-kicker in the league, he won a League Leaders medal with Leeds; he won the most coveted medal in Rugby League, a Challenge Cup winners medal at Wembley and his wife Anne presented him with his third son.

Bev Risman had for long lived under the shadow of the 'Immortal Gus' but he had, in 1968, achieved fame and distinction in his own right.

He won't during his career be able to beat his father's record of 4,054 points, but then he won't want to play as long as his father did. When Gus Risman finished his playing career he was forty-three years of age, and his last game was for Batley in 1954.

Gus Risman, a student of Rugby League, was, I thought, a natural as a manager, but he was unable to click as he had done as player-manager. He had spells at Oldham, Salford and Bradford Northern, and much of the early success at Odsal was due to Gus Risman. But Rugby League appointments in the coaching and managerial field are getting like those in Soccer - not as safe as they used to be.

I once asked Gus Risman to give me his best team in which he had played. In the Salford thirteen during his career at the Willows, where David Watkins now plays, he selected Harold Osbaldestin; Barney Hudson, Albert Gear or Bob Brown, Gus Risman and Alan Edwards; Emlyn Jenkins and Billie Watkins; Billy Williams, Bert Day, Dai Davies, Paddy Dalton or Alf Middleton, Harold Thomas and Jack Feetham.

Not all Welshmen - although there are quite a few.

The Great Ones

Barney Hudson came from the North-East and Harold Osbaldestin was a fine lad from Wigan.

In his best thirteen for Great Britain up to 1946, when Gus finished with international football, he selected: Jim Sullivan; Alf Ellaby, Stan Brogden, Gus Risman, Alan Edwards; Emlyn Jenkins, Bryn Evans; Joe Thompson, Tom Armitt, Nat Silcock, Martin Hodgson, Jack Arkwright and Harry Beverley.

And there are no prizes for the odd man out in the six forwards, for Joe Thompson of Cross Key and Leeds was the only Welshman in that pack of forwards.

In 1951 Gus Risman represented Rugby League in the parade of Sportsmen at the Royal Command performance. He played over 1,000 matches of Rugby Football and he was never sent off.

He looked, acted and behaved like a sportsman who has brought credit, as his son Bev has done, to Rugby League. Gus packed a lot into his life in Rugby League. Somewhere, somehow I shall expect him to retain his interest in the code in a practical way. Probably his return to Cumberland might inspire this.

The Rismans are not the only father and son to represent Great Britain but they are the only pair to captain a Great Britain tour team. I would like to think we shall see their like again.

3

Lionel Cooper

Six times I have been to Australia to report the fortunes of
Britain's Rugby League tourists. Each and every one of those
tours has a boatload of memories. But none can match the
first. Jetting to Australia is as easy as travelling from Wigan
to Wick, only a darned sight more comfortable! It wasn't like
that in 1946.

The bunting welcoming dads home from the war still
blazed the streets of Britain, when Dr Clive Evatt, a minister
in the Australian Government, sent his request to Rugby
League headquarters in Leeds. 'Send out a touring team to
let the people Down Under see that Britain has not been
starved to death and is still alive and kicking.' English
Rugby League officials were only too happy to oblige. The
great post-war sports boom was just getting under way.

Transport of the team was the problem. 'Hop-on-a-plane-
to-anywhere' advertisements didn't grace the glossy
magazines in those days. Getting about Britain was bad
enough. Getting a Rugby League touring party to the other

side of the globe required computerised planning. Cables flew between Canberra and Westminster. Eventually the problem was solved. Send them by aircraft carrier!

H.M.S. Indomitable steamed out of Plymouth on April 3, 1946, bound for Australia with as strange a 'crew' as any Royal Navy aircraft carrier is likely to have. Apart from the officers and men there was a complement of 122 'extras' composed of returning Australian air force members, priests from Ireland and 32 members of the British Rugby League party, of which I was one.

The *Indomitable* was going out to pick up RAF and WAAF personnel who had been serving in and around Australia. In the wake of Drake and the Pilgrim Fathers we crossed Plymouth Sound at the start of our 12,000 mile journey. Not for the first time had the Royal Navy come to the rescue.

That trip and the first post-war tour is another story, but, in addition to many things, it resulted in two Australian players being signed to play in English football for Huddersfield - Lionel Cooper and J.C. H. 'John' Hunter.

Just before leaving the North for Plymouth I was approached by two Huddersfield officials asking if I could help them to get a star winger for them.

Huddersfield at that time was without a Secretary and I was more or less give carte blanche to sign whom I could.

The Fartown club had had a great tradition of Australian players, particularly wing-threequarters. They had, of course, Albert Rosenfeld, an Australian who still holds the try scoring record of eighty tries in one season.

In the twenties they had a powerful wing pair in Ernest Mills and Ray Markham. Mills with his lithe, jerky walk was a typical lean Australian winger and had scored 289 tries for Huddersfield. Markham, strong and forceful, had scored 264 tries. Markham the winger was to stay in England to become Mr Markham of the Bradford Corporation as Markets superintendent. Others who had come from the Southern Hemisphere to play at Fartown included Edgar Wrigley who had been a visitor with the first touring team from New Zealand.

Huddersfield fans had been steeped in memories of overseas stars. Now they wanted to see action after the cold days of wartime. Lionel Cooper was a target for them, but Leeds were also interested in this strongly-built winger who had recently returned from serving with the Australian forces. A former Australian forward, Ray Stehr, told me that Lionel Cooper was the man to look at. Ray Stehr had been a strong force in Australian football and became a close friend in my later trips to Australia.

I had the opportunity of seeing Lionel Cooper in action pretty soon after arriving in Australia. He was selected on the left wing in the first Test on the Sydney cricket ground. He opposed Eric Batten the strong jumping winger. The match was drawn eight all. Joe Jorgenson (Australia) and Jack Kitching (England) clashed and Kitching was sent off after alleging he had been 'bitten'.

The English team was a really strong one. Gus Risman captained the side at full-back - and he missed a lot of goals. The threequarters were Batten, Ernest Ward, Kitching and Albert Johnson; Willie Horne and Tom McCue were at half-back and the big strong pack consisted of Frank Whitcombe (at 18½ stone), Joe Egan, Ken Gee, Doug Phillips, Les White and Ike Owens.

Australia had in the centre, Ron Bailey, who had previously been in England playing for Huddersfield. Bailey scored the first try in this Sydney Test for Australia and the equaliser came from Lionel Cooper on the left wing at the end. For the record Frank Whitcombe and Willie Horne scored tries for England with Risman getting one goal. This was the only tour incidentally where Great Britain did not lose a Test match.

The Great Ones

My eyes that day were closely on Lionel Cooper and I knew he was the man to suit the Huddersfield fans. With the help of Ray Stehr, approaches were made and negotiations started. Cooper was willing to come to England but there was one snag. He wanted a stable mate as a travelling companion. I had seen an earlier match in Sydney and was impressed with a full-back called John Hunter. He had excited me by catching a high ball over the dead ball line and running downfield with it. Was he the man to take with Cooper? They were friends and were both likeable players. They both looked footballers and they were the right positions to suit Huddersfield's requirements.

Huddersfield were happy to take my recommendations and we started talking terms with Cooper and Hunter. Leeds were the favourites. But the Leeds club were not keen to buy another player to travel with Cooper. As the Leeds deal fell through, Cooper and Hunter were set for Huddersfield.

A remarkable deal it was, too. For when terms were eventually finalised and the deal completed, Huddersfield paid out only £1,500 for the pair. A real bargain.

It was a hard winter's day when Lionel Cooper and John Hunter arrived at Huddersfield station to see snow for the first time. The station platform looked bleak with the hard snow having been beaten down on the platform.

They looked cold and a little gloomy. No doubt the sun they had left in Australia was uppermost in their thoughts as I introduced them to Huddersfield officials. The cold never really left their bones but the warmth of the reception from the Fartown fans remained with them.

Lionel Cooper was an established name, having played in all three Test matches in 1946 and scoring in the first two. He learnt quite a bit of English football tactics in the second Test at Brisbane when Britain won 14 points to 5 points.

Lionel Cooper

The Australian referees like to take touch line scrums on the blind side. Crafty English scrum-half Tom McCue from Widnes saw the value of this from his team's advantage. He used the referee well and wisely and sent Arthur Bassett in for three tries. Bassett, a Welshman, brother of Jack of Rugby Union fame, from Kenfig Hill, had his greatest day in big football with a hat-trick of tries thanks to McCue and he gave his opponent Lionel Cooper a tough time. Cooper had the consolation of scoring a good try but it was only a consolation, nothing more.

Cooper had valuable experience in this match. He didn't score in the third Test when Bassett had another two tries in his last appearance in Test football. No doubt Cooper had thoughts on Huddersfield and England.

His lesser known travelling companion to Huddersfield, John Hunter, was a bright-eyed, volatile youngster who enjoyed his travel and his football. He became a firm favourite at Huddersfield, for his infectious enthusiasm did much for them in the early formative days of post-war rugby at Fartown. His record was not as impressive as Cooper's, but the name John Hunter will be remembered for many years to come.

Lionel Cooper's first season at Huddersfield brought him 38 tries. A splendid start - for he was their leading try scorer, a record he kept for the next seven seasons with 62, 47, 58, 66, 47, 38 and 65 tries scored.

In his last season in 1955 he had hoped to pass the all-time try scoring record of his fellow Australian Albert Rosenfeld. He was fifteen tries short of it but he did have one distinction over Rosenfeld. He kicked 45 goals and in 1951 finished head of the points table with 202 points. He followed this again as leader with 212 and had the top points position with 209 points in his last season.

It was during his service at Fartown that Huddersfield

signed Pat Devery, a former Navy man from Balmain, Australia. Devery, had two very successful years at Huddersfield with 332 points and 249 points. But Devery did not stay or capture the imagination of the Fartown fans like Cooper. No Australian player can play for Great Britain and thus the only honours such a player could get was the 'Other Nationalities' side. In this and other representative matches, usually in a Green jersey, Cooper played in 21 matches. Curiously, the 'Other Nationalities' side faded out about the time Cooper returned to Australia and their last two matches were in 1955, when they beat England 33 points to 16 at Wigan and France 32-19 at Leigh. As a result, the 'Other Nationalities' were declared the International champions for the season. Then they folded-up.

Cooper's overall try scoring achievements at Fartown places him head of the list for the club with 432 tries, followed by three fellow Australians - Rosenfeld with 388, Mills with 289 and Markham 264. Quite a record for the 'Kangaroo'.

A Wembley winner's medal which is the life's ambition of all footballers came to Lionel Cooper in 1953 when Huddersfield beat St Helens by 15 points to 10. This was the dramatic match when John Hunter was taken off on a stretcher after a head tackle but jumped off the stretcher in the dressing-room to run back on the field. This was the match, too, when boos were heard at Wembley in a Rugby League Cup Final.

When season 1955-56 started at Fartown there was no Lionel Cooper to be seen. He had returned to Australia. But John Hunter stayed on to pass a 300th appearance in the famous claret and gold jersey.

Cooper's place on the left wing was taken by his stable mate John Hunter. Hunter was given a testimonial for his splendid work at Huddersfield, something I am sure he never thought he would get when he stepped on to that snow covered station platform almost ten years earlier. In that season Hunter clocked up 31 matches and scored 13 tries. J.C.H. Hunter played in 346 matches for Huddersfield, kicked 3 goals and scored 83 tries. Not bad for £500 ...

A typical Australian, Cooper was at times almost brash in the way he played football. In 1953, when Huddersfield won the Challenge Cup at Wembley, Lionel Cooper was the strong man. Throughout the reports of that march to Wembley, Cooper's name appears over and over again. Many of Cooper's four hundred tries were scored after long running efforts to show he had many items in his repertoire of obtaining points.

Perhaps I should mention that both Cooper and his Aussie pal Hunter played cricket. Hunter being the better of the two, with his big hitting and carefree attitude endearing him to the cricket followers in the area. Hunter still plays in Australia, being captain of a local cricket team in a small town where he is the local postmaster.

Cooper had a long illness which affected his favourite game of golf, but he was around to see his former club chairman, Hubert Lockwood, who toured with the 1968 World Cup party in Australia.

Lionel Cooper was no fitness fanatic and former colleagues tell me he often complained about minor ailments until one day, after a very successful match, he had a complaint which brought the comment from a colleague 'If ever you were fully fit you would knock the stand down'.

When Cooper scored a record ten tries in a match at Huddersfield against Keighley, he virtually picked up Mel De Lloyd, the Keighley player, to go over for his tenth try.

In scoring these ten tries Cooper made a new Fartown record, to beat that of nine tries scored by fellow Australian Ray Markham. No wonder they like Australian wingers at Huddersfield.

4

Alex Murphy & Jonty Parkin

When the British team toured Australia in 1958 a famous Australian scrum-half called Duncan Thompson said to me: 'That boy is a second Jonty Parkin.'

That 'boy' was Alexander Murphy of St Helens. Age: Just eighteen. Thompson's judgement was smack on because Murphy became one of the most famous scrum-halves. He was certainly one of the most controversial.

Murphy was destined for St Helens from the day he showed his brilliance as a fourteen-year-old playing Rugby League at school. The tempestuous Alex had to wait until one minute past midnight on his sixteenth birthday before he signed on the dotted line for Saints.

As the clock finished its strike of twelve, Murphy, with his Cinderella-type signing, had become a Saint. He was also destined to become a 'sinner'. Within two years he was in Australia on that controversial 1958 tour as second scrum-half to Frank Pitchford of Oldham. Rapidly he became first choice and played in all three Tests.

If he needed them, Murphy had club mates Alan

Prescott and Vinty Karalius to guide him. He even asked me on arrival in Australia if I would keep an eye on him. In retrospect this is laughable. For Alex Murphy was, and is, a footballer who could take care of himself very well indeed.

Even the first row on that tour - at a club in Wollongong - showed this wen two players clashed with officials and were threatened with being sent home. Murphy was not one of them.

This first tour for Alex opened with a rough match against New South Wales. Three men were sent off, including Murphy's club pal Karalius. Amid the storm Murphy shone brightly. After losing the first Test - the only tour defeat in Australia - he scored tries in the remaining two Tests and finished the tour with the impressive figures of 21 tries with three goals in twenty matches. Quite an achievement for an eighteen-year-old on his first tour. He continued to be first choice for Great Britain until 1963, making ten appearances against Australia.

How many more he might have made had he not clashed with authority and refused selection I can only guess. I think he would certainly have passed the eleven appearances made by the man he had been compared with - Jonty Parkin.

Alex says he owes much to his early mentor, his coach at St Helens, Jim Sullivan. 'Murph' as the tour players would call him, says that Sullivan's insistence on running between two pieces of silver paper from a cigarette packet made him the great scrum-half he was.

Sullivan made him jog to the first piece of silver paper then burst at top speed until he reached the second piece. Murphy became bored and sick of this constant training method. He wanted to do what the other players were doing in training - play with the ball. But the Sullivan silver paper trick proved so right and successful in the development of this fine player.

The Great Ones

Alex Murphy has been called most things in Rugby League football, good and bad. And I guess he still will be as long as he continues to be in the game.

When we went to Australia again on the 1962 tour he was a much more experienced footballer. Not only had he more Test match experience under this shirt, he had also sampled World cup Rugby League in the 1960s series. He played in only eleven games on this tour. An arm injury in the last club match in Australia caused him to miss the New Zealand games.

After the first two 1962 Tests had been won pretty comfortably a big effort was made to make a clean sweep - something which had never been done. It looked like being accomplished when Murphy scored the greatest individual try from a scrum I had ever seen.

Near the half-way line, playing towards the dressing-room end on the Sydney Cricket ground, Murphy took a ball cleanly from the scrum. He side stepped inside the Australian scrum-half, did a ten yard acceleration away from the loose-forward and set sail diagonally towards the posts. The Australian full-back Clifford was facing him, but with a glorious side step Murphy went past him and scored near the posts. A great try and an apparently certain clean-sweeper for the Ashes.

The score was 17 points to 11 and Britain looked home and dry. What happened after is history. Australia kicked a penalty goal, were awarded a very doubtful try, and in the last minute winger Ken Irvine kicked a dream goal to give Australia a one point victory.

The victory lap for the Ashes by Ashton, Murphy and company was somewhat dimmed by the late defeat. They had so wanted to win all three Test games.

The Tour was a great success and unfortunately the last that the Australians were to see of Murphy in the British jersey. After playing in Tests against Australia at Wembley and Swinton in 1963 Murphy left the Australian scene - at least so far as playing against them was concerned.

He was in the British team to play against France and was a likely captain for the 1966 tour. He suddenly announced he was not available for tour selection due to business reasons. A decision I think he later greatly regretted.

It was a period of general uneasiness for Murphy. He was not in the party which toured Australia although he had tremendous satisfaction when St Helens beat the old 'enemy' Wigan in the Challenge Cup Final at Wembley before a crowd of 100,000. Murphy captained the winners. But the days of Alex Murphy were numbered at St Helens. He received a benefit cheque of over £2,000 and then said he was leaving the Saints.

They had signed Tommy Bishop and moved Murphy to a mid-field position. He was all set to go to play for an Australian club and had actually put his house up for sale. While Basil Lowe, the St Helens secretary, was awaiting finalisation of the deal to transfer Murphy to Sydney a sensation was caused when the Leigh club, through their chairman Major Jack Rubin, stepped in and signed him up as coach. They couldn't sign him as a player, of course, but as usual in this sort of case they eventually did when St Helens let him go and Murphy became the player-manager at Hilton Park, Leigh.

'Murphy the Magician', 'Murphy the miracle maker', these and other titles including complimentary and uncomplimentary ones have been levelled at Alex Murphy during his remarkable football career.

A personality, a character and individual Murphy has made news when there has been little about. He has been a football writers' dream boy on many an occasion. Even when he played for the RAF on Rugby Union grounds he made news. Often outspoken, sometimes to his own ultimate disadvantage.

He looked, walked, acted and played like a great Rugby League player. On his first tour in the second Test on the Brisbane ground he offered to scrap with 6ft 3ins Kel O'Shea, the Australian forward. Murphy was never frightened of any Australian, however big they were.

He chattered, cajoled, threatened his own team-mates. His 1958 tour captain, Alan Prescott, had to say 'Zip it' many times as Murphy clashed with referees during a match.

He never played half measures when he wore the British jersey. His clean look with his dark hair rarely ruffled disguised the temperament inside the 5ft 7ins, 11 stone frame. He was a real joker, who kidded team mates and opponents alike. After St Helens had beaten Wigan by 21 points to 2 points in 1966 he had his little crack at his former tour captain, Eric Ashton, as he showed him the Challenge Cup they had just won.

For a scrum-half to be successful and live within the physical field of Rugby League he has to be 'cheeky' I suppose. Murphy had these qualities, but also a greatness of ability. It would have been interesting to have seen him operate as a tour captain in Australia. No one will ever be able to prove whether he would have been a success or failure. It would certainly have been an interesting episode.

Somebody once said that rules are only there to be broken. That somebody must have been thinking of a gentleman called Jonty Parkin. 'Jaunty' Jonty, in the words of my father, was the greatest half-back he ever saw play Rugby League. He certainly has all the records to prove it.

Jonty of Wakefield, Dewsbury and Hull K.R. was one of the greatest thinkers the game has known. He was responsible for many rules being altered because of the way he exploited them. He was, for instance, the only player ever to buy his own transfer. And he did this when he left Wakefield after seventeen years to join Hull Kingston Rovers. Jonty was on offer at a token fee of £100. He promptly paid this himself and proceeded to Humberside to join the 'Robins'. The Rugby League Council immediately stopped this self-purchasing by a player and so Parkin became the first and last player to buy himself.

Jonty was always in history-making incidents. There was the time at Headingley in a Yorkshire Cup semi-final in 1924 when the quick thinking Parkin altered the whole course and result of a match.

Wakefield were playing Leeds in the County Cup semi-final and Trinity were attacking. The ball ran towards the Leeds dead ball line with Parkin and others in pursuit. Leeds full-back Sid Walmsley picked up the ball. He said it had gone dead and instead of touching down as instructed he tossed it to the Leeds captain to drop out from the twenty-five line. Seeing this happen Parkin immediately called to the referee 'Forward pass, sir'. The referee gave a forward pass and ordered a scrum on the five yard line. While Leeds players were arguing about the decision and obviously unsettled, Jonty had the ball in and out of the scrum and was under the posts for the winning try.

With the score 5 points to 4 points Wakefield were through to the final and went on to beat Batley by 9 points to 8 points. Another Parkin victory. But then Jonty had many victories in Rugby League football, quite a few wearing the jersey of Great Britain in Test football against Australia. His first Test against Australia was in 1920 on the Sydney cricket ground and his last ten years later at Swinton. Parkin had three tours to Australia. His last tour was in 1928 and again, under his captaincy, Britain won the Ashes.

The Great Ones

It was on this tour that two great forwards made their debut in Australia - thanks to Parkin. The two forwards, Bob Sloman of Oldham and Albert Fildes of St Helens Recs, were not in the original team picked for the Test. The two managers had disagreed and Parkin was called in as arbiter.

It is said that Parkin when asked about the merits of the players in question said, 'There's no argument, it must be Sloman and Fildes. I'm a Yorkshireman, but I want these two Lancashire lads in the match. You see Bob knocks the opposition for six one way and Albert knocks them for eight coming back.' Sloman and Fildes were in and stayed there for the three Tests.

Jonty - real name Jonathan - was born in the footballing village of Sharlston, and signed for Wakefield Trinity at the age of sixteen in March 1913. He played his first senior team game in November of that year against St Helens.

At seventeen he won a Challenge Cup medal - not a winners - when he played for Trinity against Hull at Halifax.

He had played in Cup rounds against Wigan and Broughton Rangers and kept his place in the final - a sign of great things to come. Wakefield, captained by Herbert Kershaw on April 18th, 1914 were beaten by six points to nil.

With the First Word War coming shortly after, Wakefield Trinity closed down until 1919. Young Parkin, who had received £5 for signing for Wakefield, guested for Dewsbury during the war, along with players like L.Land, A. Crosland, H. Kershaw, W. Batten and J. Rogers.

When normal football resumed, Parkin soon caught up with honours again. After his first successful tour in Australia he received a special birthday gift on November 5th, 1921 when he took over for the first time as captain of England. He led his country and his county for ten years.

Parkin's last Test match was the historic clash with the Australians at Swinton in 1930. This was the match that

Australia claimed they should have won after a try by 'Chimpy' Busch, the Australian scrum-half, was disallowed.

Because of the row the Australian manager, Harry Sunderland, asked for another Test and against all normal precedents a fourth Test was given. This was played at Rochdale. England won by 3 points to nil, Stanley Smith getting the only try, but his former club captain, Jonty Parkin, was not in the team. Parkin had announced his retirement from international football.

Parkin played in eleven Tests against Australia. In some of these he was partnered by Johnny Rogers of Huddersfield. Parkin was really a scrum-half, although he played at stand-off in many games. His partnership with Rogers was an extraordinary one. In the 1920 Tests, Parkin was moved to stand-off to let in the Welshman Rogers. They had such understanding between each other that it was said that even in Test matches 'whichever of us picked up the ball first put it in the scrum'. The Parkin-Rogers partnership had all the hall marks of greatness.

Parkin's individual greatness added to his tremendous leadership. He made and scored tries with outstanding brilliance, at times most unorthodox in his application. It is said in one match, refereed by the Reverend Frank Chambers, one of the outstanding whistlers of that era, that Parkin deliberately went offside at a scrum to give away a penalty with the score margin being three points in Wakefield's favour.

Whilst Parkin told Rev. Frank that he was offside the Dewsbury scrum-half picked the ball up and scored with the referee saying it was a try. It must have been one of the very few occasions when Jonty was caught napping.

When he left Wakefield in 1930 at the age of thirty-two for Hull Kingston Rovers, after buying his own transfer, he stayed at Hull for two seasons and then returned to

The Great Ones

Wakefield to continue a successful fish business in the 'Merrie City' which had started when he joined Hull K.R. In the early fifties he became a member of the Wakefield committee, but did not stay long in this work.

In 1968 Jonty returned to the scene of his triumphs in Sydney, where he went on holiday. 'I was treated like a king' said Parkin on his return to this country.

He was met by his old adversary, 'Chimpy' Busch, who still claimed he had scored a perfect try in that Swinton Test of 1930. I gathered Jonty was inclined to agree with him, but pointed out that the touch-judge's flag had gone up and referee Bob Robinson had to accept that.

A pit worker at sixteen and a professional footballer, Jonty Parkin developed into one of the great players and a most successful businessman.

5

Lewis Jones

London's White City has seen it all. The pomp and circumstance of Military tattoos. Leaping horses amid the chrysanthemums at the show jumping extravaganzas. Athletic records by the score, the cream of galloping greyhounds, World Cup Soccer, to say nothing of international Rugby League.

After that conglomeration of events you would think nothing could makes eyes pop at this sports stadium. You would be wrong. In the summer of 1968 some strange sporting specimens stepped out across the cinders of the White City track. Standing there in the centre of the arena, they looked like a cross between lunar orbiting astronauts and refugees from outer space itself.

The circus was in town. The circus of that most extraordinary of sporting endeavours, American football - the gridiron variety that has us all baffled on this side of the Atlantic. Complete with crash helmets and all that shoulder padding, the Yanks were in London on a scouting mission.

The Great Ones

They were holding trials to find goal-kickers - somebody who could put the ball between the posts. What a pity they did not arrive four years sooner. For then they would have found the greatest 'kicker' of them all: Lewis Jones.

Like so many of the outstanding players whose pace and skill enabled them to carve out glittering careers in Rugby League, Lewis Jones was a product of Welsh Rugby Union. Perhaps the greatest of them all.

Dubbed the 'Golden Boy', Jones was just twenty-one when Leeds paid him a record £6,000 to turn professional in 1952. By the time he flew to Australia in 1964 to continue his wonderful career Down Under, no player had been so idolised. Neither had any player been so criticised.

Lewis Jones became Rugby League's most controversial figure, dividing the crowds into those who regarded him as a genius and those who claimed that he flattered to deceive. They were either 'Lewis Jones crazy' or scoffers because of the occasions when he appeared to be unwilling to shoulder his share of defensive work. But there was only one opinion on this creative ability - fantastic. His attacking flair was superb.

He introduced the acceleration 'kick'. His 'hanging pass' became the talk of the code. He could punt the ball vast distances. And he could kick a goal from the touchline or from half-way requiring no more than two strides to the ball. When it comes to timing, whether it be kicking or passing the ball, Jones has had no peer.

Throughout his twelve tempestuous seasons on the Rugby League scene in Britain this fabulous entertainer and fantastic match winner became the greatest crowd-puller of them all. The story goes that when he decided to call it a day at Headingley, and took his family to Wentworthville, seventeen miles out of Sydney - where he is still delighting the locals at thirty-seven years of age - some Leeds fans said they would quit watching the game. He left behind a target which not even that other prolific scorer of the modern era, Neil Fox of Wakefield Trinity, has been able to challenge.

For in season 1956-57 Jones became the first player to reach 500 points in a season. His total of 505 points from 197 goals and 37 tries seems likely to stand for a long, long time. Jones played in 390 matches for Leeds, landing 1,262 goals and scoring 146 tries - a total of 2,962 points - average 7.60 points a game. Add 760 points he has notched in his seasons with the Wentworthville club as player-coach and Jones has attained an aggregate of 4,236 points in Rugby League.

Only one player has topped this total - Jim Sullivan of Wigan, who played nearly twice as long in Rugby League as Jones. And before turning professional Jones was, of course, grabbing big hauls of points in Rugby Union.

Raised at Gorseinon, and developed as a Rugby Union player at Gowerton County School - which had produced such players as Rowe Harding, Hadyn Tanner and Willie Davies - Jones gained selection at full-back for the Welsh Secondary Schools' XV against France at Cardiff Arms Park.

He joined the Gorseinon team, scored 88 points before Christmas, was invited to become a member of the Neath side, and soon equalled their scoring record of 18 points in a game. His first three outings brought him 33 points and the knowledgeable Welsh rugby public realised that they had made a 'find' who was destined to rock their game.

Appearances with Glamorgan and Devonport Services prepared him for his debut with Wales in January, 1950. This was at Twickenham, where he made the only try, landed two goals, took his side to victory, and was 'chaired' off the field. That win was the prelude to Wales winning the coveted Triple Crown. Jones was still only eighteen.

Controversy was already building up around the fair-haired youngster, and arguments raged when he was left out of the British Lions side that sailed for Australia. The omission was soon to be put right. In next to no time he had been called upon as a tour replacement. And it was typical of him that he returned a hero.

Jones started with seven goals from seven attempts, and established a world Test record at Brisbane with 16 points from a try, a dropped goal, two penalty goals and two conversions. He was destined, four years later, to break the Rugby League record for Test football on the same ground with 10 goals.

Back home it was not long before he was made the scapegoat for a trouncing at Murrayfield and was dropped. Quickly recalled, he showed his all-round skill by playing on the wing against the Springboks and helping Wales to their second Triple Crown success in three seasons.

Leeds, famed for swoops into the transfer and signing market, were taking note of his remarkable youngster. Scouts from Headingley had been watching Jones, reporting on his flair for the game. When the famous Welshman let the whisper spread that he was contemplating turning professional they moved with lightning speed. They got their man for a down payment of £6,000 on a nine-season contract. That meant a £15 a week all year round for nine years before pulling on a boot, plus wages and a nicely-paid job. This was way above what any Rugby League club had previously undertaken for recruiting a player.

Jones signed for Leeds on November 6, 1952, and he made his debut on November 8 against Keighley at full-back, landing seven goals. Some debut!

It is worth noting that Jones - who played in first-class football at full-back, centre, on the wing and at off-half - preferred centre-threequarter. At all events he quickly made his mark in the middle, but at Batley on January 24, 1953, after scoring a dazzling try, he sustained a complicated fracture of the forearm. It was such a bad fracture that it was feared he might not play again - and certainly there was no possibility of his turning out again that season after a plate had been inserted into his fractured arm.

When at length the Welshman began his come-back in the 'A' team people shook their heads. 'He can be written off,' they said. Certainly at that time it did not look as if the pale-faced, whispy-haired Welshman, the inevitable cigarette drooping from his lips, would become the electrifying figure in Rugby League who was a legend in his lifetime. He appeared miles away from the man who, with his famed acceleration 'kick', scorching turn of pace over thirty yards, renowned 'hanging pass', long punting and super-marksmanship was to entertain crowds for Salford to Sydney.

By October, 1953, Jones was back the Leeds first team, scoring all the points in a big win against Warrington and he followed with ten goals and a try in the next game against Hull Kingston Rovers. Eight more goals against Wakefield Trinity took him to 80 points in three matches. He had the Leeds fans delirious. 'He's the Golden Boy all right,' they cried.

Jones gave the redoubtable Duggie Greenall, of St Helens, a fearsome tackler, a miserable afternoon in a tour trial and was picked at centre for the 1954 trip to Australia and New Zealand under the captaincy of Dicky Williams of Hunslet, a fellow Welshman. He went into action in the first Test on the wing. Both selected full-backs, Ted Cahill (Rochdale Hornets) and Jackie Cunliffe (Wigan), soon became casualties, and for the second Test the full-back berth was handed to Jones. He placed eight goals and for good measure dropped a couple.

In one game in New Zealand he put over 11 goals, succeeded a dozen times from thirteen efforts in another match, and then at Canberra topped everything by hitting the target fifteen times.

The Great Ones

Jones finished the tour with a bag of 127 goals and 8 tries - 278 points - to beat the records of the great Sullivan and equally famous French ace Puig Aubert. Returning to Headingley, he was back in the centre spot, alongside gentlemanly Keith McLellan, a schoolmaster from Australia, with quicksilver Jeff Stevenson at scrum-half.

Leeds duly won the Rugby League Cup at Wembley and, after his record 505 points that season, selection at centre for Jones in the second World Cup tourney in Australia was certain. He went as a centre but, after Ray Price of Warrington was injured, found himself playing at stand-off half and subsequently on the wing. Anyhow, Britain did not retain the World Cup, and Jones came in for heavy criticism regarding his displays Down Under.

He was a star on the club scene in England for seven years after that disastrous trip, but never again after that ill-fated summer of 1957 was Jones called upon for international duty. The main argument against him was defensive failings. He could, and often did, make a 'kill' with the best of the game's tacklers, but there were times when he faded from the defensive scene.

His main concern was attack and he made no secret of his belief that too much tackling would blunt his attacking edge. Certainly he reigned supreme as an attacker, and could prise open the tightest defence by clever change of pace, acceleration and a pinpoint pass.

How good he was in any back position can be judged from his going to off-half, taking over the captaincy when he was thirty, and leading Leeds to their first Northern Rugby League Championship success in 1961.

Shortly before this he had fractured his other arm, and having this similarly dealt with, he became the first Rugby League man with each arm 'plated'. The severe operations he underwent on each arm did not affect his skill, which grew as his speed off the mark began to decrease. His ability to spray accurate defence-splitting passes became even more deadly, and in the run-up to the Championship Final against Warrington at Odsal Stadium he outplayed two great half-backs in Alex Murphy of St Helens and Harold Poynton of Wakefield Trinity.

In the Final at Odsal he then gave Bobby Greenough, another talented and speedy player, an unhappy afternoon. Jones not only made tries for his colleagues in the final but scorched through for a solo touchdown at the post - a try that had the hallmark of his greatness stamped on it, and the crowd chaired him off the field. Quiet and reserved, Jones accepted the praise showered upon him with the same outward calmness as when his critics were in full voice.

No player in the long and colourful history of the Leeds club had such an individual following. Almost to a man the Leeds fans 'worshipped' him.

Such was his gate appeal everywhere that if Jones happened to be unfit when his club had an away game they say the opposition management more than once asked for the news that he might not play to be kept secret.

He was without doubt, a superb craftsman and master tactician, though apt to make spectators incredulous that such a gifted exponent of rugby arts could lapse into 'casualness'. One of the big attractions of Lewis Jones was the part of his make up that made him unpredictable. Nobody knew what he might do next.

More often than not he had the spectators threatening to lift off the roof of the grandstand with their cheers, but he could also send them tumbling into the depth of despair.

Revered as a youth in Wales, idolised in Leeds and nowadays a respected fatherly figure at Wentworthville - this, then, has been the great Lewis Jones, supreme artist in both Rugby codes.

The Great Ones

Leeds gave him a £2,000 testimonial after he played another two years with them at the expiration of his nine-year contract.

Wentworthville received him as their player-coach with open arms. It seemed a big step to embark upon another career 13,000 miles from his homeland when nearly thirty-three, and he intended to stay with them only two seasons. But it was inevitable that the good folk of Wentworthville came to 'love' him just as much as the Welsh and the English did. Two seasons crept to three, and then to four ....

His creative skill and kicking ability made him a player whose skill in the finer arts of rugby has never been surpassed.

I doubt if it EVER will.

6

Eric Ashton

The supremo of Wembley in Rugby League is undoubtedly Eric Ashton MBE, of Wigan. There's not a player in the world, Rugby or Soccer, who can match Ashton when it comes to Cup finals. Seven times Eric Ashton has captained a team a Wembley. And in all the short space of nine years.

Six of these visits to the twin towers of Wembley were in Rugby League Challenge Cup finals. The odd match out was the Great Britain v Australia Test match in 1963.

A remarkable record and one which may never be repeated by any player in any code of football.

Eric Ashton's story is remarkable for he has often had to live under the shadows of personalities like Billy Boston at Central Park. Yet it might surprise a lot of people, even Wiganers, to know that Ashton played more matches for Wigan than Boston.

When David Watkins the Newport and Welsh Rugby Union player signed professional forms for Salford and was reported to be receiving £14,000, Eric Ashton sat in the

The Great Ones

Wigan dressing room with his thoughts flashing back to his signing fee and start in Rugby League. It was away back in the 'fifties when he almost finished with the game after playing in one match.

His ambition was to play for his home town team of St Helens and at the age of sixteen years he got his chance. He was selected to play with the St Helens 'B' team, Ashton thought he had a satisfactory game. Apparently no one else did. For although Ashton continued to train at Knowsley Road he was soon forgotten. He did not play again and left Knowsley Road a disillusioned youngster. Ironically, five years later St Helens were to offer Wigan £12,000 for Ashton the player they could have had for nothing. That figure was still a £1,000 short of Wigan's assessment of their captain and centre, Ashton. They had placed him on the transfer list at £13,000.

There might be a little consolation for St Helens to know they were not the only club to miss Ashton. Leigh could have had him on trial but they did not answer a scout's letter of recommendation. It was during the National Service Gunner Ashton renewed his interest in Rugby.

Apart from being the Scottish Command Services 100 yards and 220 yards champion he was also one of their star rugby players. A Leigh fan in the same unit wrote to the club, but nothing came of the suggestion. Ashton became a corporal and the drill sergeant has since said he was the best and smartest drill N.C.O. he had. This probably accounts for the command on the field which he displayed when in charge of the teams he captained.

Ashton was recommended to Wigan and he agreed to six trials. One was sufficient for the astute Wigan officials, and he signed for the Central Park club for the sum of £150.

Apart from the difference in amount of this £150 and the £14,000 of David Watkins, there is a bitter twist so far as

Ashton is concerned. The Watkins fee was not chargeable for income tax. Eric Ashton, the glassworker from St Helens and a youngster doing his National Service, had to pay £35 out of the £150 he received.

'I was born ten years too soon and I should have played Rugby Union first,' once said Ashton. Ashton's success at Wigan didn't bring him the financial return from benefits, etc., like, say, Billy Boston received. Boston was rewarded with a benefit, a testimonial match and a special effort which brought him over £9,000. Eric Ashton received £1,800 as his ten years service benefit.

There was considerable controversy in the Ashton household when Eric signed for Wigan. His father, Ernie, who had played for Warrington, had other ideas of his son's value. The contract, however, was kept to and Eric Ashton started a career which was to bring him fame if not fortune in the game he loved - Rugby League.

After seven matches in the first team he received his first honour by being selected on the wing for Lancashire County. But Eric did not want to play on the wing. He almost gave up the game, but he was eventually played in the centre position as requested. But it was during his short spell on the wing, that he created a new Wigan wing style of play with his cross-kicks. David Bolton remembers many of the tries he scored from the Ashton cross-kicks. Eric did not fancy the wing position, he was too far away from the scene of activities for his agile and inquisitive football brain.

In 1957, when the second World Cup squad was selected, the name Eric Ashton appeared in the list much to his surprise. Although the series in Australia was lost, Ashton was the star and the Sydney press boys reported 'we shall see a lot more of Ashton'. They did! A year later Ashton returned to Australia under the leadership of Alan Prescott on that never to be forgotten 1958 tour.

The Great Ones

Ashton contributed much to the success of the record breaking tour in which only one match was lost out of the twenty-one played in Australia. The team drew one, and scored a record 810 points. Ashton scored 30 tries, being second only to winger Mick Sullivan with his record 38 tries.

Ashton's six foot one inch lean figure dominated the Australian scene. His stern countenance hid a quiet, yet pleasing sense of humour. Ashton used to say Test matches were not occasions for merriment, but even he could not prevent a chuckle when he watched Alex Murphy throwing his weight about against big Aussie forwards at the exhibition grounds, Brisbane, in the second Test which started Britain on the road to success in the series.

It was on this 1958 tour that Ashton captained Great Britain for the first time. He took charge in the absence of the Captain Alan Prescott and Vice-Captain Phil Jackson at Auckland, New Zealand. His team won, and Ashton proved that he was the natural successor to Prescott. He was appointed captain on his next tour to Australia and New Zealand - in 1962.

This was the tour when for the first time a record three Test wins on tour should have been achieved. It was not - by one point - and with great misgivings in the British camp. After winning the first two Tests 31-12 and 17-10, Britain sere set for the clean sweep.

Despite a troubled game, with Britain being reduced to eleven men (Derek Turner and Mick Sullivan were sent off) it still looked like being a clean sweep ten minutes from time with the score 17-11. Eric Ashton made one of his few mistakes at the moment of decision. Dropping the ball out from the twenty-five line after a missed penalty by Australia, Eric realised he had to put the ball deep in the Australian half and hold them there for the last ten minutes. Like us all, he knew penalties would most likely be given in the English half.

When Ashton dropped out, he miskicked the ball and it went straight into touch. In 1962 this meant a scrum on the twenty-five line, not a penalty as now, but it amounted to the same thing. The three-man scrum was formed and Britain were penalised, this time the goal was kicked to make the score 17-23 - and important two points lost.

In the last minute of the match Ken Irvine scored a try which the British players maintained was from a forward pass, the same player then proceeded to kick the most brilliant, but amazing goal of his career to give Australia a one point victory by 18 points to 17 points. There were tremendous scenes even though it had no bearing on the Ashes destination. There were a lot of complaints and grumbles from the victorious British team members, particularly Alex Murphy, as the team ran round the Sydney cricket ground with the Ashes cup.

On the Monday following the Test, there was an important discussion at the Australia Hotel where I was staying in Sydney. Manager Stuart Hadfield, Eric Ashton and Alex Murphy called to see me. During football talk, manager Hadfield asked Eric and Alex to play in a match on the Wednesday against the crack Australian league team, St George. Both were feeling the effects of the final Test match, but the defeat had emphasised a desire to thrash the St George team and to do this the leadership of Ashton and the skill of Murphy was needed. They had two days to get reasonably fit, or at least half fit.

It was sufficient, for St George the king-pins of Sydney, were thrashed - but with serious repercussions for Eric Ashton. The British captain had led the team so well that Norm Provan and his men were rarely in the picture. Near the end of the match, Eric Ashton ran to score a fine try on the right wing corner at the Sydney Hill end. After he had touched down with ease he was tackled, fell awkwardly and

The Great Ones

broke his leg. He was taken to hospital, and I went along with him. As we waited in the hospital for the x-ray plates he told me how it had happened and how so many similar broken bones occurred when a player was not ready for the impact. He blamed himself for not being aware that someone might come and tackle him even after putting the ball down for the try. I felt he was hard against himself.

This injury prevented him playing in New Zealand, and he returned home from the 'shaky Isles' before the tour was over. I saw him fly off from Auckland carrying the biggest Koala bear I had ever seen, taking it home for his first daughter.

This was the last tour Ashton was to make 'Down Under', but it was not the end of his international career. He probably wished he had not played again for in two Tests in England in 1963 both were lost. In the pouring rain at Wembley, the first Test ever to be played at the Stadium, Britain lost by 28 points to 2 points. In the second Test at Swinton, the half-century of points was knocked up for the first time ever. Australia scored 12 tries in a total of 50 points to Britain's 12 points. It was Ashton's farewell to Test football. Although this was his last appearance, there were a number who thought that he might have made the 1966 tour as captain.

He had announced his retirement from the test scene but some Rugby League officials suggested he might be made captain if he would withdraw his retirement message. This he did, but to his surprise he was not chosen and the job of captain went to Harry Poole.

The title of 'Wigan Wallopers' was given to the Wigan players who played deck-hockey on the aircraft carrier *Indomitable* on the tour to Australia in 1946. Tough as they were they could not beat a team of Irish priests, who were on board. The 'Wigan Wallopers' could be renamed the

'Wembley Wallopers' so far as the Wigan R.L.F.C. are concerned.

If you ask Eric Ashton for his greatest Wembley moment I am sure he will say 1958 - when they beat Workington Town by 13 points to 9 points. If 1958 was not Ashton's first choice, then it would be 1965 - when one of the best ever Wembley finals was won by Wigan with 20 points to Hunslet's 16 points.

This was a special success for Ashton, for he was then Wigan's player-coach. In addition to his captaincy, this threw a lot of worry on his shoulders. The Wigan captain was, and is always ready, to give praise to his colleagues. He paid a big tribute to Brian McTigue for his part in the 1958 Wembley win for the way Mighty Mac dealt with Brian Edgar the Workington star forward in addition to the try which McTigue scored when the Town defence were waiting for him to throw one of his renowned long passes out. McTigue's 'dummy' threw the Workington defence off-balance and the try settled their fate.

In 1959 Wigan - led by Ashton, of course - put up a record Wembley win when they beat Hull by 30 points to 13 points.

But amidst the joy of champagne corks popping for the Wembley wizards from Wigan there has been great disappointment too, for Eric Ashton on the Wembley scene.

His home town team St Helens provided the two biggest blows. In 1961, when St Helens won with a margin of 6 points, Ashton was not only disappointed but upset when the defeat was followed by payment of only £7 for losing and the loss of coach Joe Egan, who left Wigan for Widnes.

After the Wembley defeat, Egan's contract was not renewed and no coach ever had more respect from players than Egan had from Eric Ashton and his team-mates. Wigan had been the Champions in 1959-60, beating Wakefield at Odsal easily, but that did not stop the move of Joe Egan from

The Great Ones

Central Park. Although Ashton later became coach at Central Park, he always had the Egan case in mind.

Even harder to take than the 1961 defeat by St Helens was the 1966 success by the Saints, who scored 21 points to Wigan's solitary goal. This was a bitter blow for Ashton and Company, not just the defeat itself but the way it was done, and the situation was not eased when that ubiquitous Murphy, then captain of the Saints, took the silver cup to the Wigan bus, to let the players wives look at it. Sunday May 22nd, 1966 was the worst weekend Eric Ashton ever spent in London. Although in 1963 Wigan had been well beaten by Wakefield, with a score line of 25 points to 10 points, Ashton was not as disturbed with this defeat as the St Helens one.

The leadership of Ashton was all that his drill sergeant had intimated. I remember the occasion in Australia when Dave Bolton went off injured. Ashton looked round for Bolton and saw him on the touchline. When he reproached Bolton, the stand-off said: 'I told you I was going off.' Ashton said 'Did I answer you? Next time don't go off until I say you can.' Ashton had great respect from all his team-mates, but he wanted to know exactly what went on.

Eric Ashton could rise to the occasion. He once played at Leeds in a cup-tie when he had the 'flu. He looked pale and wan and was not fit to play. His team mates said: 'Come out if only to boss us around the field.' He did that and Wigan drew 5-5 each; they won the replay. In a cup replay against Leeds at Central Park he was sent off for protecting Billy Boston. 'Burly Bill' had clashed with farmer forward from Leeds, Jack Fairbanks. Ashton moved him away from the inevitable retaliation, but Fairbanks and Ashton then clashed instead - and both were sent off.

Alex Murphy used to say that Eric Ashton had the longest legs and arms in the business. 'Never throw a wild pass when the long arms of Ashton are near you' said

Murphy before one cup final. 'If you do, you'll have me to settle with' added Murphy.

Not many centres scored tries as often as Ashton did. His centre mentor was Ernie Ashcroft at Wigan and he had a great regard for the training he received from him. It was Ashton who broke the Wigan centre try record of Ashcroft's when he scored 32 tries, and this was in the days when Wigan had good wingers who scored tries. 'Best tutor I could have had' said Ashton of Ashcroft.

Eric Ashton could kick goals. When he kicked 11 goals in a cup tie in 1969 he was asked if he had ever scored 11 before. In that quiet sense of humour, typical of the man, he replied 'No, but I've missed 11'. He once missed one in a game at Leeds in front of the posts and Wigan lost by two points. I don't think Ashton has any illusions about the problems of Rugby League.

Players only get paid when they play, and the injury problem is always there so far as payment is concerned. Yet Ashton wanted a life of Rugby League and even gave up a grocer's shop to concentrate on full-time employment at Central Park.

When St Helens offered the £12,000 for him at least one St Helens official felt they made a mistake by not going to the transfer-listed price of £13,000.

Around 500 appearances for Wigan, twelve Tests against Australia, seven against New Zealand and a similar number against France, in addition to many County games etc., still does not fully give the picture of the greatness of Ashton.

A master strategist, cool, calm, phlegmatic, well respected in all R.L. playing countries, Eric Ashton has had his share of success and troubles. Whenever I see the film of the 1961 St Helens-Wigan cup final at Wembley I think how close Ashton was to saving that sensational try by Tom Vollenhoven. But not close enough. And the saying in Rugby

The Great Ones

League 'that winners can laugh and losers please themselves' is one which Eric Ashton well knows. I once heard a Wigan official say, 'We pay our players well at Wigan, but we pay them to win...'

In one benefit collection at Central Park Ashton received only £43, yet a hooker with nothing like Ashton's records had £218 from a collection at a nearby club. Ashton is philosophical about these things, and, as he thinks about the David Watkins £14,000 reward for turning pro he probably thinks about the £150 he got for turning professional and compares that with the many £10 players Wigan have signed like Joe Egan, Tommy Bradshaw, Ken Gee and no doubt many more with other Clubs.

The Wigan tradition, strange as it may seem for a native of St Helens, has meant much to Ashton.

The teenager youth, who took a bus ride from the council house in St Helens to Wigan to start a remarkable career in the thirteen a side rugby code, became a household name. But, knowing Ashton, possibly his first try in August, 1955 - the first of many - was as big a thrill has his illustrious career provided for him ... Possibly as much as the day in June, 1966 when he was given the honour of the MBE, for services to Rugby League Football.

Before Eric Ashton decided to bring his Rugby League career to a close in season 1968-69 he was hoping to reach a personal scoring chart for Wigan of 300 tries and 300 goals. On Saturday April 19th, before millions on television, Eric Ashton did just that when he scored his 300th try for Wigan at Central Park against Whitehaven. It was his second of the match and a try worthy of the occasion. He had to run a long way for the try but he did and the crowd gave him a standing ovation for his effort.

7

Victor Hey & Other Stand-Off Halves

I have often wondered what all those cricket lovers, who thunderously applauded Don Bradman's record 354 'clout' for Australia against England at Headingley in 1934, would have said if they had known that Rugby League would stage one of its most exceptional matches on that very same patch of sacred turf just a few years later.

Headingley is the only ground in England where both International cricket and International Rugby League is played. Many famous cricketers from all over the world have played on the Headingley cricket ground, while many test matches between Australia and England have taken place under the professional code of Rugby, on the adjacent football pitch.

The exceptional rugby league game was played at Headingley in 1938. Not on the rugby ground, but on the sacred cricketing turf itself. The match was transferred from the football pitch to the cricket ground almost at the last minute because of the football ground being frozen and unfit for Rugby. In these days this could not happen for the Headingley football ground has underground heating, and when other matches have to be postponed because of frost, rugby goes on at Headingley.

The Christmas fixture of 1938 was against Salford, who were then a mighty side in the rugby world. It was a history-making game and one of the great players who played - and indeed scored the only try of the match - was Vic Hey. Vic, of Yorkshire extract (Dewsbury, in fact) was born in Australia but had been signed by Leeds in 1937. A tremendous stand-off half-back of great ability and physique, Hey's signing by Leeds caused a sensation in the league.

He had as his partner at this time Dai Jenkins, a Welsh player from Trecorchy, South Wales, who had played for Acton and Willesden - one of two London clubs who played in the Northern League in the mid-thirties. Jenkins and Hey quickly settled into a good half-back partnership, and many of the Leeds movements originated from this pair. The only try in the Christmas match of 1938 was the sort Leeds fans loved to see.

Vic Hey told the story of the try against Salford 'We were attacking on the Salford 25-line, when Dai Jenkins received the ball from the scrum, darted diagonally away from the pack. I went with him for a few yards and then straightened up behind him on the burst. Just at the right moment Dai bobbed the ball into my arms. I was through, with only Harold Osbaldestin the Salford full-back in front. I took him to where I wanted him and side-stepped and that was it - another try from the old back pass.'

Vic was happy to think he had scored a try where the famous Don Bradman, a fellow countryman, had made his record Test match score. Later, when Vic coached the Australian R.L. team, he told me of his happiest Christmas in football through this try and his part in the 5-0 victory on the cricket ground. Vic Hey continued to play for Leeds until 1944, when he signed for Dewsbury.

The first stand-off I signed for Leeds was a ginger-haired student from London University, a native of Mountain Ash, called Dick Williams. Dick had been recommended by another Leeds player A.T. Cornelius and he was given a trial at St Helens partnered by Hector Gee. The brilliance of Williams was quickly evident and I knew I would have to get him signed before St Helens, who had been impressed with him, tried to fix him up. On the way back from Manchester I agreed terms with Dick and he later joined the Leeds club when he signed a seven years contract.

One of his first games, after signing for Leeds, was against Dewsbury with Vic Hey as their stand-off. Returning to the scene of many of his triumphs, it was obvious Vic, a great favourite would not only want to please his many Leeds fans but show the club they were wrong in letting him go. With this in mind, I prepared the early stages of the game to avoid getting the lighter 10 stone Williams bumped by the $15^{1/2}$ stone Hey. From the first scrum the theory came unstuck. Williams was given a pass and I saw Vic Hey tearing up in such a way that I had seen many times to take the man and the ball. I just shut my eyes at the point of impact, afraid of what would happen. The tackle was made, but to everyone astonishment the man who got up first was Williams not Hey. The Australian stand-off hurt himself - and Williams successful career was duly launched.

Williams not only played for the seven years I had signed him for at £550, but he signed a new contract at four times that amount later - to stay another three years at Headingley. He later moved to Hunslet and in 1954 had the honour of being appointed captain of the Great Britain touring team to Australia and New Zealand, he had previously toured in

The Great Ones

1950. Before Dick was made captain he had to be selected. There was almost a repetition of the Hey clash, for in the final trial at Swinton for the 1954 tour selection Williams was subjected to a tremendous onslaught from a fellow Welshman, Ray Price, one of Britain toughest stand-off halves ever to play so far as tackling was concerned.

As I went to Southport with some of the selectors there appeared some doubt of Williams being selected. The fact that he stood up courageously to the heavy tackling of Price, however, impressed the selectors and, once he was in the party, his selection as captain was a natural follow-up, for his experience and leadership were amongst his many attributes.

The majority of Welsh players return to the Principality after their playing days are over, but Williams stayed on in the city of Leeds after his career ended at Leeds and Hunslet. He played in 233 matches for Leeds and scored 69 tries.

In his International appearances, Williams played in a number of Test matches. Against Australia, his first was at Swinton in 1948 and his last in 1954.

Many great stand-off halves have, of course, come from Wales. Salford must have thought of this when they signed David Watkins in 1968. They had had previous successful days at Salford with all-Welsh partnership of Billie Watkins and Emlyn Jenkins. The fair-haired Jenkins from the valleys had impressed Salford's manager, Lance Todd, and he was looking for a replacement of yet another Welsh stand-off at Salford Eddie Matthews. The Watkins-Jenkins partnership replaced the other Welsh pair Matthews and Meek.

Emlyn Jenkins 'Went North' as they used to say in Wales and became an important part of the Salford club and the British International scene. He had a short Test match career against Australia, but it was a successful one. It started in 1935 at Swinton and ended in 1937 at Huddersfield. Emlyn now a teacher, but a cinema manager in his playing days in Salford, had one tour Down Under with the 1936 team. He played in all three Test matches in Sydney and Brisbane. His scrum-half partner on that tour and in the other Test matches against Australia was Billie Watkins the short-haired, lively scrum-half.

Going back to the unusual match on the Headingley cricket ground in 1938, there was another unusual venue for a big match that same year. Leeds and Hunslet were due to meet at Wakefield in the final of the Championship. It was obvious that a big crowd wanted to see this final and Belle Vue, Wakefield, would not be big enough to accommodate the spectators wanting to see the game. League officials under pressure from club officials changed the venue from Wakefield to Leeds - no not Headingley, but Elland Road the home of Leeds United. And the decision proved to a wise one for a record 56,000 spectators saw this match, with Hunslet loaning the goal posts and then rubbing their generosity in by winning the match and taking the Championship trophy. A member of the Hunslet team that day was Oliver Morris, a Welsh capture by Hunslet. He starred in this match but was later transferred to Leeds, who wanted him to replace Vic Hey. Oliver was not to play many games for Leeds, 61 in fact, for he joined up, became Lt Oliver Morris and was killed in action. The great potential of Morris was indicated by his 44 tries in only 61 matches for Leeds. Hunslet officials who signed him, reckoned he would have been the greatest but for the war. When Morris was signed his father insisted on cash instead of a cheque, for his £400 signing fee. Without so much cash on them Hunslet officials had to stay over in Wales for the weekend until the bank opened and they could get their cash to sign Oliver.

Rochdale Hornets officials tell a different sort of a story when they signed the great Welsh singer, J. Wickam. 'Wick'

The Great Ones

Powell. He kept refusing the tempting offers from the Hornets officials, but suddenly one of the officials pulled a wad of £800 in pound notes, flung them on the table and Powell was tempted.

This Cardiff flying winger had many offers, but he had solidly refused to turn professional. It was reported by the Hornets officials that he later said it was the sudden dramatic action which broke down his resistance to the offer to play in the Northern Union.

Backs, not forwards, are the positions where Welshmen have succeeded mostly in R.L., particularly stand-off halves.

Bradford Northern made one of their many fine Welsh signings when they broke up the R.U. partnership of W.H.T. Davies and Haydn Tanner.

William Thomas Harcourt Davies came from the cockle village of Penclawdd on the Mumbles coast. A cousin of Haydn Tanner, the pair of halves had many successes in the Rugby Union world - both with Swansea and Wales.

It was an unexpected signing when Bradford Northern persuaded the dark-haired, quiet-spoken Davies to turn professional. This was in 1939 and with the declaration of war in September of that year and the cancellation of the season's programme, Davies like many others had limited football during the following years. He did play, however, whenever possible on RAF leave, and I remember one great performance by Davies on a very muddy ground at Huddersfield when Bradford Northern won the Yorkshire Cup against Halifax by 24 points to nil. Many of the critics had said Davies was purely a dry ground player and would not be able to take punishment. This brilliant, wet ground display put paid to the tag of Davies being only a dry ground player.

Davies went to Australia on the 1946 tour, but did not play in a Test, having to play second fiddle to Willie Horne.

Davies' triumphs were in club football - not at an International level. In the 1947 Wembley final Davies was the man of the match, receiving the best player award.

Davies was opposed by the new Welsh star, Dick Williams. This match, incidentally, was a great day for the Welsh - with W.Davies, Emlyn Walters, Frank Whitcombe, Trevor Foster and Hagen Evans representing the principality in Bradford's Red, Amber and Black jersey, and with Leeds having seven players from Wales: A.Cornelius, Gareth Price, T.L. Williams Dick Williams, Dai Jenkins, and in their pack Con Murphy, Dai Prosser, and Ike Owens.

I never could make out whether W.T.H.Davies really loved his Rugby League. He did not seem to enjoy his 1946 tour, but he was a quiet man and a clear thinker on and off the field. He had to contend with Willie Horne on the 1946 tour. Of all the stand-off halves in R.L. none had a bigger following from the North West that he had.

When Dick Williams was appointed captain of the 1954 tour there were many and varied comments from Barrow, where their fans thought Horne should be the captain. A lean, pale-faced man, Horne did not look the footballer he was. A dour sort of man, Horne was a natural ball player. Golf, tennis, table tennis, soccer, any ball game, you name it, and Willie Horne played it - and most successfully too. He played in seven Tests against Australia, including all three in 1946 and all of the 1952 Tests in England. Although he toured in 1950, he did not get a Test place, and played in only five matches, having injured his achilles tendon in a country game. Horne did much for Barrow during his time with the club. His goal-kicking style was completely unusual and against all normal methods of good kickers. He side-kicked his goals in an arc run, but he kicked goals, he dropped them and he made and scored tries. He was almost a phenomenon in the way he played football.

The Great Ones

When Barrow won their first and only Challenge Cup in 1955, they were led by Willie Horne. He kicked six goals for them against Workington Town. Some of Horne's dropped goals were real match winners, and it was a sad day for Barrow and the code when he retired to spend more time on golf and in a sports shop.

Before I leave the story of some of the stand-off halves who left their mark in Rugby League I must write about two more. One, a New Zealander from the West Coast where Rugby League is very strong, and a Yorkshireman.

The New Zealander, whom many West Lancashire fans will claim as the best was Cecil R. Mountford. Mountford just beat the ban imposed on signing overseas players when he signed for Wigan and arrived in England by boat in July, 1946.

He came on a three year contract and had been recommended by an exiled Wiganer, who had gone to work in this exposed mining part of New Zealand. The South and the West Coast had produced many great footballers - both union and league. Mountford was one of three brothers, and in a very short season with Blackball, he scored 31 tries and kicked 67 goals. A sign of things to come, it was a good signing for Wigan. He was small, 5ft 5ins, but stocky with a pretty varied repertoire in his attacking play. He soon had won a winner's medal for a Challenge Cup success, when he helped Wigan to beat Bradford 8 points to 3 points. This stopped Bradford doing a hat-trick of Wembley wins something which has never been done. Two out of three by Bradford and two in succession by both Wigan and Wakefield - but never a hat-trick. Wigan won a championship title in Mountford's first term at Central Park when they beat Dewsbury 13 points to 4 points at the home of Manchester City.

When his three year contract was up Mountford, married

to a Lancashire girl, returned home to Blackball for a holiday before he came back to England. He later joined Warrington as manager.

Before joining Warrington, Mountford had the honour of being the Wigan captain when they won the Challenge Cup at Wembley in 1951 - and being voted the best player. After a successful spell as Warrington's manager, Cecil R. Mountford returned for good to his native New Zealand and became an official member of the New Zealand Rugby League - first in a coaching capacity and later in an administrative role.

Before leaving the tale of the stand-off halves I must mention the most modern one in his benefit year in 1969. It is Alan Hardisty, hero of a great Castleford cup win on February 15th 1969, when millions of TV viewers saw a sensational interception try scored by Hardisty which killed the hopes of Wigan, the Wembley wizards, for 1969. Keith Hepworth, scrum-half, and Alan Hardisty, the stand-off, have been the local heroes around Castleford for many years. Their careers have taken almost an identical course, both starting with the club in season 1958/59, and still going strong - as that Wigan win showed. Castleford, a fairly new member to the Rugby League, admitted to the Northern R.L. in 1926 and under the leadership of that tremendous centre-threequarter Arthur Atkinson, won the Challenge Cup in their greatest moment at Wembley in 1935. Atkinson, a local boy who played for England in Test football, was of Castleford mould in every ounce of his solid 14 stone.

In the same mould, although a much smaller mould, Alan Hardisty, born at Castleford in 1941 and known as 'Chuck', hit International headlines in 1966 when he scored or was awarded a remarkable penalty try on the Sydney cricket ground in the third Test match. Twelve months later the Castleford supporters and just about every one of the

The Great Ones

40,350 inhabitants who talk about the club's affairs if they don't follow the team, were shattered to hear that Alan Hardisty might be signing for St George, the big 'money bags' club. His success on the hard ground of Sydney was assured had he gone to Australia. He did not - much as he would have like to, and he stayed on with his pal 'Heppy' to give Castleford fans - and others I might add - much enjoyment for the enterprising type of rugby the pair displayed. The sharp burst from the scrum by Hepworth and the short grubber kick or the interception by Hardisty are items in their repertoire which have brought grace and some glory to the code.

8

Neil Fox & Ernest Ward

It takes all sorts to make a world. Take a look around and you are forced to agree with the Yorkshireman who coined the classic phrase: 'There's nowt as queer as folk.' It wouldn't surprise me one bit if he had sports fans in mind the day he thought up that one.

They certainly are a rare species. Who else, after a week's work would pay to stand on wet and windy terraces to cheer a team and get a kick out of it? I admire those lads - and lasses. Where would professional sport be without them? They are the bread and butter of all the big-time sports.

There is nothing I like more than to get among the fans, and meandering down memory lane is the pleasurable pastime of anyone who is a thoroughbred sports lover. The only snag is that you have to possess a good memory. Visions soon get clouded. It seems that memory is kind in later years to remember only the good things a player did. Successes are retold more frequently than failures. Goals a player kicked get longer and better. His speed gathers momentum as the years go by. I see nothing wrong with this. Pleasant memories are there to be treasured!

For this reason I have no doubt that Wakefield Trinity fans in particular will in due time forget December 1968 when they trace the fortune of Neil Fox.

From its very beginnings the Neil Fox career had had its fair share of shocks. Now, as Trinity fans put the finishing touches to their Christmas shopping, the evening paper placards yelled out in their loudest print the news that was to spoil many a seasonal party. Wakefield had placed their glamour boy Neil Fox on the transfer list. For many years centre-threequarters Fox *had been* Wakefield Trinity. The thought of him leaving was sacrilege. The Belle Vue fans could not picture him stepping out in any other than the famous white jersey with the red and blue band. He had worn those colours with distinction for thirteen years.

They remembered so well the day when as a young sixteen-year-old, he made his senior debut for the club as a full-back. It was April 1956 when he trotted out against Huddersfield - a big strapping lad with the confidence to match. Neil Fox kicked six goals that day with the left leg that was to set-up and knock down rugby scoring records like nine-pins.

The fact that he ever played for Wakefield was remarkable in the first place. Neil was the youngest son of school caretaker, Tommy Fox, in the Yorkshire village of Sharlston. The nearest club to the village was Featherstone Rovers and father Fox had played for them in his younger days. It was natural that his three sons, Peter, Don and young Neil should want to play Rugby League. It was natural that once they proved they had the makings of professional players that they should join their father's old club. Peter and Don Fox did just that.

When 'baby' Neil reached the signing-on age of sixteen

the village of Sharlston had every confidence that he would follow in father's footsteps and join Featherstone Rovers. He didn't. Neil's choice was Wakefield Trinity - and what a string of successes he was about to put Wakefield's way.

The lethal left leg of Neil Fox has become rugby lore. I once described him as the Don Bradman of Rugby League. He was! His scoring feats have been remarkable - not only in the number of points he has scored but the consistency with which he got them. One statistician showed me figures where Fox had a much higher average of goal-kicking successes than any other international footballer with a 70-per cent accuracy. That's some kicking!

Fox started to collect scoring records in 1957/58. That one season, at the tender age of nineteen, he had scored MOST goals in a season with 124, MOST points, 344, MOST points in a match 31. And this was only the start! A season later he broke is own records, scoring 370 points - including 146 goals - and added a new one by scoring in every match in which he played. He made forty club appearances, one for Yorkshire and one for Great Britain.

Fox could not be stopped as he gathered manhood, and in season 1959/60 he had a total of 453 points for 46 appearances with 171 goals and 37 tries. His own club record was beaten in the process, and he played in six representative games. He never missed scoring except in one match, the Northern R.L. final at Odsal and ended a run of 95 first class games in which he scored.

Wakefield are one of the clubs who have enthusiastic statisticians and whose records leave nothing to chance. Those Trinity scoring charts show that Neil Fox passed his 4,000 point mark in 1968 at the age of twenty-nine. There were ten glorious years for Wakefield Trinity from 1958 to 1968. It is more than coincidence that these were also the great years of Neil Fox.

The Great Ones

Wakefield had never appeared in a Championship final from the year the competition started in 1901 until season 1959/60. From then they appeared in four finals, winning two Championships, with Neil Fox being the only player to appear in all four finals.

Possibly the most disappointing of all the finals in which he appeared was the Championship final at Odsal Stadium, Bradford, on May 18, 1962. Wakefield were bidding for the tremendous 'all-four' Cup wins. They had beaten Huddersfield, their championship final opponents at Wembley the previous week, by 12 points to 6 points and Trinity were definitely the favourites that day at Bradford. The feat of winning all four cups had not been achieved since 1928.

The chairman of Wakefield was Stuart Hadfield, who had been given permission to delay his departure as manager of the Australian touring party. Mr Hadfield dearly wanted to be at Odsal to see his team follow up their Wembley success with a Championship win.

Conditions were difficult for the Championship final, with plenty of rain swirling around the big Odsal bowl. Despite winning the toss and playing with the wind, Wakefield made mistakes and were down at half-time by 7 points to 5 points. They never recovered. Huddersfield went on to score more second-half points ... and Wakefield's 'four cups' dream was shattered.

I travelled to Australia with the Wakefield players Gerry Round, Neil Fox, Harold Poynton, Jack Wilkinson and Derek Turner and the solitary Huddersfield tourist Ken Noble. Noble didn't let the Trinity lads forget who were the champions. Neil Fox, I might add, scored all the five Wakefield points in that Championship final. This was the second Championship defeat for they had lost to Wigan at Odsal by 27 points in 1960.

Wakefield's ill luck in the Championship finals changed

in 1967 and 1968 when they won the big silver trophy. Before the Neil Fox era Wakefield had won the most coveted of all Rugby League trophies - the Challenge Cup - only twice - in 1909 and 1946. The first against Hull and the second against Wigan. 1960 was Royal Wembley. The Queen was in the Royal Box to present the players with their medals. It was also a right royal Wembley for Neil Fox and his merry men. The score of Wakefield 38 points, Hull 5 points, was a Wembley record. Fox had a personal tally of 20 points with a record number of seven goals.

Neil started the Wembley scoring record with a penalty goal after two minutes and finished it in the 79th minute when he converted Keith Holliday's try. Neil Fox earned his title of 'Prince of Points' that day!

Two years later Wakefield were back at Wembley and Fox had another honour in that win against Huddersfield. This time he was awarded the Lance Todd trophy for the best player. He scored a try and kicked three goals. And the remarkable thing was that they were all 'dropped' goals.

In the pre fourth-tackle rule days dropped goals were unusual but this was a deliberate Trinity plan to stop Huddersfield. A year later Wakefield were back at Wembley - glorious years indeed for Trinity.

This time Wigan were their stiff Lancashire opposition. Neil Fox was in his usual goal-kicking form and kept up his good average with ten points from five goals. For the third time 'Rocky' Turner carried the Cup high from Wembley after a match which Wakefield won by 25 points to 10 points.

Neil Fox was a big match player. He became known as the 'Big Fella'. This was not only due to the extra poundage he had added to his early thirteen-stone Rugby frame. In every sense he was a big man for the occasion.

He began his Test career for Great Britain when he played against the Australians at Headingley, Leeds, in 1959.

The Great Ones

His Test appearances were not as many as they might have been. Injury started to plague him later in his career and he had a particularly bad year in 1968. He was unable to play for Wakefield in the memorable Cup Final where Wembley looked like an aquatic show and he had to withdraw from the World Cup squad.

Neil Fox rarely showed his feelings. He was not emotional. The possible exception was that 1968 Wembley 'water' final when his brother Don, who had moved from Featherstone to Wakefield, missed a last minute goal-kick under the posts that would have not only given Wakefield the Cup, but also the elusive Cup and League double. Neil Fox was heartbroken. But nowhere near as distressed as the Trinity fans when they heard Wakefield had place him on the transfer list six months later. For them it was the end of an era. The Neil Fox era.

Grand National day March 29th 1969 brought Neil Fox back into the R.L. picture with a vengeance. Although turf accountant Fox had an interest in the winner of the National his mind that afternoon was on another sporting subject, that of the Challenge Cup semi-final at Headingley Leeds. Wakefield Trinity were playing Castleford and Fox back in favour with the club was not only back in the side but was captain of the team.

Five minutes from time Wakefield were just 300 seconds away from Wembley and the life ambition of Neil Fox to lead his team on the Empire Stadium. In that five minutes his dream was shattered. Mike Redfearn kicked a sensational goal for Castleford to wipe out the one point lead held by Trinity and when Hardisty scored a try bang on time it was Castleford who were given the right to represent Yorkshire against Salford for Lancashire. The semi-final was the 500th game of R.L. in which Fox had played. He scored four points to bring his total to 4,156, the remarkable average of over 8 points a match in his illustrious career.

Neil Fox & Ernest Ward

Neil Fox was in a different mould both physically and in his style of play to two other international centres who wore the red, white and blue jersey of the Great Britain team a decade before Fox was on the Rugby League scene.

I refer to the two Ernies - Ward and Ashcroft. Both classical centres, Ashcroft was with Wigan and Ward with Bradford Northern. Because Ernest Ward was a tour captain I shall concentrate on him, but this does not in any way diminish my regard for Ashcroft who was not only a fine footballer but a fine fellow with whom I spent many pleasant hours en route and in Australia when I was choir master to the team's choir. And there were none better than the Wigan mob when it came to choir practice and fun.

Ernest Ward was a boy prodigy. His father - also called Ernest - played one game for England and was trainer for a spell at Crown Flatt, Dewsbury. Young Ernest at fourteen years was a tall schoolboy with a classic style of playing Rugby League. He played with a team called the Dewsbury Boys later to become famous as the 'Black Knights'. It seemed obvious that on his sixteenth birthday Ernest Ward would sign for Dewsbury. His father left the Dewsbury club and, to the great disappointment of the club, young Ernest signed professional forms, not at Crown Flatt but at Odsal for Bradford. His fee was a mere £150. It was the start of a remarkable career for Ernest Ward.

He was six foot, lean with a straight back, and a brilliant tactician. Whether he could have achieved the same sort of fame at Dewsbury as he achieved at Bradford would be mere speculation. His twelve Test match appearances against Australia would certainly have been many more but for the intervention of the Second World War. By the same token, Ward would not have played in as many big war-time Service matches as he did.

The Great Ones

It would be easy at this point of the Ward story to ask who was the player who captained teams at Wembley four times in three years. It would not be an easy trick question to answer by even the most rabid of Rugby League fans. The answer obviously is Ernest Ward but how did he do this? His three years as captain were with Bradford Northern, who beat Leeds 8 points to 4 points in 1947, then lost to Wigan 8 points to 3 points in 1948 and for the hat-trick beat Halifax 12 points to nil in 1949. That accounts for three. The fourth appearance at Wembley was Ernest Ward's leadership of Great Britain against France in March 1949.

Ernest Ward had two tours to Australia - the first with Gus Risman's 'Indomitables' in 1946, when he played at full-back, and as captain of the 1950 touring team which sailed on the *SS Himalaya*.

A captain's duties with a Rugby League touring side are pretty hard and I feel on the 1950 tour Ernest suffered with many extra responsibilities and found the speech part onerous. The off-stage duties have affected other captains in other sports in Australia and I gather that Sir Len Hutton found problems in his tour leadership for the MCC.

The 1946 tour brought many honours to Ward and the team and it was a happy and successful tour. I suppose being the first of my six tours I found it most enjoyable. Ernest Ward revelled on the hard Australian grounds, with his specialised kicking and fine football. In a match in Mackay in New South Wales which Great Britain won by 94 points to nil, Ward kicked 17 goals.

The hard ground on the Sydney cricket ground in 1946 - with the bulli soil which makes a quick recovery from football to cricket in one week - had a different look on Ward's second tour in 1950.

If anyone ever tells you the sun always shines in Australia just say 'July 2nd 1950'! That was the date when the Sydney cricket ground was the biggest morass of mud I have ever seen - and that includes some of the worst that Bradford's Odsal produced at one period.

The significance about the July date of 1950 was the fact that the vital third Test was being staged between Great Britain and Australia. Great Britain had won the first Test on the Sydney cricket ground by 6 points to 4 points on a ground of mud. The Brisbane second Test was lost, a match in which Ken Gee and Tommy Bradshaw were sent off for 'talking', and this July 2nd date was for 'winner take all'. The British players and manager did not want to play. After a week of incessant rain the ground was truly horrible.

Australian officials had their problems, too, for the British party were due to take a boat to New Zealand soon after the Test and it was not possible to return to Australia after the New Zealand part of the tour. After hard words and objections the match was declared on and Australia won it by the only try of the match 5 points to 2 points. The British players were not in a happy mood and although they had a far superior side to Australia they lot the Ashes.

The hero of Australia was the try-scoring winger Ron Roberts, who had the overlap in a move in which the English centres for once did not position themselves right. Providing Roberts took the pass he would score, he took the pass alright and with it the Ashes. The Australian fanatics in the crowd scooped up handfuls of bulli mud from the Sydney cricket ground. For a long time I kept a piece given to me - it was as hard as a cricket ball.

When Trevor Allan, the Australian Rugby Union player, signed for Leigh he complained about the cold English weather. I reminded him of the conditions on the 1950 tour. His answer to me was 'There is one vital difference, the English mud is cold and the Australian mud is warm'. He had a point, however, but this was nullified by the fact that the Australian mud, due to the bulli soil, had a shocking smell which almost suffocated the players when they were tackled and had their noses pushed into it. The British players had a lot to say about the odour from the muddy Sydney cricket ground!

There was some compensation for Ward when he played in all three Tests against Australia in the next series in England in 1952 when Britain won back the Ashes.

Just about the best-ever New Zealand team to tour England was the 1947 party, led by captain Pat Smith. They were unlucky to find Ernest Ward at his brilliant best in the deciding Test at Odsal before a record gate of 45,000. In addition to kicking four goals, Ward was the master of the match with cool poised rugby. The 'Kiwis' had been great tourists with only a one point defeat in the first Test at Leeds and a good 10 points to 7 points win in the second Test at Swinton.

Ernest Ward was partnered in the centre by Ernest Ashcroft, but had fine opponents in the New Zealand centre pair, Morrie Robertson and Ron McGregor. The New Zealand pack was possibly the best ever to wear the black and white jersey with the Kiwi badge. They are worth recording here: Pat Smith, Bob Aynsley, J. Johnson, Jack Newton, Charlie McBride, and Ken Mountford. A great pack and some fine fellows including the rugged Newton. A former Rugby Union 'All Black' Jim Haig was at scrum-half with good goal kicker Warwick Clarke at full-back and Len Jordon and 'Nippy' Forest on the wings.

After his triumphs with Great Britain and Bradford Ernest Ward ended seventeen years at Odsal when he was transferred to Castleford for £2,500 in season 1953/54. Three years later he had trials with Batley, but as the Mount Pleasant club wanted to pay his transfer fee of £500 in instalments the deal fell through and Ward finished his remarkable career in most unusual circumstances just two miles from where it all started twenty years earlier.

For the record, Ernest's brothers, Donald and Stanley, played professional football - Donald at Bradford very successfully in Northern's post war cup successes as a scrum-half and Stanley with Dewsbury.

Ernest's son Trevor played Rugby Union and later joined Dewsbury as a professional.

9

Jim Sullivan

South Wales has always been a happy hunting ground for Rugby League clubs. Long before the breakaway of 1895, players came from South Wales to work and play with Northern teams. I don't know who was the first to arrive, but certainly amongst the early 'immigrants' were the James brothers from Swansea who played with Broughton Rangers in Manchester.

Batley, who won the first two Challenge Cup finals in 1897 and 1898, brought stalwarts from South Wales in Wattie Davies and Dai Fitzgerald. Their near neighbours, Dewsbury, had Bill Stadden playing in their Rugby Union side, and I believe it was Stadden who scored the only try when Wales beat England for the first time in a Rugby Union International at Crown Flatt before Dewsbury, like others, joined the Northern Union.

The list of Welshmen joining Rugby League is a long one. Wigan must be well up in the list in numbers of the Welsh signings. They certainly had the greatest Welshman ever to be signed. The name: Jim Sullivan, full-back supreme, who to this day holds the all-time record of the greatest number of points any one player has scored in Rugby League football. His total number of points, in a career which lasted from 1921 until 1945, was 6,206 points, 2,959 goals and 96 tries.

Records flowed from Sullivan with his accurate right foot. In season 1922 he kicked 172 goals beating the record of Huddersfield's Welsh kicker, Ben Gronow. On Sullivan's first tour in 1924 he shattered previous tour records when he kicked 84 goals. On the 1932 tour - his third - he scored 223 points. What a phenomena. From his first season in 1921/22, he hit a century of goals every year for nineteen successive seasons until the outbreak of war in 1939.

Jim Sullivan, son of a Cardiff butcher, was born on December 2nd, 1903. He was sixteen years of age when he played for Cardiff Rugby Union first team after only half a dozen reserve team games. The South Wales Rugby League scouts soon spotted the potential of this tall, upright full-back. At eighteen he was on Wigan's professional register and played his first game at Central Park on August 27th, 1921, kicking five goals against Widnes. Some start!

With computer-like precision Sullivan continued throughout his great career to kick goals from all angles. He was human, of course. He missed them too. One of his misses, I remember, when he played for a team I managed, was in front of the posts.

Jim loved to score tries as well. Many of them were scored on the short side of the scrum. It was his own created move and his strength - he was a big fellow - was sufficient to take him past a winger or, if necessary, draw the opposing winger and give it to his own winger to score.

The whole chapter on Sullivan could be devoted to his amazing goal-kicking prowess. In 1925, for instance, he kicked 22 goals for Wigan in a Rugby League Cup-tie against Flimby and Fothergill, a junior side from Cumberland. For twenty-four years he held the season's goal record of 204 goals until it was beaten by Bernard Ganley in 1957/58.

Sullivan was unique in everything he did. He loved to play rugby and when on tour he was reluctant to be rested - which gave the managers a headache. He made three tours to Australia - in 1924, 1928 and 1936 - and would have made a fourth as captain but refused the invitation because of family illness.

He was a great favourite in Australia with his ponderous kicking. The story is told of him playing at Sydney before a packed crowd when a roar went up in the first minute. One fan who couldn't see what was happening asked what was going on. 'Sullivan's kicked a goal from the half-way line' was the reply. 'Oh, I thought he must have missed one with that cheer' said the small spectator.

In Anglo-Australian Test matches, Jim Sullivan still holds the record with fifteen Tests starting with his first in Sydney in 1924 and ending in 1933 at Swinton. He was dropped just once - in 1929 for the first Test at Hull against Tom Gorman's Kangaroos. England, as the team was then known, were thrashed by 31 points to 8 points. Sullivan was soon restored!

Statistics can be meaningless. But not the sort that Sullivan turned out, particularly in the big matches ... and the biggest matches in Rugby League are Test games against Australia. 'Big Jim' played in five Test series against the Aussies. He was usually on the winning side in the series, with eleven matches won, one drawn and three lost, and three of these successful series were in Australia. In only three games out of the fifteen he played did he fail to kick a goal. His total of goal successes was 31 which still stands supreme amongst his many records. His consistency is remarkable, for his scoring chart shows 7 goals in the 1924 series followed with 8 ... 3 ... 4 ... and finishing with 9 in the 1933 series including five in his last Test.

That was not the end of Sullivan's by any means - although he did not play again against the Australians. He continued, season by season, to kick his century of goals, and he was on the forty years mark before he started to think about packing up the game.

Wigan thought he had reached the end of his career, and I stepped in as manager of Dewsbury and got the loan of Peerless Jim. Within a few months he was in the Dewsbury side which reached the Yorkshire County Final. And he continued to play in many memorable games for Dewsbury during their many successes.

Wigan suddenly realised his worth again and recalled him to Central Park to play in the cherry and white jersey.

He had worn that jersey with great distinction for a long time. He led Wigan out in the first-ever Wembley Challenge Cup Final in 1929 and was the victorious captain against Dewsbury. These were the years when Wigan were known as the 'League of Nations' team. They had New Zealand players, like Len Mason and Lou Brown, and South Africans, like Van Heerdon and Van Rooyen, who found their way to Central Park in addition to the many Welsh players who went to Wigan.

The indestructible Sullivan continued on - and truly earned the title of the immortal. He was a perfectionist in fitness, a powerful kicker, a good tackler and brilliant fielder of the ball. He was always in the news, but stayed with Wigan until he played in the red amber and black jersey at Crown Flatt. I certainly learned a lot as a young manager with Sullivan as leader of the team. His tactics changed with every game to suit the occasion and the opposition.

Gus Risman tells the story of how a Salford move was

born out of a Sullivan creation in a Wales v France match at Llanelly in 1935. Sullivan was up to his favourite trick of going down the blind side, shouting for the ball, and sending his wing man in for tries. The Welsh scrum-half, Billie Watkins, was being put off his game by the 'Sully' shout and he asked Risman what to do.

'Give him the dummy next time and send the ball to your midfield backs.' This happened and, with the defence drawn to Sullivan, another try was scored on the other side of the field by Wales. It was a move which Risman adopted for Salford's benefit thereafter. Gus Risman, himself no mean performer at full-back, like all others regarded Sullivan as the king pin of full-backs.

After his playing days, Sullivan had successes as a coach at Wigan, and in taking St Helens to Wembley, having much to do with the development of Alex Murphy.

The six-foot two-inch frame of Sullivan put on a lot of weight after his playing days when he weighed fourteen stone. He later joined Rochdale Hornets as coach returned to Wigan and then had a serious illness.

He life was in danger for a long time, but with that resilience and determination which had characterised everything about him throughout his playing days, he steadily pulled round. His coaching days were over, of course, but one Saturday afternoon many months later he was brought down to Central Park to see a 'seven-a-side' match. The match was being televised and another Welshman, Cliff Morgan, then editor of BBC *Grandstand* saw the figure of Jim Sullivan walking slowly to meet the winning captain. Millions of TV viewers saw 'Sully' again - and no doubt many memories were recaptured, incidents of Sullivan's great moments.

How would he have fared under the present day rules I'm often asked? He was such a great player - he would have found a way to be the success he always was.

10

Tom van Vollenhoven & Eric Harris

It is said that during a bible lesson at a St Helens Sunday school a class of children were asked to name their favourite Saint. To the astonishment of the teacher one bright-eyed youngster immediately jumped up and said 'Alf Ellaby, Miss'. Such was the impact of Rugby League players in the West Lancashire town that some school-children knew the names of the St Helens Rugby League team better than the Christian saints!

No doubt other names of footballers have been given in answer at bible classes, and I imagine in recent years the name of Tom Vollenhoven was very much the answer from time to time. Before writing about the greatness of Karen Tom Van Vollenhoven, the St Helens winger, who came from South Africa, I should write about the Saint named those many years ago - Alfred Ellaby. A name equally as well-known in Australia as in England, and still remembered when great wingers are written and talked about.

Alf Ellaby was a soccer player who showed great promise of making a career with the round ball in the

The Great Ones

Liverpool area. A tall, well-built footballer, with a diffident style which at times might have been mistaken for dourness.

He joined St Helens at a time when he had leg trouble - a nerve complaint which was cured by a very capable trainer called Ted Forber. The season was 1925/26 and right wing-threequarter Ellaby made his debut in the St Helens jersey against Keighley in March 1926. An easy win resulted, and before the season was out the dark-haired, quiet-spoken but expressive Ellaby had scored nine tries ... a start to his career which eventually reached the massive total of 487 tries, including 40 tries on two Australian tours. His best season was his second in 1926/27, when he scored 55 tries - a record which stayed until Vollenhoven appeared on the right-wing at Knowsley Road ground some thirty years later.

Ellaby played in the great days of St Helens when stars like Leslie Fairclough, George Lewis, Ben Halfpenny, Billy Mercer and Alf Frodsham were in the team. It was also a time when St Helens had two teams. The other team was St Helens Recreation, and some of the clashes between the two teams, I'm told, were something which have never since been seen between any two clubs. St Helens Recs disbanded in the late thirties.

In 1926/27, a great Rugby League season in the town, it was St Helens Recs who reached the final of the championship, losing against Swinton and en route having beaten St Helens by 33 points to nil. What a night out that must have caused in the town, for St Helens Recs had characters, both on and off the field, with one player having protection from his mother ably assisted by an umbrella when required!

Alf Ellaby was soon a star in the code, and two years later, in 1928, was on the boat to Australia with the fifth touring party - a team which won the Ashes, helped by tries by Ellaby in the first two Tests. Four years later, Ellaby was again the first choice winger in the Test which helped

England to win by 8 points to 6 points. He played in all three Tests when the Ashes were won. Alf Ellaby played in 9 Test matches against Australia, his last being in 1933 at Belle Vue, Manchester when England won by 4 points to nil, through two goals by Jim Sullivan.

Between the two tours, however, there was a match which brought Ellaby's biggest disappointment of his career. St Helens reached the final of the Challenge Cup in 1931 against local Lancastrian rivals Widnes. The star-studded Saints had a collection of great names and players that are worth recalling: Crooks, Ellaby, Mercer, Lewis, Hardgrave, Fairclough and Groves; Hutt, Clarey, Houghton, Hall, Halfpenny and Harrison. A wealth of talent - with three New Zealand players in Hardgrave, Hutt, and Hall. Their opposition were twelve local lads from Widnes and a South African, big Van Rooyen, a second row forward.

The match looked a walkover for the Saints. It was just a matter of how many points they would score said the critics. It did not turn out that way, and in the most sensational of all Cup Finals Widnes won 10 points to 3 points. Alf Ellaby made the only try scored by Houghton for St Helens, who were shattered by the defeat.

Some time ago I received a letter from Mrs Mercer, wife of the St Helens captain of 1931, who told me of her trip with other players' wives to the final. They left St Helens in a motor coach on the Saturday morning, had a breakdown en route and arrived at the Stadium to hear the final whistle sounded. By the time they got inside the Stadium, the players had gone to the dressing-room! 'I never even saw my Billy on the field' said Mrs Mercer. It was a day without glory for the Saints.

Alf Ellaby never had any other chance to win a Cup Final medal. He was unlucky where Cup medals were concerned, for when the Saints won the League Championship Cup against Huddersfield in 1932 Alf Ellaby was on his way to

Australia. He had, however, done his share in the team reaching the final with 33 tries for the club. They added to the 20 he scored during the summer Down Under.

Alf Ellaby finished his career at Wigan, being transferred to Central Park from St Helens. He became mine host of a public house in Blackpool, where he spent many years before taking up residence in Yorkshire. He later joined the Castleford Board, and was often out-spoken on Rugby League matters - particularly about the roughness which had crept into the game.

He left the Castleford Club but continued to attend matches - although he now winters abroad in search of the sun. Few modern wingers score tries in the Ellaby style. He was fast, with a body swerve which had a variation of pace and stride. Hat-tricks were commonplace to him, and once he scored six tries in a match. He was the supreme winger - and sole star of the St Helens right wing until Tom Vollenhoven appeared on the scene.

Unlike Ellaby, 'Tommy Voll', as Alan Prescott always called him, came with a great reputation from South Africa Rugby Union. He was a 'Springbok', playing in all five Tests against the 1955 British Rugby Union 'Lions'. He toured Australia and New Zealand besides winning other Rugby Union caps. He was later persuaded to sign for St Helens, in 1957. He cost the club £4,000 but never was that amount of money better spent for a Rugby Union player. After one season, or part of one - when he scored 40 tries - he beat the all-time record of Alf Ellaby by scoring 62 tries. He got close to the Ellaby total try record by scoring around 400 tries in eleven illustrious seasons.

He became an idol of the Saints followers who will for ever say: 'There will never be another Van.' In October, 1957, he was thrown in at the deep-end in his first game against Leeds at Knowsley Road. He gave a try away, but a minute from time scored one - and the critics were satisfied. His coach the shrewd Jim Sullivan said: 'We have seen nothing yet, he'll be a sensation.' 'Sully' was right. Vollenhoven became a Rugby League star almost overnight.

He arrived at St Helens a year after the Saints had beaten Halifax at Wembley, but he was at Wembley himself three years later - in the 1961 final, which has many references in his book. It was the 'Vollenhoven try' final, scored on the Royal box side started by Dick Huddart, helped by Ken Large and finished in most glorious style by the 'Van' himself. This try - to most people - will probably go down as his greatest. The occasion was right, so was the setting, and so was the timing of the try which enabled St Helens to beat their fiercest rivals Wigan.

To me, however, the greatest Vollenhoven try was scored at Odsal Stadium, Bradford, in the 1959 Championship final - a final which had everything, including sixty-six points scored with magnificent football by both St Helens and Hunslet. St Helens finished with 44 points to Hunslet's 22 points, but it was a tremendous match.

Hunslet were on top for the early part, until they were shattered by the sheer brilliance of Vollenhoven. The Yorkshiremen had set up an early attack and kept hammering away at the St Helens line. They looked good and confident until a rather wild pass was given on the St Helens twenty-five yards line on the old stand side at Odsal. Before Hunslet could say 'St Helens', Vollenhoven and snapped up the ball - like a dog after a ball - and set off down the touchline side. It did not look dangerous, there was such a long way to go and Hunslet cover defenders, were in position. However, Vollenhoven kept going ... and at the half-way line Hunslet players realised there were danger signs.

With a concentrated effort three players descended on him to cut him off and attempt to knock him into touch. He

skated along the touch line and one defender got near him -
a hand-off from Vollenhoven settled that - and with all the
Saints fans yelling their heads off Vollenhoven reached the
line. He went as far as he could towards the posts - about 25
yards - where he grounded the ball for a most remarkable
try. It was superb football, with Vollenhoven at his very best.

There were glorious years for St Helens around this time.
Seven Lancashire County Cup appearances on the trot from
1958 to 1964 with five winners in succession. Lancashire
league title winners for four successive seasons - and
another Cup Final win at Wembley in 1966.

Vollenhoven was from Pretoria, and was an ex-
policeman. He had varied jobs at St Helens - including
working in a record shop. That was understandable, with
the records he achieved at St Helens! He was the best South
African to come into Rugby League. Many came ... only a
few succeeded. St Helens had another success, although not
as good as Vollenhoven, in Jan Prinsloo.

Wigan signed full-back Fred Griffiths, who kicked 702
goals and scored around 50 tries before going to play in
Australia. Wilf Rosenberg was, in my view, the best Leeds
signed - and they had quite a few South Africans.

Alan Skene, Oupa Coetzer and Colin Greenwood
succeeded at Wakefield, where a player like Ivor Dorrington
did not. Even the star 'Springbok' scrum-half, Tommy
Gentles did not make the grade at Wigan, where Trevor Lake
from Rhodesia was the leading try scorer in two successive
seasons. There were far more failures than successes from
South Africa and this makes the tremendous success of
Vollenhoven all the more remarkable.

He won every honour the game could offer, but he had
his disappointments too. Hull Kingston Rovers stopped St
Helens, led by Vollenhoven, from reaching the
Championship final in 1968. He badly wanted that win to

finish off his career. He played his last match at Knowsley Road on April 25th, 1968, when a 16,000 crowd saw him receive the 'Player' award against Warrington.

He received a testimonial cheque for £2,800 from St Helens for 'services rendered'. He then returned to his native South Africa, but I am sure he will not forget his days in West Lancashire - where he won the hearts of the football fans.

Eric Harris was known as 'The Toowoomba Ghost'. A live ghost, too, which haunted R.L. players for nine years and provided Leeds fans with thrills galore.

The Toowoomba Ghost was the title given to Eric Harris, a 6ft 2in Australian, who was the idol of Headingley from 1930 to 1939. A time of success for Leeds, a time when Eric Harris averaged a try a game covering the amazing spell of 391 tries in 383 games in the Leeds jersey.

Eric was given his ghost description for two reasons. The Toowoomba part was his birthplace in Queensland, Australia, where he came from to Leeds; the ghost part was the phantom way which he ran and deceived opponents who looked certain to tackle him.

Such was the case in the Challenge Cup Final in 1932 - when the normal Wembley venue was changed to Central Park, Wigan, because the Stadium was not available on the date desired - April 9th. Leeds met Swinton and it was one of the famous ghost-like tries by Harris which enabled Leeds to win the Challenge Cup.

Joe Thompson, the forward who kicked a record 826 goals for Leeds, never had four more important successes than he had that Saturday afternoon. He had to contend with four goals from the mighty boot of Martin Hodgson of Swinton, and then it was left to Eric Harris to score the only try of the match. It was in a lucky thirteenth minute of the second half that Harris got the chance he wanted.

The Great Ones

In a joint all-Australian move, with Jeff Moores and Frank O'Rourke taking part, Harris received a pass at the right moment. He slipped past the Swinton left-winger Kenny, and then had almost half the field in front of him and eventually Swinton full-back Scott to face. With his cool calculated approach, Harris stayed on the wing. He had to - because of the covering defenders. As he neared Scott, the chance looked completely closed with Scott ready to bundle Harris into touch.

Within inches away from the touchline, Harris approached Scott and then, with an amazing acceleration of speed, he was past the Swinton full-back and on his way for his try. The ghost was through - and not for the first time in that competition. In the semi-final against Halifax the same thing had happened with full-back Davies at Wakefield, when Harris slipped by almost unnoticed.

This was the sort of run which the Headingley fans had to cheer about from the season he joined the club in 1930 until wartime football in 1939. No player ever had a better entry into English football than Harris.

He was brought to this country by fellow Australian Jeff Moores, who was then captain of Leeds. Leeds had opened the season in a disastrous fashion - four defeats in six games - when Harris arrived to play his first game against Featherstone Rovers on September 27th, 1930. What a transformation scene it was too. Harris started on a run of seventeen league matches without defeat - and a bagful of tries. Two against Featherstone, two the following week, three against St Helens, five against Keighley, four more hat-tricks ... and in his first ten matches Harris had scored 29 tries. That first season brought a total of 58 tries and a Yorkshire Cup winners medal. What a start to a magical nine seasons.

Toowoomba is a beautiful city in the Darling Downs of Queensland. It produced many great footballers, like

Duncan Thompson and 'Nigger' Brown, but never one so acceptable to Leeds and English football as Eric Harris.

Tall, lean, graceful, he ran with ease and had the power of acceleration which brought him so many tries. He headed the try-scoring list at Leeds in every season he played for them. He also kicked 16 goals. After three seasons in Yorkshire, Harris returned home to Australia, but on October 21st, 1933, he was back in the Leeds blue and amber jersey. Despite missing eight opening games, he was immediately back on the scoring beat on the right wing, and ended the season as usual at the top of the scoring chart.

1936 was the Leeds year in the Challenge Cup; it was also a record year for Harris, who established a new try scoring record with 63 tries. In one spell of seventeen successive matches he scored in every match for a total of 36 tries.

Leeds beat Warrington, at Wembley, in a match which brought much controversy - with Harris in the story. Warrington were the first to attack, but seven minutes after the start Eric Harris got his awaited pass and opening. The Leeds crowd were on their toes, expecting Harris to streak away on the sunny Wembley turf. To the astonishment of the 51,000 crowd Harris suddenly stopped in his tracks - and kicked towards the centre of the field. Warrington were totally unaware of this planned move and Leeds loose forward Ike Isaac ran straight up the middle, took the ball a few yards from the Warrington line, and scored a try.

Leeds fans were delighted; Warrington fans and players furious, for they claimed - and I might add still do, that Isaac was offside. Did Eric Harris continue running to put his loose forward onside? Leeds say 'yes', Warrington fans say 'no'. This was in the days before television so there was no chance of the marvellous instant replay TV to settle arguments.

Referee Albert Dobson never had any doubts and this try

- to which Evan Williams kicked the goal - gave Leeds a lead they never lost, eventually running out winners by 18 points to 2 points. One remarkable feature of this match was the scrummages.

In all, there were 64 scrums - of which Warrington won 46 scrums, yet they could not score a try. Eric Harris scored in this final so did his namesake Fred Harris (no relation), a centre from Leigh. The Harris combination on the right flank was truly successful at Headingley. They had a perfect understanding, and Fred scored many tries with scissors dummy which they worked brilliantly. Fred scored 71 tries for Leeds - and he made many for Eric.

Each season brought some success for Eric Harris - another Yorkshire Cup winners medal in 1937/38 and Championship medal and a losers. This was the Championship final played at Elland Road. Leeds were never to win that elusive Championship cup until the Lewis Jones days of 1961.

Harris and Leeds expected another Wembley appearance in 1939, but Halifax stopped their gallop at Odsal Stadium. A try by Arthur Basset for Halifax after seven minutes brought arguments and defeat for Leeds. This was Harris's last chance for an appearance at Wembley. By the start of the next season war clouds were looming.

Eric Harris scored one try on September 2nd - the day before the outbreak of war. It was against Bramley, and Leeds won by 36 points to 4 points. This was the last Leeds fans were to see of the famous Toowoomba Ghost. He returned home to Queensland, but did not play much football there. He had lost the ghost-like qualities of acceleration, and he soon retired from the game.

When he made a visit to England thirty years after his successes he was given a warm reception, and is still a loved figure by the older Headingley supporters.

11

Mick Sullivan & Allan Edwards

All those headlines of football violence bring quite a smile to me. Not that I agree with it. Far from it. But I often wonder if those who dramatise these sad occasions have ever witnessed real sporting violence.

For crazy crowd reaction there is nothing in my book to touch the explosive Aussies who inhabit the Sydney Hill end of the Sydney Cricket Ground. What a turbulent performance those boys can put up. It's enough to terrify the bravest of the brave. But one guy they could not scare was Mick Sullivan, without a doubt the greatest post-war left-wing-threequarter in the game. It was 'Sully' who scared them!

I well remember him on his second tour of Australia in 1958 - and did he enjoy himself! The tour was packed with incidents which crescendoed to the third and deciding Test at Sydney. There was enough atmosphere to generate a power station as Britain lined-up to face Australia. The referee was a Queensland man, Mr Casey, and he upset the

The Great Ones

Aussie supporters to such an extent, that they bombarded him - and the British players - with oranges, apples, bottles, the lot. The man who enjoyed it all was Mick Sullivan. It was his try which sparked off the bombardment. It all started like this.

Australian winger Ian Moir had the crowd yelling on their toes with some strong running on the left-wing. He had one run which looked like being a try when he was obstructed. The obstruction did not completely stop his progress and referee Casey allowed him to go on, no doubt expecting him to score and therefore take advantage. But it didn't happen like that. Moir failed to take the bouncing ball, and the advantage went to Great Britain. From their own line British players started a movement which ended in Sullivan going right down the left wing to score a peach of a try. A great try and a vital one.

When Sullivan returned to the Sydney Hill end of the ground all hell broke loose. The bottle, orange and apple bombardment started in full force. Then 'Sully' struck.

Cooly, calmly, cheekily, he picked up an orange. And as the missiles whizzed about him he peeled it - then ate it! The crowd went mad. But 'Sully' hadn't finished yet. He then picked up a bottle, took off the top, and drank the contents. Every single drop. The crowd roared and roared to the end of the match. 'Sully' didn't worry. Neither did his team-mates. Britain won by 40 points to 17 points - and with it the Ashes. This was Sullivan at his best. And he collected 38 tries in nineteen appearances on that tour.

It was Harold Wagstaff who said the true test of a player's standard was his ability to be successful against Australia in Test match football. On this reckoning Sullivan tops the table for he was a constant scourge to the Kangaroos.

No player holds the record in international post-war

football as Sullivan does. In 47 Test games against Australia, New Zealand and France he has scored 43 tries and not even the great Billy Boston comes within that record.

There have been two Sullivans in top class Rugby League, but completely unrelated. Mick had nothing like the physique of his namesake Jim, but he was a player of the same amazing physical capacity.

Mick Sullivan from Pudsey, a product of the famous Shaw Cross Dewsbury junior club, was never out of the news once he started his football career. He was a character who had been called almost every known name, good and bad, during his remarkable career. He argued with officialdom, he fell out with clubs and once told the top officials in the holy of holies on the Sydney cricket ground just what he thought of Australian referees and officials. He was booed on many grounds. Sent off others. When he couldn't get a clearance to join an Australian club, he joined a rebel Australian club at Wagga.

'Sully' was a bit of a rebel himself, but he was a courageous footballer who never played badly for his country and could quieten the toughest of opponents - particularly if wearing the feared Australian green and gold jersey.

Sullivan's career in big time football started in 1954, when he joined up with the Great Britain squad to play in the first ever World Cup series in France. Most of the British 1954 touring party to Australia had turned down an offer to play in the World Cup squad and it was a new party which went to France. It included the young Huddersfield winger, Mick Sullivan. Australia were the favourites for this competition, having taken on the Ashes three months earlier. The favourites soon toppled - and young Sullivan had much to do with it.

His courage and ferocity of play were soon evident. He

received a badly cut eye and was taken off the field. He was soon back and tearing into the big tough players.

'Sully' was the surprise packet of the team which won the massive trophy. From that moment, Sullivan was in the big time - and he made his presence felt. Sixteen matches against Australia with incidents abounding.

Sullivan was on the Wigan books when he went on the 1958 tour. He was on the St Helens books when he returned to Australia four years later to score 15 tries in nineteen matches.

In 1962 Sullivan was in another stormy third Test scene ... but this time with a different ending. Britain had won both the first two Tests and were set for a clean sweep. Sullivan, however, did not see this game out, at least not on the field. He was sent off. So was Derek Turner. Australia lost Dud Beattie, who got tangled with Turner - and they both received 'marching orders'. After this match, Sullivan was called into the Sydney cricket ground offices to answer the charges leading to his sending-off. He clashed verbally with Australia officials, and his future looked in jeopardy. But in true Sullivan style, he rose again and re-appeared on the Test scene - to play in the second Test at Swinton in 1963. But there was no glamour ending. The Kangaroos won, and with the win went the Ashes.

Sullivan was a big-time player. He was only slight. Weighed around 11 stone, but played to 14 stone; was 5ft 8ins, but stood six foot tall whenever he wore a football jersey. He had a sense of fun and cheek which he rarely lost. His flashes of toughness came suddenly, and he never flinched a tackle. His temperament could not make him a one-club man. He was always in big money deals when he moved.

He was with Huddersfield when he went to Australia with the second World Cup party in 1957, but a year later was playing for Wigan at Wembley and won his first

Wembley cup medal. Workington were Wigan's opponents and scored first, with a try by Ike Southward after a Brian Edgar break-through. But Wigan's back speed was too much. Sullivan scored a try, his fiftieth of the season, which put Wigan in the picture and on the way to victory.

Immediately after the sensational 1958 tour, Sullivan was back the following year at Wembley with Wigan, and in the scoring list against Hull. 1959 brought more Test honours for 'Sully' when he played in all three home Tests against the Kangaroos.

Sullivan's next Wembley appearance was in 1961, but he had changed jerseys again and played for St Helens against Wigan. Three visits to Wembley - and three winning medals - was not bad for Sullivan. That was his last appearance at Wembley, but he still had his greatest moments to come with the success of the 1962 tour.

After his forty-seventh Test game, Sullivan left the big scene and was attached to York and Dewsbury, before going to Australia to play club football. At the request of the Australian League, Sullivan was suspended for joining the rebel league club of Junee. This suspension was lifted - and the Dewsbury club spoke in his favour.

It was a pity that Sullivan's career finished as it did, but his tour colleagues and team-mates would always say that 'Sully' was a 100-per-cent plus player ... and he certainly enlightened the days of Rugby League when he was playing.

On the 'planes he loved to be the steward to his team-mates. He was serious on the field ... and fun off. Sullivan's big match record was remarkable. Three trips to Australia, two tours and a World Cup. He heads the list of Test try scorers against Australia, New Zealand and France with 43 tries from forty-seven appearances, eighteen tries more than his nearest rival Billy Boston. Sullivan was truly a remarkable footballer.

The Great Ones

There is a third Sullivan now on the international scene in Clive Sullivan, no relation to the other two, but like Jim, a Welshman. A coloured player, he was voted the best player on the 1968 World Championship tour and topped the try scoring list. He played for Hull - and is a fast wing-threequarter. He has been troubled by injuries which have affected his appearances on his return from Australia. In season 1965/66, he scored 23 tries and moved up to third place a year later with 31 tries.

If Clive Sullivan can do half what his two namesakes did on the international field we are all in for a very lively time.

Most of the big names of wing-threequarters have curiously been right-wingers. Certainly far more tries have been scored by the top six right flank men - like Boston, Vollenhoven, Bevan, Ellaby, Mills and Harris. Top class left-wing threequarter are more of a rarity.

I have written about overseas wingers, like Cooper and Markham, who were left-wing players, while Bradford signed a great left-wing-threequarter in Jack McLean from New Zealand. Our own home products on the left, over the many years of Rugby League, have been rather scarce compared to the right flank men.

One top class wing-threequarter, who was a real left-wing star was Alan Edwards, a Welshman from Aberavon, who joined Salford in 1935 and quickly made his mark in Rugby League. Clichés don't always fit the player. In the case of Alan Edwards most of them did. He did 'thunder' down the wing. He could side-step 'off a penny'. And he ran like a 'hare'. But none of these did full justice to the merit of this lean, pale-faced youngster from South Wales, who became a great favourite in the Salford heydays.

Alan Edwards scored many tries that are still talked about. He scored some brilliant ones when he played for Dewsbury.

Yet the one try he scored that people talk about was in the 1939 Championship final at Maine Road, Manchester.

Salford were playing Castleford - virtually at 'home' for Maine Road was only a few miles away from the Willows. Castleford had a really great side and they travelled over the Pennines, with a big following full of confidence. Salford had been at Wembley the previous week and had gone down unexpectedly to another Yorkshire side - Halifax. With ten minutes to go in the Championship final, Castleford were still full of confidence. They led by 6 points to 5 points. Star of the match, 'Juicy' Les Adams, who was later killed on war service, had created a try for Fred Brindle, the Castleford loose-forward, and centre-threequarter Jim Robinson had scored another try.

Salford had scored a try through stand-off Tom Kenny and Gus Risman had kicked the goal, but Castleford's one point lead was being held. And Castleford had the greatest tackler in the business in Jimmie Robinson, who once told me 'I love to tackle'.

As the minutes ticked by with the 70,000 spectators screaming their heads off, it looked as if Castleford might take their first ever Championship title. Then came the lithe, hungry-looking Edwards on the opposite side to the main stand at Maine Road. Swift passing reached his eager hands on the half-way line. He got round Bernard Cunniffe, and thundered, as only Edwards could do, to approach full-back George Lewis. With a most remarkable side-step off his left foot Edwards was away to score - and Salford were the Champions. It was a try that few could have scored and those who saw it would not easily forget it.

That was not the only Championship match Edwards played in. Three years later, while guesting for Dewsbury, he played centre-threequarter against Bradford Northern at Headingley and helped Dewsbury to a 13 points to nil win by dropping a tremendous goal from the half-way line on the North stand side towards the Kirkstall Lane end.

Edwards played many fine matches in the centre position for Dewsbury, and I recall him playing at York in that position and sending Sid Williams in for four tries with Williams on the left-wing. Williams had been signed by Salford, really to replace Barney Hudson on the right-wing, but he was never able to give Salford the service due to Army war service.

Curiously, Hudson, who might have been out of football at this time, continued to play whilst in the RAF and captained Dewsbury in many of their successes. Edwards thought a great deal of Hudson, and there were few better club pairs than Hudson from the North East and Edwards from South Wales. Edwards was an immediate success in Rugby League, and seven months after signing at Salford was on the boat to Australia with the 'Lions' touring party. He was the 'baby' of the team, but still managed to be the leading try scorer with 12 tries.

Edwards' last Test appearance against Australia was at Huddersfield in 1937, when a gate of 10,000 saw Britain defeated. Many people thought Edwards should have gone on the 1946 tour for by this time he had made a great come-back after a shoulder injury. So much so that Bradford Northern signed him for £700 from Salford. Edwards continued to score tries, and was in Bradford's Wembley side defeated by Wigan in 1948. He scored in this final and was back a year later, this time to receive a winner's medal when Halifax were beaten by 12 points to nil.

Alan had quite a Cup Final record. He played for Salford in two Cup Finals, one for Dewsbury, and two for Bradford - and collected a winner's reward with each club. Edwards was an exciting winger with over 300 tries to his credit. He played in many wartime internationals - and with the RAF service side. He was a professional from the day he joined Rugby League, and his spirit was tremendous.

The tenant of the English team jersey on the left-wing before the days of Edwards was Stanley Smith, a boy from Wakefield. Indeed, Smith and Edwards toured together on the 1936 trip to Australia and whereas Edwards scored 12 tries, Smith scored two tries.

Stanley Smith, scorer of 187 tries in 261 appearances for Leeds, was signed from Wakefield Trinity in season 1929/30 at a big fee. Smith had hit the newspaper headlines when he scored the only try for England in the fourth Test at Rochdale against the Australians. His centre partner that cold grey winter's day was another Stan, also in his first Test, destined to hit the headlines in many years to come. This was Stan Brogden, a Bradford junior who became a name in the rugby land.

Stanley Smith wore the English Test jersey until 1933, and the Leeds jersey until the outbreak of hostilities in 1939. Smith was unlucky in Cup-ties. Twice Leeds played in a Cup Final during his stay at the club, but he did not get a team place. In the Wembley final of 1936, the left-wing berth went to the other Stan, who had partnered him at Rochdale - 'Broggy' as Brogden was warmly regarded. In Smith's last year with Leeds in 1939, again Cup luck robbed him of the Wembley chance he so much wanted. In a controversial semi-final match at Odsal against Halifax, a try scored by Arthur Bassett from a kick by scrum-half Goodall was hotly disputed, Bassett being alleged to be offside, while later an inside pass from Stanley Smith to Denis Madden was ruled forward. It was Smith's last chance of a Cup Final medal for Halifax went on to Wembley and beat Salford.

A clean, polished player, Smith had 13 tries on the 1932 tour. Like many other former players he had a spell as coach, but later left the game completely.

12

Billy Boston & Brian Bevan

Billy Boston cried the day he quit Rugby League. All fifteen stone of him! And his were not the only tears at Central Park, Wigan, that night in April 1968 as 11,000 watched his farewell.

When Cardiff-born Billy burst into the game in 1954, 8,000 clicked through the turnstiles to see him play - in an 'A' team game. In fact, Billy Boston was a big name before he turned professional.

Three clubs felt certain he was booked for them. Hunslet, probably the first club really to chase Boston, were satisfied he would end up at Parkside. Workington Town, with Gus Risman as their manager, were equally sure he would sign for them. Boston spent many days in the Cumberland district - and they had no doubt he would settle with them.

The third club was Wigan - and they kept his signing secret for many months.

I recall going up to Catterick camp, where Boston was stationed with the Royal Corp of Signals, with the Hunslet

Chairman, Hector Rawson, where we talked to Boston. There was no hint that he had already signed for Wigan, and we expected him to join Hunslet.

I was somehow sure, however, that Boston had already signed for Wigan and the following day, at the Rugby League conference, in Scarborough, told Tom Hesketh, the Wigan Council member, that the chase was over.

However, the 'secret' was kept until Boston was able to play Rugby League football, which he did in 1954 - and continued playing until April 1968 when he left the game.

It was a period of great times for Wigan with Boston ever in the news. He was nineteen years of age when he played for Wigan, and a year later he was on his way to Australia and New Zealand with the Great Britain touring side.

He scored 36 tries on that tour to beat Tom Danby (ex-Harlequins and English Rugby Union) 1950 try record. I gave Boston a birthday party in New Zealand on his twentieth birthday, soon after the start of his international career. Before he left the international scene he had played thirty-three matches wearing the Great Britain jersey, including eleven Tests against Australia. He scored 25 tries - less than the Mike Sullivan's total.

Big, burly Boston attracted constant interest and attention by his crash tries and crash tackling.

He weighed 15 stone, more at times, and he used every ounce of his weight. Yet he was agile enough to side-step his way through the smallest space. He was not always popular, even with the Wigan fans. Wigan once suspended him - and twice put him on the transfer list. But he ended his career with the club where he started, after scoring 475 tries - a record which beat the record of Johnny Ring, another Welshman, at Central Park.

'Billy B', as most of the Wigan players and touring mates called him, had many items in his repertoire. His crash tackles on a centre at the moment of receiving the ball had jarred many a centre and saved overlap tries.

The Australians always felt he had one vital weakness, the inability to field a high ball. With this in mind, the Australians in the second Test at Lang Park in 1962 decided to concentrate on this weakness ... as they thought. Travelling in the 'plane to Brisbane a newspaper article was shown to Boston, giving the Australian tactics. This riled Billy, and he left no doubt as to his intentions. He took every ball which was put in the air that Saturday at Lang Park, a field which had once been a cemetery, and turned the tables which helped Britain to a win and the Ashes success.

After the match, there was a champagne celebration in the dressing-room - and the sight of Boston having champagne poured over him was one I shall not easily forget. This was the last-but-one of Boston's Test appearances in the British jersey. Billy Boston was the first coloured player to wear this jersey in Australia - and he had his problems. He did not tour South Africa with the 1962 Great Britain party, and at New Zealand, on arrival on the 1962 tour, he was asked to go into a room to be questioned.

This embarrassment resulted in Boston asking to be immediately sent back to England. He was not as it turned out, but there was an apology later, given by the New Zealand authorities. There were many matches in England when Boston had to stand up to crowd comments about his play and colour - and more than once he went towards the crowd.

He was a great favourite at Central Park. He had that magnetic quality that had the crowd on its toes when ever he received the ball. He was a crowd-puller without any doubt.

Boston scored four ties in a Test match against New Zealand at Auckland on the 1954 tour, and twice scored seven tries in a match. His full record of tries, including representative matches, came to the grand total of 563. For Wigan, in 472 appearances, he averaged a try a match.

In April, 1968, the soldier-boy of 1954 had gone the full circle. A testimonial match at Wigan was watched by 10,000 spectators who came to honour Boston at Central Park. He scored a hat-trick of tries and kicked a goal. The tremendous sight of seeing Boston, head forward, his big chest and broad shoulders swinging away, was over. He did have the urge to play, even at loose forward, and both Salford and Blackpool had high hopes of Boston joining them. The League, however, ruled against such a move in view of his testimonial match, for Boston had had a ten years benefit award earlier.

'Bill B' had worn the cherry and white jersey for the last time. He had had a variety of jobs in Wigan. He had been a publican, traveller, groundsman, and a post office worker - amongst other employment. He had had his Wembley triumphs and failures. Boston had done well for Wigan.

He was the Wigan Peer!

Club officials often tell the stories of the players they captured who made good in Rugby League. They are not so keen to relate the story of the players they missed who made good.

Such was the case of the Leeds club, who had the chance of signing a wing-threequarter who turned out to be one of the greatest ever wingers in the game. And if the number of tries scored is a criterion then he WAS the greatest ever. The man, Brian Bevan, the football freak of the decade.

'Bev' approached the Leeds club on the recommendation of Bill Shankland, a golfing pro at Potters Bar club, himself a fine footballer with Warrington and also from Australia like Bevan. Dressed in navy uniform, I can well imagine the Leeds official concerned did not think he looked much like a footballer - let along a crack winger. A lean, serious-faced man with a jerky walk, Bevan obviously failed to inspire the Headingley club officials, and he walked away from Leeds disappointed that he was not wanted. But he moved away over the Pennines to join Shankland's old club, Warrington, and started a career that has become a piece of history in Rugby League.

Up to Bevan's arrival at Wilderspool, home of the Warrington club, a player called Jack Fish was the greatest winger the 'Wire' fans had to talk about. It all changed when Bevan walked into the wooden office under the stand at Warrington and asked for a trial.

Born in Sydney in 1924, Bevan learnt to play touch rugby on the beaches of Bondi and Tamarama. He was the eldest of a footballing family and his father used to teach him side-stepping by running round telegraph poles in the Paddington area of Sydney.

He tells the story of coming out of the Sydney cricket ground after watching his favourites like Bill Shankland and Dave Brown play, and side-stepping his way past the white poles leading into Moore Park opposite the Olympic Hotel where the Great Britain teams always stay.

Bevan's football started later than most wingers - which makes his amazing try scoring record of 834 tries all the more fantastic. He came to England in 1945 as a stoker with the H.M.A.S. *Australia* when the ship came for a repair to Portsmouth. During the nine months in England Bevan saw a lot of Rugby League when he went North to contact his father's friend Bill Shankland, who was then golf pro at Temple Newsam, on the outskirts of Leeds.

After his failure to impress the Leeds officials he was advised to try his luck with Warrington, and was there offered reserve team games. Warrington liked what they saw and after his discharge from the Navy, soon after his return to Australia, Bevan was back in Lancashire, ready to start his career at the age of twenty-two years.

He told the story that he found the conditions very grim, and after the sun of Bondi, Warrington was indeed a very cold place. He must have thought many times of returning to his native Sydney, but his early successes soon established him as the find of the forties.

In his first winter in what he once described as the cold dark days, he scored 48 tries and, this might surprise a lot of people, kicked 35 goals. Bevan was not known to be a goal-kicker, and he later gave up the goal-kicking job first to Harold Palin, a good loose forward and later to his fellow countryman, Harry Bath. Bevan's consistency in scoring tries was remarkable.

In 1947/48 season he scored sixty-two tries, followed by 57, and then had an injury session in 1949/50 - but still managed to score 40 tries. He was soon on the try scoring sixties again when he notched up 69 in 1950/51, and then kept on scoring at a prolific rate. His try scoring record alone was remarkable, but some of his tries were fantastic - almost freakish. He could score from any blade of grass on the field. Most things he did were unorthodox, and whenever he had the ball a try was possible. He once scored one against Wigan from his own line. He would start on one side of the field and prance his way to score on the other corner.

His balding hair and his toothless look, coupled with bandages on both knees, gave no impression of the brilliance in his eleven stone frame. He was fast, very fast, and was reported to have clocked 9.9 seconds in football gear. He reckoned his quickness off the mark was due to his training on the sandy beaches of Bondi.

He looked a nervous man. When he played, he did not smile easily. But 'Bev' was a kindly man, not the brash Australian, often typified in some of the players who come to England from Sydney. He was a brilliant pianist and he had a variety of jobs. Insurance agent, hairdresser, shopkeeper etc.

He was a genius in most things he did for they were flashes of inspiration which more often than not proved to be right. He would kick if he wanted to and he usually found the wide open spaces and was on the ball before the defences knew what was happening.

He won his first medal in 1948 when he scored a try at Maine Road, Manchester in the Warrington championship win over Bradford Northern. Two years later he was a Wembley for the first time with a Cup winner's medal against local rivals Widnes, but he did not score.

There has only been one drawn game at Wembley in a Challenge Cup Final - and that was in 1954. The match between Warrington and Halifax ended in a tryless game, with four points each. Even Bevan could not produce one of his miracles in this match, but he got his second Cup winner's medal in the replay at Odsal Stadium, Bradford.

The reply, on the Wednesday following the final, was played amid fantastic scenes. The official crowd of 102,000 was regarded by many as being 20,000 short of those people who got in the ground - many without paying. Numberless Warrington fans never saw their team win this trophy, for the traffic jams over the Pennines were so long that police were advising the car drivers to return to Lancashire even before they had arrived at Halifax - eight miles from Odsal ground.

There were scenes that could never happen again at this vast bowl, and many were still leaving the match at midnight. I know, I was one of them!

Bevan was not in the scoring chart for this match, the star that day being the Warrington scrum-half, Gerry Helme. These were great days for Warrington and Bevan. Their favourite ground was Manchester City, for it was here in 1954 where they had another Championship win this time against Halifax, by only one point. It gave them the coveted double of Challenge Cup and Championship trophy.

A year later in 1955 Warrington had a 7 to 3 points win in the Championship over Oldham, again at Maine Road, but this was the end of the road for the time being of both Warrington as Champions and for the Championship being played on a soccer ground.

After the 1956 final on the Manchester City ground, the Football League officials objected to the use of soccer grounds for Rugby League games and they were then staged at Odsal Stadium for the next six years.

Brian Bevan continued to delight Rugby fans and stayed with the club for fifteen seasons. He left Warrington for Blackpool, but did not stay there long. He wanted to be a coach - and he was flown to Australia for a special match so that Sydneysiders could see the great 'Bev'.

He thrilled the fans on the Sydney cricket ground, but it was on the grounds of Lancashire and Yorkshire clubs where Bevan had produced his wizardry so often.

13

Alan Prescott & Arthur Clues

The green, green grass was getting thin. Britain's most pampered piece of turf had definite signs of wear and tear. Around it was the finest collection of floral hats. Fancy dresses. Thousands of eyes and a million hopes. The time was the summer of 1958. The scene was the Centre Court of Wimbledon.

On to court, with the customary curtsey, stepped a serious-faced young lass from Torquay. Britain was backing her this July day. It had been twenty-one years since a British woman had won the Wimbledon title. Angela Mortimer was one match away from it. Before her stood the queen of the American tennis world, Althea Gibson. It was quite a sporting day in Britain that day ...

Two hundred miles north at Headingley, the cricketing head-quarters of Yorkshire, England had skittled New Zealand for a mere 67 runs. Those Surrey spin twins Laker and Lock had done the damage with nine wickets for 31 runs.

Across the Pennines, Australian golf wizard Peter Thomson was battling with the sand dunes of Royal Lytham to beat Welshman Dave Thomas in a 36-hole play-off for his fourth British Open title. Down at the Hove they heard the news that Angela Mortimer had been beaten at Wimbledon as Doug Insole hit 108 for Essex against Sussex.

But the real sporting drama that day was taking place 12,000 miles from Britain's shores. The real action was happening in Brisbane.

In the bright Australian sunshine Alan Prescott walked slowly at the head of his team as Great Britain prepared to do battle with Australia in the second Rugby League Test. One hour-and-a-half later Prescott limped off in what he describes as 'the greatest moment of my life'. It surely was nothing less than that.

What happened in those ninety, power-packed minutes is a book in itself. Very soon after the start of the match Prescott was injured. An arm injury which he decided could be properly attended to at half-time. Shortly after Prescott's injury Dave Bolton, the stand-off-half, was tackled hard and he had to leave the field holding an injured shoulder. It was broken - and Bolton was the first to be taken to hospital. Yet despite the $11^{1}/_{2}$ stone men, Britain were 10 points to 2 points up at half-time.

I left my Press seat in the stand and went to the dressing-room to be confronted with an amazing scene. An Australian doctor was examining Prescott's arm. As the players queued for quick treatment for cuts and bruises they kept throwing glances at the injured British skipper. Suddenly the doctor straightened up and turned to the manager Tom Mitchell.

'Prescott's arm is broken. He's finished for the day.' The remaining eleven players greeted the news with utter silence.

The Great Ones

Varying stories have been told about what then happened. Apart from the tour officials and players, I was the only other man in the dressing-room. Prescott, with his ginger-hair standing upright, looked at his startled colleagues and said: 'I'll play on, say nowt to nobody.'

At that moment the touch judge came in to say it was time for the restart. Not a word was said. They didn't want the Australian players to know the extent of the injury.

It was soon evident that the brave Prescott had no use at all in his injured arm. He passed with one arm and took a strategic defensive position by just being in the way of the Australians. He survived. How, I will never know. But survive he did - and so did the British team.

When Mick Sullivan scored a try in the second half, to make the score line 15 points to 2 points, Britain were still not safe. The Australians were out for the kill and at one period it looked as if the British line would not hold out. Prescott shouted, threatened and cajoled his team-mates. His very presence drove them on to amazing deeds.

Vinty Karalius played like two men at stand-off, and when young Alex Murphy scored a try late in the game it was all over although Australia, at the final whistle, were only seven points behind Britain, with the score 25 points to 18 points. The match was saved ... and, as it later proved, the Ashes too. But at a cost.

Prescott and Bolton did not play again on tour and after the match I paid a visit to the Brisbane hospital where quite a few of the British team had to receive treatment.

At an hotel celebration after the match the phrase 'Prescott's Epic' was suggested by Ted Harris, a good friend to the British team. Although Ted was an Australian, he had given a lot of time and hospitality to British touring teams since I first met him in 1946.

Two weeks later Prescott, with his arm in a sling, walked

on to the Sydney cricket ground at the end of the third Test which Britain won by 40 points to 17 to receive the Ashes trophy, after a tour which had been full of everything - including early rows and incidents.

Even including the New Zealand part of the tour, where the interest wanes, only two matches out of 30 games were lost on this 1958 tour, equalled only by Sullivan's 1932 team - and then this 1932 team played only 26 matches.

The sight of Prescott in full flight was quite something. His flaming red hair, red face and heavy frame made him an unforgettable sight. He could run too. In fact, he was a runner in his early schooldays and won many prizes for sprinting at Warrington Road school.

Born in Widnes, young Prescott at eight years of age started to play Rugby League. This is not unusual in Lancashire. At sixteen he was a professional with Halifax as a wing-threequarter. This was in 1945 - when he little dreamed of the future ahead. He did not stay long in the threequarters, as he put on weight. At one period he weighed $16^{1/2}$ stone. A move to the forwards was inevitable - and he made it successfully. Like many Lancastrians who start with a Yorkshire club, Alan moved back to his native Lancashire at St Helens. From a back three forward, he became a prop forward and the 'fifties were his most successful.

His first Test against the Australians was in 1952, at Headingley - a win for the Lions by 19 points to 6. Prescott played in all three Tests in that series, and this paved the way for a trip with the 1954 side which lost the Ashes. He played in 20 tour games and scored one try. Success was running Prescott's way and the crowning glory, from a club point of view, was in 1956 when St Helens, led by Prescott, beat Halifax to win the Challenge Cup at Wembley. A try and the Lance Todd 'best player' trophy was a fitting reward.

The Great Ones

Prescott himself regards his try in this 1956 final as his greatest. And he scored many.

Prescott had a place in the World Cup squad in 1957 which lost in Australia, and then twelve months later he played his last and amazing Test at Brisbane. His Test career ended with the broken arm but he continued to play club football up to retirement.

During the 1954 tour, Britain had a hooker called Tom McKinney. A Scot-cum-Irishman from Salford, Tom was quite a character. In one match, McKinney was brought out by Referee Darcy Lawlor, Australia's most controversial referee at the time, and accused of biting. The flabbergasted McKinney just opened his mouth to show he had no teeth at all, said Prescott.

Alan Prescott includes McKinney in his best St Helens side. And his thirteen contains some interesting names: Glyn Moses at full-back, threequarters, Vollenhoven, Greenall, Finnan, Llewellyn, Metcalfe and Murphy, Prescott, McKinney, Terry, Silcock, Huddart and Karalius. 'Precky', as his tour-mates called him, regarded McKinney as the best hooker he played with and Joe Egan as the best hooker he played against.

When Prescott eventually decided to hang up his boots, he took over as coach at St Helens. He was there a few years before moving to be coach at Leigh. Prescott moulded much of his training methods on those of his first trainer, Peter Lyons from Widnes, who coached Prescott at St Helens in his playing days.

Prescott's epic Test at Brisbane will remain in Rugby League history for a long time. He was a cheerful tourist who enjoyed his trips to Australia - and made the most of them. Not all footballers do that, for some get homesick and spend far too much time at the pictures and in the pub.

Many of the purists in rugby will tell you that a

threequarter can never make a top class prop forward. You have to start in the pack in the early days to be a successful scrummager, say these purists.

In the main they are possibly right - in Prescott's case they would be wrong. For he made the change from a winger to a prop forward with a first-class honours degree.

When he left football he went into a Wigan public house where his shining red face still beams cheerfully ... especially when you talk Rugby League to him.

A player was sent off in each of the three Tests in the first post-war tour of 1946. In the first Test on the Sydney Cricket ground, Jack Kitching of Bradford was sent off after he had alleged that Australian centre, Joe Jorgensen, had bitten him.

In the second Test at Brisbane, Joe Egan of Wigan was sent off, and in the third Test at Sydney an Australian, Arthur Clues, was sent off. The story behind the dismissal of Clues is interesting.

The referee was Tom McMahon, a very good Australian referee. When Clues swung a punch at Joe Egan, the English forward, he failed to connect with the target and the blow went wide. Immediately Tom McMahon ordered Clues off the field. 'I didn't hit him, I missed,' yelled Clues. Mr McMahon replied 'That is why I'm sending you off - for missing!' That tour was the first association which Arthur Clues had with English football. He didn't play again in the green and gold jersey of Australia, for he was brought to Leeds in 1947 to play the first of his 236 games with the club.

From the Sydney sun to a Yorkshire blizzard signified his arrival in one of the worst ever winters, with fuel shortage and rationing. He must have liked what he saw, for Clues stayed on to make his life in England, married a Leeds girl, and after his playing career had ended - at Hunslet incidentally - joined the Leeds football committee.

The Great Ones

The heavy winter of 1947, when no grounds could be covered because of straw shortage, made fixture fulfilment extremely difficult. The Clues debut against Hull, on February 1st, was the only match Leeds played between January 25th and March 8th due to the bad winter.

'Big Arthur' was a second row forward, standing 6 ft 1 in and weighing 15 stone. He had played with the club sides - Parramatta and Western Suburbs - before getting his place in the Australian thirteen in 1946. He was a Sydney policeman. He had almost a delicate side step for such a big fellow, and his left leg kicking was another important part of his equipment which brought him 74 tries for Leeds - bettered, incidentally, by only two other Leeds forwards, Billy Ward with 99 tries in 318 games and Fred Webster with 96 in 543 games.

Clues started in Rugby Union in Sydney and tells the story of being suspended for life by the Australian Rugby Union. Not as one might understandably be inclined to think for roughness, but for his interference when acting as a touch judge.

In a match in which his local club were playing, Clues had taken over the touch flag when the opposition broke away and a try looked certain. That was too much for Clues, particularly when he saw none of his own players were in a position to stop the try. He dropped the flag and dived to make a try-saving tackle ... and brought down the wrath of officialdom on his head. The R.U. suspension which followed did not entirely stop him playing the game, but he turned to R.L. and to his advantage, as his future told. After seven years at Headingley Clues moved south across the river Aire to join Hunslet and played for three years in the Hunslet jersey - until he announced his retirement.

Soon after he had arrived in England, Clues had his first honour - an appearance in a Challenge Cup final at Wembley - and remarkably after only seven games with his club. Great players have waited a lifetime but have never appeared at Wembley. Arthur Clues was there so soon after his entry into English football when Leeds played Bradford Northern. The Leeds road to Wembley was a record one for the team had not one point scored against them on the way to the final. In the final, Bradford scored the first points against them and eventually won the Challenge Cup.

The Clues story would really not be complete without some reference to another footballer from Down Under in Bert Cook, a full-back who came from New Zealand to have almost an identical career as Clues. The pair became firm friends during their stay at Headingley.

Cook played his first game at Leeds on January 18th, 1948 and his days at Headingley ended in the 1953/54 season when he joined Keighley as a player-coach after kicking 556 goals in 210 appearances. He played in a size three football boot. One of his most memorable goals was in the Leeds Cup run of 1947. The match was against Wigan at Central Park in the third round of the Cup. It was the best of Cook, for on a muddy ground his size three boot lifted a ball out of the morass and hit it 50 yards for one of the greatest goals ever seen at Wigan. In addition to a try by Gareth Price, it put Leeds through to the semi-final where they beat Wakefield Trinity with Bert Cook kicking three goals. He had kicked nine goals in the competition - missing scoring in only one round, the second leg of the first round against Barrow.

Bert Cook, like Arthur Clues, played many matches for the Other Nationalities team which had a lot of success during a period when many overseas players were in the country. The first Other Nationalities game was against France at Bordeaux in 1949 and the last, also in Bordeaux, in 1953 when the side were the unofficial league champions. Clues played a great part in the green jerseys of the Other Nationalities.

The Great Ones

He will not easily forget his clashes with another great second row forward, Eduard Poncinet of France. In a match in France, Clues and Poncient had clashed and the French forward had been taken off with a head injury. In 1951 at Hull the teams again met on November 3rd. The two big brawny pack men met straight from the kick-off when Clues fielded the ball. As a result of what followed Clues was taken off the field and to hospital.

Clues had a pretty consistent try-scoring record at Headingley and in season 1949/50 actually shared the top position with Dicky Williams with 16 tries each. During his stay at Headingley he opened up a sports shop which he still has. He was a cricketer of some merit. He returned to Australia for a spell, but came back to England despite his early experience of that winter of 1947.

Another forward of that era, who created his own hall of fame, was David Donald Valentine. He was a Scot from Hawick in the Border country, where many men have come from to play Rugby League. 'Val' was a tourist in Australia in 1954, and played in eight Tests from 1948 to 1954.

His great moment, however, was in the World Cup in 1954, after many players had said 'No' to the invitation to play in France. The 1954 tour team were a tired lot on their return from Australia and New Zealand and did not want to know much about the World Cup being played in France. What was described at the time as a team of 'no hopers' was assembled under the captaincy of border Scot, Dave Valentine - the only Scot ever to captain a Great Britain team to date.

With a Scottish border song as the inspiration, Valentine led his team to success never dreamed of by even the most partisan English R.L. fan. It was Valentine's greatest moment when he was carried off shoulder high in the Parc de Princess stadium in Paris, having won the massive French trophy - a trophy so big that when we carried it to Birmingham to appear on a TV sports programme three policemen stopped us both to see what we were carrying under a blanket.

David Valentine was a good courageous loose forward and a sound leader. He later became coach at Huddersfield and made a come-back after retirement to play in a Yorkshire cup final at Headingley.

The Huddersfield club often raided the Scottish borders for footballers. They brought many back, but none better than Valentine.

14

Joe Egan

The first player to receive the Rugby League Challenge Cup from a reigning monarch was Joe Egan of Wigan and Great Britain fame. The occasion was in 1948 when Egan, a hooker, was captain of Wigan, the team which successfully beat Bradford Northern and received the trophy from H.M.King George VI. Royalty had graced Wembley before this occasion - when H.R.H. The Prince of Wales presented the R.L. cup to Len Bowkett of Huddersfield in 1933 - and fourteen years later H.R.H. Duke of Gloucester presented the cup to Ernest Ward. Yet it is Joe Egan who has the honour of being the first to receive the Cup from a reigning monarch.

Wigan have produced many great wingers and full-backs, but have not found many great hookers. The best and greatest they have had is Joe Egan, who was found on their own door-step - and although he did start as a full-back with the well-known St Patrick's schoolboys team in Wigan, Egan's ability, not only as a footballer but as a future captain, was quickly seen by the Wigan board.

Joe Egan

As a newcomer to senior Rugby League, Egan was a shrewd footballer. He signed for Wigan in January, 1937, at the age of seventeen years and a year later he was soon amongst the medals with a Lancashire Cup winner medal in 1938 when Wigan defeated Salford. The outbreak of war prevented what must have been a lot more honours for the young hooker, Egan. He had to wait until the 1946 tour before he was in the International side and on tour. Egan toured Australia again in 1950 when he was vice-captain of the touring side.

Egan's hooking ability was supported by some skillful play in the loose. Hookers, of course, normally like to run with the ball, just as fast bowlers fancy themselves as batsmen. In Egan's case, he was a good ball player and I saw him in brilliant style play in the second row in one country game in Australia. Of course, he liked and loved to play football. His 'dummy' speciality was amongst the best I have ever seen, certainly the best-ever from a hooker.

Joe Egan played in many Lancashire cup finals, County games and Internationals. He captained his country and his club, and after ten years' service had a joint benefit along with Ken Gee. Players don't normally like to have joint rewards, but in the Egan-Gee case this was understandable. The pair had so much in common, for their careers had a very similar course. Both started and ended their Test career against Australia together, they had packed down in the scrum together for thousands of scrummages - with Ken as the open side prop and Joe the hooker.

The story is that Wigan found Ken Gee because he had a reputation at the Windy Arbour colliery, near Wigan, of throwing pit props around with great strength. Where two men were required to handle the big props, Gee could handle them on his own. The combination of Gee and Egan was quite remarkable. On the 1946 tour Egan played in seventeen matches and all Tests and Gee played in eighteen matches and the three Tests. Four years later, when they toured together and played in all the Tests, Egan played in fifteen matches and Gee fourteen. I have seen Gee do such amazing feats of strength with people on tour, and yet he had a quiet sense of humour, loved to join in the team's choir and was always around to help when things were going wrong.

The French R.L. people thought a lot of Gee and invited him to France to present him with a special trophy, for they thought he symbolised English Rugby League. I once heard him describe a little forward as a 'knocked-up thumb'. Gee could kick goals, not in a classic style, but he puffed away as he kicked and managed some pretty good ones. When he finished with the League game he later became a publican and his name is remembered in Wigan for a competition called the Ken Gee cup.

Joe Egan was not a big man in height, but he was big in every other way. He was a solid 5ft 9inch, and a pocket Hercules. He did not talk a lot but when he did, he meant what he said. He was able to get the best out of his fellow scrummager, Ken Gee, and he could read a match with surprising accuracy. He was an able leader and a skilled captain - a job he did many times for Great Britain and, of course, Wigan. His bow legs - one player on tour called him 'Cowboy Joe' - were known on all Rugby League grounds. He had many representative honours against all rugby playing countries, but decided to call it a day in big time football in 1950.

Joe Egan was a natural to take over a job of coach when he retired from playing, but that moment had not yet arrived. The time, however, arrived in 1950 for him to part company with Wigan - something that the Wigan fans could not believe when they saw the newsboy placards saying Joe Egan had signed for Leigh.

His whole football life, from his early days with the St Patrick's schoolboys (old boys and juniors) had been with Wigan, and Lancashire R.L. fans spent days talking about this move to nearby Leigh. Why did he go was the question many fans asked. It was certainly a sensational transfer for the fee of £5,000 was a record at that time.

Leigh, under the leadership of Chairman Mr James Hilton, was determined to put the club on the map. Mr Hilton later persuaded Trevor Allen, the Australian crack Rugby Union centre, to join them - a deal I had much to do with - and he had helped to build a new ground at Leigh, now named Hilton Park in his memory. Joe Egan was put on the transfer list at £5,000 by Wigan. Within no time at all, Egan had taken the few short miles from Wigan to Leigh to become their player-coach. Leigh, in the process of re-building the club, were not only willing to pay £5,000 but would have gone to £6,000 to sign Egan as their player and coach. He settled down at Leigh, and then the club and fans were stunned one day when he broke his leg. The crowd gasped when they heard the crack - and it looked as if Egan as a player was finished. With the resilience he had, he started training again as soon as possible by running for hours up and down the Central Park ground terraces - and eventually returned to Leigh. He was grooming a young star to take over the leadership of Leigh, in loose forward Peter Foster, but Foster was tragically killed in a car accident.

In 1956 Egan returned to Wigan as coach, and began a run of successes. He was coach when Wigan beat Workington in 1958 at Wembley, again the following year against Hull, and in 1960 Wigan had a great Championship win under Egan's guidance, against Wakefield at Bradford. In 1961, with another Wembley appearance, his luck gave out - and Wigan lost against St Helens.

Shortly after, Egan left Wigan again and went to nearby

The Great Ones

Widnes. In R.L. the coach is possibly equivalent to soccer's manager so far as responsibility is concerned. It is rarely a secretary manager is sacked in R.L. - it is usually the coach who takes the blame for bad results. However, Egan for the second time, left Wigan, but he had success at Widnes when the 'Chemicals' - as Widnes are known - went to Wembley in 1964. There, they beat Hull K.R., who were making their first Wembley appearance.

Egan had signed Karalius from St Helens and Collier from Wigan - and the pair did wonders for the team. Egan's spell at Widnes ended in 1968 and at that time he considered giving up the game for good.

He lived very near the Wigan Athletic ground at Springfield Park and he could never understand people paying five shillings to watch soccer when they could see Rugby League for the same price. Joe Egan was finished with Rugby League and took over a newsagents shop. But, of course, it turned out that Egan was not yet finished with the code which had been his whole life for so many years. He was offered the post of coach to Warrington R.L.F.C. in the 1968/69 season - and accepted and began once again wearing his football boots to coach footballers.

He had tried hard to coach E. McDonald Bailey, the crack springer, when he was at Leigh. He spent many hours hoping to turn the sprint ability into rugby ability. Leigh players put in many hours of overtime to get 'The Brown Flash' under way and after long and patient help, McDonald Bailey did step out in a Leigh jersey against Wigan in a friendly.

There was tremendous publicity for the premiere, TV cameras (still a novelty in those days in 1953) were in full force and London National press writers left their warm seats in Fleet Street to come up to unknown and cold Leigh, in Lancashire, to see the joint-holder of the 100 metres world record play his first game of Rugby League.

It was his first and last game - but he did score a try and lasted the game out. Leigh paid out £1,000 for the signing fee, with more to come if 'Mac' succeeded. The club covered the signing fee with the gate, the publicity value was enormous, but even the great Joe Egan could not make McDonald Bailey into a R.L. player.

His signing, however, did start a move of athletes into the game - for later Berwyn Jones, Europe's fastest sprinter, signed for Wakefield Trinity, Alf Meakin, Olympic sprinter, signed for Oldham.

Joe Egan had hoped his son, also called Joe, would take over the mantle of the famous name in International football. Young Joe, like his father, was a hooker and played for St Helens. Like many sons of famous fathers, it proved a hard path to follow - particularly in Rugby League.

Most of Britains' best hookers have come from the breeding ground of R.L. in the North of England. Joe Egan would name another Lancastrian as his first hooker choice - Tommy Armitt of Swinton. There have been one or two R.U. hookers who have made the grade in the thirteen-a-side code.

Not many, but such as Tommy Harris and Frank Osmond, had the honour of touring with a Great Britain side. If you talk of hookers, however, amongst the ardent fans of the north there will be one name constantly cropping up; the name, of course - Joe Egan.

15

Vinty Karalius, Derek Turner & John Whiteley

The longest and loneliest walk in the world of sport is the one a footballer has to take to the dressing-room after he has been sent off. Some of the walks are longer than others.

Grounds like Central Park, Wigan, Knowsley Road, St Helens, and Fartown, Huddersfield are so situated that the dismissed player does not have direct contact with spectators en route for the early bath.

Recently the Mount Pleasant rooms at Batley were altered and built under the stands after seventy years of players having to walk across a cricket field to get to the dressing-rooms. I recall, as a boy, seeing two players sent off at Mount Pleasant ... and the scrap continuing as they walked across the cricket ground.

The longest trek is from the Sydney cricket ground. From the Sydney Hill end to the dressing-room is a long lonely walk, and before reaching the dressing-rooms, rows and rows of members have to be passed before reaching the haven of seclusion. It is a path many English players have taken.

Vinty Karalius, Derek Turner & John Whiteley

Former tour manager Bob Anderton used to tell the story of such a walk during the 1936 Test series. One of Australia's best and toughest forwards was Ray Stehr, a good friend of mine, but in 1936 not a good friend to the English forwards.

Particularly not one named Big John Arkwright of Warrington and England fame. Stehr always reckoned the English forwards were the toughest in the world. Ray tells the story of his 1936 clashes with the English pack members and in the deciding Test said to one of his forward mates that he was going to clock Arkwright at the next scrum down.

'I swung a punch which would have put paid to any normal man' said Stehr. The Australian pack men held their breath expecting a real Donnybrook to stir. Arkwright rubbed his chin and said to Ray Stehr 'T' mosquitoes are bad today lad' ... Bob Anderton said this was not the end but the start and eventually Arkwright and Stehr were sent-off.

As Arkwright went on that long lonely walk the bank on duty that day at the Sydney cricket ground struck up 'Goodnight sweetheart'. When eventually Ray Stehr came round, on the ground, he too walked to the strains of the music.

The thirties were the days of the big tough forwards, the English pack in that 1936 series were all good big handy forwards. The pack of Nat Silcock, Tom Armitt, Harry Woods, Jack Arkwright, Martin Hodgson and Harry Beverley were fit and mighty men. Martin Hodgson, a great goal kicker, holds the unofficial record of the longest goal kicked in Rugby League at 78 yards.

He was a six-footer plus, like the genial giant Beverley, who started at Hunslet as a centre and finished as a loose-forward at Halifax with immense success. All the six I have named were fifteen stone plus and they played in an era when there were a lot of big good forwards ready to take any vacant International spot.

The Great Ones

Two other forwards who know what it is like to take that long, lonely stroll on the Sydney cricket ground are 'Vinty' Karalius and 'Rocky' Turner.

Vinty Karalius despite his Lithuanian name is Lancashire born and bred. Although he only made one tour to Australia, he made his mark so much in the short spell he had there that his name has gone down with greatness, just as much as it has done at Widnes and St Helens - his two teams in England.

'King' Karalius, as one critic described him, was dubbed 'The wild bull of the Pampas' by the Australian writers. 'Vinty' didn't mind this, in fact he didn't much mind what the Australian critics said of him ... providing his team won. The tour he made was in 1958.

He missed out in the first Test for he had been sent off in the NSW match, rather unluckily. He received a three-match suspension after a clash with Australian Peter Dimond. Thus, the craggy Karalius had time to watch and prepare for the second and vital Test in Brisbane.

Karalius made no effort to hide his dislike for the Australians on the field. He didn't want to shake hands with them. I can vividly remember him waiting in the dressing-room like a caged lion before going out on to the Brisbane ground in that Prescott Test match. When one Australian player - Ken Kearney - came in to talk to the British players 'Vinty' stayed firmly in his seat in the corner just waiting for the battle to commence.

The Australian Press, with their love for cliches, moved their pens most poetically. One writer referred to Karalius as 'the St Helens boiler-maker with classical taste in music who could stiff arm to the lilt of *Il Trovatore*. *Carmen* and *Toreador* were often tied up with Karalius. But he wasn't a stiff arm merchant, he was a tackler with a bear hug. He had big hands, and could effectively stop an opponent from wanting to take the ball with his hands and arms with body tackles. The job that Karalius had to do in that Brisbane Test was to quieten the Australian pack. It turned out differently because of the Bolton and Prescott injuries. Karalius was moved to the stand-off half position and the Aussie fans laughed. They had laughed thirty-four years earlier at Sydney when another great loose forward, Frank Gallagher, was moved to play in the stand-off position in a Test match. But in 1924 the great Gallagher did what Karalius did in 1958. He threw their laughs back in their faces and paralysed the opposition with brilliance and strength.

Karalius enjoyed himself at Brisbane, he threw opponents about and ran with the ball. His timing to catch the team's bus along with his tour mate Dick Huddart was never good, but his timing of his passes was perfect. He made the short burst - sent colleagues on their way. When Alex Murphy scored a long running try Karalius said: 'It's all yours, Spud, just run.' It was this sort of football which gave the depleted British team their greatest hour on that tour.

That 1958 NSW battle in which Vince Karalius was sent off was one of the many incidents on tour. In that match Rex Mossop, a former Leigh R.L. and Australian R.U. player, was also dismissed for a tackle on Eric Ashton, and Greg Hawick another Australian was sent off for an incident involving Phil Jackson. It was certainly a day for the long, lonely walk.

Although Karalius didn't have a long Test career against the Australians, he played in two more Test games in 1963 and the World Cup in 1960, in addition, he had a very successful career with St Helens.

Off the field he could be quiet, with an enigmatic smile, but he was always ready to join in the fun. He had a great dislike of flying. One one occasion, up in remote Prosperpine in Queensland, he did all he could to get out of flying further North. He liked to be on the ground - I suppose that is where he liked his opponents too!

'Vinty' Karalius had a hat-trick of successes at Wembley. His first when St Helens beat Halifax in 1956, his second when captain of the Saints in 1961, and his third, again as captain, but this time when he led his town team Widnes in 1964.

Vincent Peter Patrick Karalius, to give him his full name, was a player's man. Yet his brushes with authority were not of the vicious sort. He had great respect for Alan Prescott on the 1958 tour, and was certainly the sort of player a captain wanted in his team.

He was a leader of men and he grew in stature and ability when he was in charge. Such an occasion was in 1964 - when Widnes reached the final of the Challenge Cup. 'Vinty' knew what sort of a job was on hand so he took the week off from his demolition business to decide how he could demolish Hull Kingston Rovers at the Empire Stadium.

He was able to recall the preparations at Surfers Paradise Queensland in 1958 when the tour team and reserves went to bed at 10pm with no curfew having to be imposed and no one breaking any orders. They were put on trust and not one of the players went out of step.

Karalius was impressed with the preparations and he remembered this when he joined forces with coach Joe Egan to prepare Widnes, very much a local team for the final.

Widnes had paid St Helens £4,000 to sign Karalius and, with a big burly forward called Frank Collier also signed, the 'Chemicals' took the song out of the Yorkshire 'Robins', and it was a very proud Vince Karalius who was the first up to the Royal box to receive the Challenge Cup.

Vinty Karalius, Derek Turner & John Whiteley

DEREK TURNER

Four years after Vince Karalius had shattered the 'dignity' of the Sydney members another tough-as-teak man arrived on the scene to stir the Sydneysiders.

This time it was dark-haired, wide, fierce open-eyed Derek Turner from Wakefield Trinity. Australians love to give a player a nickname if they cannot abbreviate his Christian name. They didn't have to bother with Turner, for already English fans had given him the name of 'Rocky'.

In that 1962 bid for a complete three Test win, Turner was on the marching end after a clash with Dudley Beattie, an Australian forward. This was one of the occasions when I thought Turner was unlucky to be sent-off.

Beattie had been injured in the first half but was put back on the field and kept tussling with Turner. The British loose-forward knew he had to keep out of trouble, but eventually there was a close contact and the inevitable happened - referee Darcy Lawlor, an unemotional man in contrast to the volatile Derek Turner, was pointing to the dressing-room and away 'Rocky' went, followed by Beattie.

It was the last time the Australians were to play against Turner, but they never forgot him. John Raper, the greatest loose forward Australia has possibly ever had, apart from Frank Burge, always said Turner was the toughest and hardest man he had played against.

A Dewsbury junior find, Turner started with Hull Kingston Rovers, moved on to Oldham and returned to Yorkshire to play and captain Wakefield Trinity for a transfer fee of £8.000 in 1959. Prior to Turner's arrival at Belle Vue, another great loose forward, Ken Traill, had been in command in that position and continued as coach to give off-the-field leadership in Wakefield's glorious ten years which were to follow. Ken Traill knew the way to Wembley.

151

The Great Ones

He had been there successfully as a player with Bradford Northern and had toured Australia twice in 1950 and 1954. Traill was a different type of player to Turner although, curiously, both were left leg kickers.

'Rocky' Turner started his International career against the Australians in the 1956 Test match at Bradford - when he was on the Oldham books. He had five Test matches against the Kangaroos and played against them in two World Cup competitions in England and Australia.

Strength for strength, there was little difference between Karalius and Turner. They had one thing in common - they both disliked the Australians. Karalius was probably a better ball player than Turner, at least Eric Ashton always felt this, but Turner had one big advantage - he could kick the ball with strong left leg punting with remarkable accuracy. From a play, he could move play long distances by kicking the ball to touch. Karalius didn't and couldn't kick much.

The arrival of Turner coincided with Wakefield's start of Cup chasing. The combination of two loose forwards, Turner on the field and Traill off, proved effective for in 1960 Trinity had their first ever Championship final against Wigan at Bradford.

Two years later they were back at Odsal, but once again the Championship Cup needed to give Trinity the four cups was missed against Huddersfield. Turner was having his best footballing years, however, with the Royal Cup Final at Wembley in 1960 (when he received the trophy from the Queen) and in 1962, when he flew to Australia for the second time.

It was all go for Trinity at this period and in 1963 Trinity fans were yet again driving down the A.1 to Wembley. Turner's championship defeat by Huddersfield the year before was forgotten when he walked up to the Royal box for the third time, to receive the Cup. Three out of three for

Vinty Karalius, Derek Turner & John Whiteley

'Rocky'! There was a lot of cup drinking being done around this time for Trinity.

Trinity's triumphs were taking it out of Derek Turner, and injuries began to mount up for him. He 'retired' - as many R.L. players do - but came back to give Trinity a helping hand in season 1964/65. His experience was valuable, but *anno domini* was telling although he moved up from the position he had made his name at, loose forward, to being a prop forward. A dislocated collar bone - his first of his long career - a badly torn ear and another dislocation troubled both Turner and Trinity. However, he soldiered on, but at the opening of the 1966/67 season Turner was away on a different sort of lonely walk, another dislocated shoulder in the first match against Castleford. It was time really to call it a day, and he wisely did so. During this injury period Turner was knocked out by a New Zealand player, something I never thought I would see happen to this tough-as-teak player.

When 'Rocky' left the game he continued to assist Ken Traill on the coaching staff at Wakefield. He refused offers to join other clubs until 1968 when he suddenly packed his bags at Belle Vue and moved over Heath Common to Castleford, to become their coach. He had lots of playing experience to help in his new post.

He had a successful career which brought him many honours. An outspoken player who will no doubt continue as an outspoken touchline watcher. He certainly thinks the forwards are much softer now and the game much easier and softer. There may not be any more Vinty Karalius's or 'Rocky' Turner's coming into R.L. They provided a lot of good rugby and increased blood pressure for friend and foe.

Both players had the sense to realise R.L. is only part-time. Turner moved in successfully to become head of a Haulage and Furniture Removal firm, while Vinty continues successfully his Iron business in his native Widnes.

153

The Great Ones

JOHN WHITELEY

In sharp contrast, at least in style of play to the loose forwards I have written about, is John Whiteley of Hull. A Humberside favourite for many years, Whiteley was a classic style of footballer who believed in the ball doing the work.

His passing was beautifully timed and his long raking stride had a quality all its own. When Hull were a power in the mid-fifties the Hull pack, led by Whiteley, brought the famous 'threepenny stand' followers alight with enthusiasm. Hull born and bred, Whiteley, now coach to the club, moved from the Hull Boys Club to the Boulevard in season 1950/51.

Four years later he joined up with that first World Cup squad and went over to France. He was junior member to David Valentine on that tour, but had his first outing in the British jersey against Australia in the next World Cup in 1957. One year later he was back with the Great Britain touring side, and was a very popular and successful member of the 1958 tour party. I saw a lot of Whiteley on this trip, particularly in the preparation for that vital second Test when the team were down at Surfers Paradise on the Gold Coast of Queensland.

His enthusiasm for fitness and his general cheerfulness brought him much praise from his fellow tourists. The Australians thought a lot of Whiteley, but they never really forgave him for the part he played in Britain's winning of the Ashes in the home series in 1959. Whiteley had missed the first Test, played at Swinton, which Australia won by 22 points to 14 points. It was the great Reg Gasnier's match, with a hat-trick of tries for the Kangaroos. Australia were one up when they entered the Headingley ground on November 31st, 1959. Amongst the players recalled into the side were Tykes Jeff Stevenson and John Whiteley. It was this pair which nailed the Australians - and produced cries of wrath from them.

In a tense match, Britain took the lead with tries by Don Robinson and Neil Fox, but the mighty Australian side, with Gasnier producing flashes of brilliance, were leading by 10 points to 6 points with the end in sight.

Brian Carlson, the Australian goal-kicker taking over from Keith Barnes, the Welsh born Australian captain, missed an easy conversion from his try and this was to prove vital. Near the end, a scrum was ordered in front of the Headingley posts at the Kirkstall Lane end and the ball heeled successfully by Tom Harris, the Welsh born Hull hooker.

Stevenson eagerly snapped up the ball, taking the Australian breaking forwards with him, and flipped a backward pass to the long, waiting arms of Whiteley. With the big crowd urging Whiteley on he crashed over the Australian line for the try which followed with a successful goal by Neil Fox and Britain were through, only just, but through by one point.

Whiteley retained his place in the final Test at Wigan and so did Stevenson. The Hull loose forward had an important part in the 18 points to 12 points win at Central Park and ended his Test career against Australia on a triumphant note.

'Long John' had successes and disappointments - such as never receiving a winner's medal in a Challenge Cup Final. They seem rarely to come Hull's way, for the only thirteen players who ever won them did so way back in 1914. Whiteley did, however, have cup successes in the County cup competition and in the Championship - in which he played in three finals, all for Hull of course.

Whiteley played in an era when Britain had a lot of good loose forwards - he was a great amongst greats. The irregular black and white jersey of Hull had no better wearer of the No. 13 jersey than John Whiteley.

16

Final Word

It all started 74 years ago in a Huddersfield hotel - the wonderful game of Rugby League.

Since then, wherever and whenever crowds have gathered to watch the game, arguments have raged over the qualities of the men who have played Rugby League.

Who was the greatest of them all? Who was the best goal kicker? Who was the toughest guy to step into a pair of rugby boots? In this book I have tried to solve those questions. I only hope my selection of players does not spark off even more arguments! No doubt there are many who would have liked me to include other Rugby League greats. But it's always a hard job pleasing everybody!

My father would have wished me to include his all-time favourite, Richard Evison 'Dicky' Lockwood. I haven't. I have even had to leave out some of my own boyhood favourites.

What I have tried to do is give a picture of the men who have helped to put Rugby League on the map. Men who play a man's game. Men who have left their mark in the man's world of Rugby League.

Appendix

13 TEAMS THAT TOURED AUSTRALIA

Britain has sent thirteen touring teams to Australia. Nine times the British team have returned with the Ashes.

1910 - Won Ashes

J. Lomas, J. Sharrocks, F. Young, C. Jenkins, F. Farrar, J. Leytham, W. Batten, J. Bartholomew, B. Jenkins, J. Riley, F. Smith, J. Thomas, J. Davies, T. H. Newbold, T. Helm, G. Ruddick, F. Shugars, R. Ramsdale, E. Curzon, W. Winstanley, F. Boylen, H. Kershaw, W. Jukes W. Ward, F. Webster, A.E. Avery
Played 14, W 9, L 4, D 1

1914 - Won Ashes

H. Wagstaff, A.E. Wood, G. Thomas, A.E. Francis, S. Moorhouse, J. Robinson, F. Williams, W.A. Davies, B. Jenkins, W. Hall, J. O'Gara, W. S. Prosser, J. Rogers, F. Smith, L. Clampitt, D. Clark, F. Longstaff, W. Roman, D. Holland, J.W. Smailes, W. Jarman, J. Chilcott, J.W. Guerin, A.P. Coldrick, A. Johnson, R. Ramsdale
Played 12, W 9, L 3, D 0

1920 - Lost Ashes

H. Wagstaff, G. Thomas, A.E. Wood, W. Stone, S.Stockwell, C. Stacey, J. Bacon, D. Hurcombe, E. Davies, J. Doyle, E. Jones, J. Parkin, R. Lloyd, J. Rogers, J. Cartwright, A. Milne, J. Bowers, W.Cunliffe, G.A. Skelhorne, B. Gronow, A. Johnson, W. Reid, G. Rees, H. Hilton, D. Clarke, F. Gallagher
Played 16, W 12, L 4, D 0

1924 - Won Ashes

J. Parkin, E. Sullivan, E. Knapman, F. Evans, J. Ring, C. Pollard, W. Bentham, S. Rix, T. Howley, C. Carr, J. Bacon, W. Mooney, S. Whitty, D. Hurcombe, B. Gronow, H. Bowman, J. Darwell, R. Sloman, W. Cunliffe, J. Bennett, J. Price, D. Rees, J. Thompson, W. Burgess, A. Brough, F. Gallagher
Played 18, W 14, L 4, D 0

1928 - Won Ashes

J. Sullivan, W. Gowers, A. Ellaby, E. Gwynne, A. Frodsham, T. Askin, J. Oliver, J. Brough, M. Rosser, J. Evans, J. Parkin, L. Fairclough, W. Rees, B. Evans, W.A. Williams, N. Bentham, O. Dolan, H. Bowman, J. Thompson, W. Burgess, A.E. Fildes, W. Horton, R. Sloman, W. Bowen, B. Halfpenny, H. Young
Played 16, W 11, L 4, D 1

1932 - Won Ashes

J. Sullivan, A.J.Risman, B. Hudson, S. Smith, A. Ellaby, J. T. Woods, A., Atkinson, S. Brogden, W. Dingsdale, G. Robinson, I. Davies, E. Pollard, B. Evans, L. Adams, J. Thompson, N. Silcock, W.A. Williams, J. Wright, L.L. White, J. Lowe, A.E. Fildes, N. Fender, W. Horton, M. Hodgson, J. Feetham, F. Butters
Played 18, W 15, L 2 D 1

The Great Ones

1936 - Won Ashes
J. Brough, W. Belshaw, J.C. Morley, B. Hudson, S. Smith, A. Edwards, F. Harris, A. Atkinson, A J. Risman, E.G. Davies, E. Jenkins, S. Brogden, W. Watkins, T. McCue, H. Field, T. Armitt, N. Silcock, J.H. Woods, J. Miller, H. Jones, L.A. Troup, J. Arkwright, M. Hodgson, G. Exley, H. Beverley, H. Ellerington
Played 17, W 14, L 3, D 0

1946 - Won Ashes
A.J. Risman, A. Bassett, E. Batten, G. Curran, W.T.H. Davies, J. Egan, T. Foster, K. Gee, W. Horne, W.F. Hughes, D. Jenkins, A.E. Johnson, J. Jones, J. Kitching, B. Knowlden, J. Lewthwaite, T. McCue, D. Phillips, M. Ryan, E. Ward, E. H. Ward, F. Whitcombe, L. White
Played 20, W 16, L 3, D 1

1950 - Lost Ashes
E. Ward, J. Egan, E. Ashcroft, T. Bradshaw, J. Cunliffe, T. Danby, A. Daniels, J. Featherstone, E. Gwyther, K. Gee, F. Higgins, H. Murphy, D. Naughton, D. Phillips, R. Ryan, H. Street, K. Traill, F. Osmond, A. J. Pepperell, W. Horne, R. Williams, J. Hilton, W.G. Ratcliffe, R. Pollard, M. Ryan, J. Ledgard
Played 19, W 15, L 4, D 0

1954 - Lost Ashes
R. Williams, E. Ashcroft, A. Burnell, J. Bowden, W. Boston, B. Briggs, E. Cahill, J. Cunliffe, F. Castle, T. Gunney, P. Jackson, G. Helme, J. Henderson, T. Harris, L. Jones, T. McKinney, T. O'Grady, D. Greenall, R. Price, A. Prescott, C. Pawsey, N. Silcock, A.Turnbull, K. Traill, J. Wilkinson, D. Valentine
Played 22, W 13, L 8, D 1

1958 - Won Ashes
A. Prescott, A. Ackerley, H. Archer, D. Bolton, E. Ashton, F. Carlton, J. Challinor, A. Davies, B. Edgar, E. Fraser, D. Goodwin, T. Harris, R. Huddart, K. Jackson, P. Jackson, V. Karalius, M. Martyn, B. McTigue, G. Moses, A. Murphy, F. Pitchford, I. Southward, M. Sullivan, J. Whiteley, W. Wookey, A. Terry
Played 21, W 19, L 1, D 1

1962 - Won Ashes
G. Round, E. Fraser, W. Boston, E. Ashton, N. Fox, M. Sullivan, I. Southward, F. Carlton, G. Cooper, D. Fox, A. Murphy, D. Bolton, H. Poynton, P. Small, N. Herbert, B. McTigue, J. Sayer, B. Edgar, K. Noble, J. Shaw, J. Wilkinson, R. Huddart, J. Taylor, R. Evans, D. Turner, L. Gilfedder
Played 21, W 18, L 3, D 0

1966 - Lost Ashes
K. Gowers, A. Keegan, W. Burgess, B. Jones, G. Shelton, A. Buckley, J. Stopford, I. Brooke, C. Dooler, A. Hardisty, T. Bishop, W. Aspinall, G. Wrigglesworth, F. Myler, B. Edgar, C. Watson, K. Roberts, G. Crewdson, C. Clarke, D. Flanagan, J. Mantle, T. Fogerty, W. Ramsey, W. Bryant, D. Robinson, H. Poole
Played 22, W 13, L 9, D 0

CAPTAINS ON TOUR
1910	James Lomas (Salford)
1914	Harold Wagstaff (Hudders)
1920	Harold Wagstaff (Hudders)
1924	Jonty Parkin (Wakefield T.)
1928	Jonty Parkin (Wakefield T.)
1932	Jim Sullivan (Wigan)
1936	Jim Brough (Leeds)
1946	Gus Risman (Salford)
1950	Ernest Ward (Bradford N.)
1954	Dick Williams (Hunslet)
1958	Alan Prescott (St Helens)
1962	Eric Ashton (Wigan)
1966	Harry Poole (Leeds)

ENGLAND TO
AUSTRALIA AND NEW ZEALAND

Original Foreword (1947)

The next best thing to going from 'England to Australia and New Zealand' is to read this live and vivid presentation of the trip by Eddie Waring.

Before you have read the first dozen pages you will be one of the party - you will be an 'Indomitable'. Their joys will be your joys, and their sorrows your sorrows and, believe me, as one who has been over the ground, that while the joys are many - very many - there are also sorrows.

The Author is a keen observer and records his observations with a frank, breezy enthusiasm which is as refreshing as it is entertaining.

You will sight-see with him in the Mediterranean, the Canal, Aden and Colombo, play deck games East of Suez, Cross the Line, and suffer the discomforts of that awful train journey across the Nullabor Plain.

All these however, interesting as they are, are merely the *hors d'oeuvres*, the real feast is the Rugby League football games played in Australia and New Zealand.

The thrill of watching your team on the packed Sydney Cricket Ground in a Test Match (and tell it not at Old Trafford or Headingley, they play Rugby League football across the cricket Test Match wicket!) the joy when they win,

161

and the depths of sorrow and despondency when they lose, can all be experienced by Mr. Waring's graphic writings.

The opening pages on the formation of the Northern Union Rugby Football fifty-two years ago are just introductory and not really part of the story.

This is a 'Foreword' and not a criticism, but the writer joins issue with the Author when he says that the breakaway from the Rugby Union 'is so well known.' The history of the great breakaway is, to-day, well known to probably less than twenty persons and as, of course, Eddie Waring is not one of them - he is too young - he shows wisdom in 'leaving it at that.'

Reading 'England to Australia and New Zealand' brings happy, if nostalgic, memories to ...

JOHN WILSON
Secretary, Rugby Football League, 1920-46
August 14th, 1947

OUT OF THE WILDERNESS

If by any chance this title mystifies you, I make no apologies whatsoever.

Throughout the years International sport of all phases has been recorded so that the worthy deeds of athletic pioneers may be made known to future generations.

But one great sport - Rugby League football - has been out in the wilderness. For what reason I cannot say, because this game, known in its infancy as Northern Union, has been, in recent years, the only British sport to maintain World superiority.

Rugby League football has received little attention from the pens of authors. Why? Please don't ask me. There have been good writers and even better legislators who could have compiled a most interesting collection of anecdotes and reminiscences. But all, so far, have fought shy of the task.

Now I propose to take Rugby League football out of the wilderness - a desire that originated in 1946 when I had the privilege of visiting Australia and New Zealand with the British Rugby League team, and having a round-the-world adventure writing for the *Sunday Pictorial* and the *Yorkshire Evening News*.

On my return to England I began a series of lectures on the Tour, and hundreds of listeners urged me to put the subject on paper, so the idea of this book took shape. There have been tours between England and Australia and New Zealand for many years, but none of them has been recorded in book form.

The 1946 visit was the first time a journalist had travelled with any touring team from England, and as John Wilson (then the R.L. Secretary) wrote in his initial instructions to all members of the party ... 'It's a trip of a lifetime'.

I hope this record will serve not only as a memento to those with whom I had the pleasure of sharing a great adventure, but that, in a wider sphere, it will do its little part in creating a fuller understanding and a further strengthening of the ties that hold the extreme ends of our British Commonwealth of Nations.

CHAPTER I.

THE PIONEERS AND THE 'INDOMITABLES'. DR.
EVATT'S PLEA. THE NAVY TAKES BOARDERS.
GIB. AND MALTA.

The history of Rugby League football and its break away from Rugby Union is so well known that I do not propose to dwell on it. Suffice to say that in the year 1895 twenty-two rebel clubs left the Rugby Union and formed a body called the Northern Union, later known as the Rugby League. The first President was Mr H.H.Waller, of Brighouse. As one of the Press members present at the Jubilee dinner at Belle Vue last year, I was disappointed not to hear this founder-member speak of his experiences in those rebel days.

From a small beginning - and the critics said the new League could not go very far - it has progressed until now it is on a sound footing in every way. Curiously it has never moved for any length of time out of the Northern Counties of Yorkshire, Lancashire and Cumberland. The soundness and vision of the early legislators was very evident, and we are constantly reminded of this in various ways. Only this year - 1947 - the New Zealand Rugby Union authorities have recommended certain alterations to the rules of the Amateur code. Practically all of them are changes which in principle, were made by Rugby League officials when they changed from Amateurism to Professionalism as far back as 1895. That alone gives an indication of the wisdom of the early guardians of the most democratic game in the world.

Financially, the League has always been sound. This has been due mainly to the tours of Australia and New Zealand, Australia providing the largest part of the revenue. Yet it was a New Zealander who paved the way for these successful tours. I refer to a 25-year-old star footballer named A. H. Baskerville.

What faith this boy had! He gathered around him a number of players willing to stake money, reputation, and everything on a 12,000 miles trip to England with no guarantee that when they arrived they would even be given a full list of fixtures. On leaving New Zealand for England they called at Australia and played a game at Sydney. This was one of the first brilliant moves, for they tempted an Australian players, in the person of Dally Messenger, to join the party. The team arrived in England, and their results do not count or enter into recognised official inter-country statistics.

But this was the pioneering way, and to A.H. Baskerville goes the credit of not only being the first, but of lighting the torch. How tragic it all was that on the journey home this young pioneer was to meet his death at Brisbane! What a sorrowing party it was for the young healthy footballers, who had achieved fame and little fortune, that they should lose their leader. The body of this grand sportsman was taken back to New Zealand and interred in Wellington.

But the flame was alight, and the first official Test in England was played in London on December 12th, 1908. It ended in a draw of 22 pts. each. The second Test was played at Newcastle, and the third in Birmingham. Curious that the game is not played in any of these three centres.

England To Australia and New Zealand

The first tour by England was in 1910. The opening game was played at Sydney, and England won by 27 pts. to 20 pts. As I give the full detailed statistics at the end of the book, I do not propose to dwell on that match at this juncture.

From 1910 to 1946 is a long jump, and the eighth team to go out to represent England was named the Indomitables, a title which stuck to this side throughout the tour. It was obvious from the day the Admiralty said the party could travel on the aircraft carrier *H.M.S. Indomitable* that this name would be adopted.

On the resumption of normal football activities in 1945-6 season the Australian Board of Control quickly sent an invitation to the Rugby League to send a side out to the Antipodes in the summer (or winter, in the case of Australia) of 1946. There were many doubts and many queries before this was even seriously thought of, and not until Dr. H.E.Evatt (Minister for External Affairs) visited Manchester and talked to the Rugby League Council members did the Tour look possible. Eloquently, he described the great welcome the tourists would be given, or they would be the first party to go from England after the war. Dr. Evatt stressed the importance of these 'Ambassadors' from a bond angle, and the Rugby League officials were half won over before the Minister had finished his address. Even after the decision to go, the transport question looked like providing the one obstacle that could not be surmounted. However, with Australian and British Navy co-operation a party of 32 were given berths on the *Indomitable* and had to be ready by April 1st.

There were natural disappointments to some officials and would-be visitors that the number was limited, and for the first time it was a purely business party. In fact, it was nearly less than 32, for on arrival at Plymouth, the point of embarkation, the number given for allocation was eight fewer than the number present. With typical Navy action, the thought of players being left behind was overcome, and on April 3rd the Indomitable left on her trip to Australia, carrying a most unusual bag of civilian passengers. Half-a-dozen priests from Eire and a number of returned Servicemen from overseas were among the list.

How well the Captain and Commander stood up to the intrusion of civilians! Many times the disciplinary code was broken both by the footballers and other non-service personnel, but this was taken in a spirit that gained the praise of the 'unofficial party'. Even when some of the party trespassed they were only politely told of their intrusion. This was instanced when some of the 'visitors' thought they were entitled to use the high ranking Officers' bathroom and repeatedly held up business when the real occupant desired its use. In the end an official notice was put on the door to the effect that this particular bathroom was for use of V.I.P.s only.

The players were berthed in various parts of the ship, and it took some of them days to find out exactly where everyone was. A cosy Warrant Officers' mess was placed at the disposal of the boys, but eventually 35 people in a place usually occupied by about eight got a little too much for the W.O.s and an annexe was erected, which proved most satisfactory to all.

The smokers of the party enjoyed the privileges of cigarettes at 500 for 12/6, and spirits at Navy rate proved advantageous. How often I have heard returned tourists speak feelingly of the *Indomitable* mess since the cigarette shortage arose!

The first land sight was at Gibraltar, but none was allowed on shore. I obtained permission to send Press cables to London, and I acted as shopper for the party - mainly fresh fruit, which we had not eaten for years. The boat hawkers had a busy time round the ship with their goods, but, smart as they are, they were not quicker than some of the Yorkshire lads, whose method of purchase is a secret for ship travellers only. The Navy boys, experienced in such matters, were free with their advice, and when they were desirous of moving on the salesmen a hose did what words could not do.

The first official on-shore stop was at the George Cross Island of Malta. With a good and quick dhow ferry service and that remarkably long - and, to me, unsafe - lift to the town, we were in the midst of this attractive battle-scarred spot. Harry Murphy, the loose forward, called it a place of eating houses and barber's shops. The popular rendezvous for entertainment and eating was known amongst the matelots as 'The Gut.'

The amount of food available was amazing and caused much comment. Chocolates and confectionery were plentiful, and the owners of the eating houses in 'The Gut' vied with each other for quantity and cheapness. A pleasant bus run to Valetta was among the day's activities. Many of the Maltese to whom I spoke were keen to know about football - but not the handling code, for they were soccer advocates and their Stadium, which I visited, was a very fine one. How keen they are for English teams to visit them! Their papers gave English League results.

CHAPTER II.

WIGAN WALLOPERS GO OUT. TOUGHER THAN
RL. THROUGH THE SUEZ CANAL. TOO MUCH
HEAT. FRUIT FROM THE CROWN PRINCE.
NATIVES' HONESTY CONTEST. THE COOLIE
FROM LANCASHIRE. THE MANAGERS LOSE
THEIR BREAKFAST.

Through the Mediterranean deck games were got into full
swing, giving the players plenty of room in which to train. The
top flight deck, free from aeroplanes, was long enough to do
any amount of work, although the hard deck proved rather
too much when we ran into really hot weather. Deck hockey is
the principal Navy game. It is played with seven a side, with
sticks not to be raised above shoulders, and a formation of
goalkeeper, two backs, one half, and three forwards. A knock-
out competition was organised and the Rugby League party
entered four teams called 'The Wigan Wallopers', 'Cudworth
Cripples', 'Tourists' Terrors' and 'Welsh Wizards'.

The Wigan Wallopers were the best of the four teams,
and we thought they had a good chance of success in the
tournament. They went into the second round, but then the
Stokers - tough lads - know how to play deck hockey, so the
Wallopers went out. One of the best 'outside' teams was the
'Sky Pilots' - these were the boys from Eire. And were they
rough, too! The semi-final between the Stokers and the 'Sky
Pilots' was tougher than any R.L. match I had seen.

Handball was another form of training, but the Mediterranean sun was the most attractive of pastimes.

Our approach to the Suez Canal - we did not land at Port Said - was most interesting and full of colour. A visit from a Cable and Wireless official for my Press cable, a Police visit, and a bouquet of flowers 'from 'Irish Jim' for the Captain,' were all out-of-the-ordinary affairs. We saw the Simon Artz store, where, supposedly, you can purchase anything. The Police and Government buildings looked very ornate.

Settling down on the Canal journey - 100 miles, taking about eight hours - I was fortunate in having the use of very good binoculars. The modern age of steam seems to run into the olden age of transport. With jeeps running on the road further in the sanded desert I could see lone riders with their camels; further still in the distance were the old shrines, with black-frocked people apparently waiting for some kind of service to begin.

Mid-way through, at El Ballah, we were reminded of home when a crowd of Army bathers, hailing from the Northern counties, called out their home towns and awaited for response. Word had gone ahead that the British team were passing through the Canal, and at shops en route we had visitors. The Canal can be boring or fascinating. To me it was the latter, and I was loathe to leave it for one moment, even for meals. There was much to remind one of Biblical terms and phrases in seeing the natives following their various age-old pursuits, apparently oblivious of the modern war monsters. The *Indomitable*, with its 25,000 tons, took up most of the Canal width. The eight hours' 'slow march' was all too quick and we anchored in Bitter Lakes for the night, after a day full of unforgettable scenes. Bitter Lakes offers opportunity for ships to pass each other, so does Ismalia. Leaving Suez, the town, we went down the Red Sea, where the weather was the hottest we experienced.

It has since amazed me that an itinerary is never issued to a touring team. Most of the party were unprepared for the extreme hot weather, and shorts and an outfit suited for this climate was just not part of the equipment we had taken. Take note you future tourists when going through the Red Sea, take a Red Sea outfit!

Fortunately, this omission of clothing was rectified by purchases from the well-equipped Navy store. No doubt, many articles of clothing were bought which, in many cases, will never be used again. However, it saved us from complete annihilation by the sun, for the cabins - yes, I had a single cabin - were intolerably hot. I had a fan which occasionally worked, but was advised not to put it directly on to a sweating body, and as this was the only way one could keep the heat away, it was an almost hopeless position.

Cinema shows were staged out-of-door, but even with such good films as 'Brief Encounter' and 'Scarlet Street', the hard still seats were too much until one got the idea of taking a pillow or, better still, a cabin chair, if you had one.

The heat stayed with us and we reached Aden a bronzed lot of hefty footballers. What can be said of Aden? Do I do it an injustice when I say 'not much'? Whether our party saw only the worst of this Arab town I do not know, but a visit to the native quarters certainly left us with the impression that what we had been told about Navy personnel being sent there as a form of punishment, was true. A well-appointed Officers' Club provided a good shore meal, but the highlight was the visit of the Crown Prince of Yemen to the ship.

I was ashore when he arrived at the launch which took him across to the ship. No Prime Minister has ever had a more colourful or careful bodyguard than the Crown Prince had. Their outfits were not military as we know them, but their guns were impressive, and the local police took no chances with the local populace. He certainly enjoyed his visit, for he later sent 25 cases of melons, 25 cases of peaches, cases of raisins, sacks of nuts and tomatoes.

The Police Chief told me their biggest trouble was the local guide. He was certainly right, for once the guide saw one was willing to have him around it was impossible to get him away. All the 'Imshis' and any other native phrases picked up just would not move him.

It was queer to see tennis balls and sporting equipment unobtainable in England at that time filling the shops of this place. Probably the sight of an old leper colony as you enter Aden disturbs a bit, and to see the coal dockers filing up a ship from a barge was another sight not pleasant. In ant-like formation they climbed up the side of the ship with a coal bag on their shoulders and walked down the other side. It looked like a regimentation of busy little ants. Later, in Colon, I saw some ants carrying grass in almost the same way.

The effect of Aden was that the whole party were back on board before the allotted dead line, which was an indication of their feelings.

From Aden, our last calling place before we reached Australia was Colombo. Ceylon, 'the gem in the Indian Ocean,' certainly has spots which live up to their description. We had hoped to go up the hills to Kandy, but a smallpox epidemic put us off, and so we had a trip out to Mount Lavinia. This gave the first opportunity of real sea bathing. Murphy had tried it at Aden and severely injured his back. But it was surf riding at Mount Lavinia. Natives erected their tarpaulin tents on the shore, and with a numbered key for our clothes they were quite safe. The testimonies of previous bathers, shown by letters, surrounded the place to prove their honesty. There was competition between them, and this appeared to rest on the one who had the most letters to show. Their remarkably built fishing boats of long narrow craft - how they kept upright was amazing - was the method of sea transport.

Back in Colombo the shops with their unmarked gold rings, ebony elephants and jewellery proved the most popular attractions. Drinking in the famous Palace Hotel, a group of British sailors came over to talk to some of the boys. Nearby they saw a sun-tanned 'local' with a fez on his head. After watching the 'local' taking a great deal of interest in their conversation they eventually turned on him and told him to mind his own business. To their utter amazement the 'local' said: 'It's alreight, lad, I come fra' Bradford!' It was Eric Batten, the winger. He was always much browner than anyone else, and was known as Abdul to his pals.

A social call was made at Colombo when a party visited the very fine Town Hall for a dance. Unfortunately, the social side was all on the 'locals', and the dance flopped. Deciding to make a quick return to the ship, coolies brought along their gharries and a dozen or so of the players decided to have a race back to the docks. Away the coolies went, almost level for a long while, until one of the rear competitors suddenly came up with a terrific burst. Looking in amazement at this turn of speed we found the driver was Martin Ryan, and the coolie sat serenely in the back! What these Lancastrians will do to win! But Martin still had to pay his two rupees for the use of the vehicle. He said it was his idea of training!

The longest spell without sight of land - nine days - took us to Fremantle, and on April 30th we arrived in Australia. The trip had taken 27 days. We had still, officially, another six days round the Bight to go. Sea sickness had been very rare. The ship had done about 22 knots on an average, and to see the *Indomitable* riding a rough sea was a really grand picture.

Owing to war conditions the famous 'Crossing the Line' ceremony had been more or less done away with. It was decided on this trip to renew it with all its old pageantry and vigour. The night before the imaginary line was reached the Herald came on board, gave the usual tidings about entering the domain and that the Court would be held the day following.

There was much dressing up, with Neptune, Aphrodite and their Court. The bears and Police appeared, and later came the procession with the gun plainly marked 'Stop me and buy one.' On the platform, where the 'King' and 'Queen' sat, were the three stools for the initiation ceremony. The Court barber lathered and shaved each person, who was then tipped into the first (dirty) bath and thrown out into the second (clean) bath, and finally passed out a fully qualified member.

Various ruses were adopted to escape this business but the Stokers, who were the Policemen, made sure of the football party. I conceived the idea of taking a film of the scene and so escaping punishment. But whatever the sailors thought, the R.L. players were determined otherwise. Having disposed of my camera and following the turn of Walter Crockford and Wilf Gabbatt, both fully dressed, I was given 'the usual', and in I went. On coming up from the first bath I espied in the second bath men who should not have been there. I realised they were six hefty R.L. footballers, obviously set for me.

I tried to get out by the side but was unlucky, and over I went. I was very forcibly given six instead of the recognised two duckings when I heard some kind players say 'I think he's had enough'. Coming up for a breather, some other not-too-kind players said 'Oh give him another two for the *Sunday Pictorial*!' and down I went, emerging exhausted. And I will give would-be crossers a hint. Don't change into dry clothes. The Court think you have not been in and you get a double dose despite your protestations.

During the 27 days voyage the clock had been advanced at intervals, which caused more than one member to miss his breakfast through not hearing the loudspeaker announcement - 'Clocks must be advanced thirty minutes to-night.' The two Managers of the British R.L. team were Wilfred Gabbatt (of Barrow) and Walter Popplewell (of Bramley) and they were the first two to miss a meal, forgetting to alter the time on the first occasion necessary.

CHAPTER III.

WE REACH AUSTRALIA AND OUR PLANS GO
ADRIFT. THE AUSTRALIAN GAME. 2,600 MILES
BY RAIL. SLEEPING WITH THE LUGGAGE. THE
NAVY SENDS A BILL. ADELAIDE, MELBOURNE
AND SYDNEY.

Arriving at Fremantle, the huge interest in sport was very evident, for waiting at the quayside were Sydney Press representatives who had travelled 2,600 miles to go the last stretch with the side. I had been contracted to write for the *Sydney Telegraph*, so no reporter came from this popular journal, but they sent a photographer, who must have taken hundreds shots before he arrived back. The *Sydney Morning Herald* sent Tom Goodman, and the *Sydney Sun*, W.F. Corbett, whose brother, Claud Corbett, had made trips to England for this paper. In addition, a cartoonist for the *Brisbane Courier* made the trip across.

An expected short stay in Fremantle was extended to seven days. This was due to the aircraft carrier *Victorious* running into trouble coming through the notorious Bight and suffering such damage which necessitated going into dry dock at Fremantle. For five days our plans of further movement were held up until the Admiralty from London issued instructions for the *Indomitable* to disembark her own passengers, embark the passengers from the *Victorious* and return to England.

This hold-up gave us the opportunity to take a good look at Perth, 10 miles out of Fremantle. No better introduction to Australia could be given a first-time visitor than to spend a few days in this beautiful City of Western Australia. It was autumn and the colouring of some of the famous plants was not so profuse as in other seasons. Kangaroo paws in their reds and greens, and the golden wattle were passing their best.

Overlooking the Swan River is the glorious King's Park with its thousand acres of natural bushland. It was from King's Park that I watched the Head of the River race. This is the big day for the college oarsmen, and the sight of the four teams rowing from the Brewery to the finishing post is unforgettable. Western Australia is justly proud of her remarkable University. The building looks very modern, yet possesses natural beauty that is as great as its scholastic records.

As some return for the hospitality received from the *Indomitable* crew a Charity Match was arranged at Fremantle for the Ship's charity. This served as a loosener for the boys and it gave the Australian Press the opportunity of assessing the players.

I refereed the game, which had its problems, due to lack of fitness on the part of some of the players, but it was the best training they had.

One R.A.A.F. member travelling home with us was Ken Farmer, who created a record for Australian rules football by kicking 1,000 goals. Ken Farmer, a grand type of sportsman, discussed at length the advantages and disadvantages of the Australian game and our own code. The stay in Perth gave him the opportunity of showing us a match at Subiaco. We agreed to differ which was the better game, although we agreed that both games had parts which were superior.

So far as this Australian game is concerned, 18 players

form a team. The field is about 190 yards in length and 160 yards wide. Two tall uprights with no cross-bar and two small uprights constitute the goal-posts. Basically, the idea is for the oval rugby ball, rather smaller than the one used in Rugby League, to be punted between these uprights. For each goal between the tall uprights six is awarded. The ball can only be punted after a mark, which means a clean catch. This sounded easy, but after seeing the obstruction allowed, I decided it was not so easy. The thrill in the game is to see players make a flying leap into the air to catch the ball, literally with their finger tips. In 1940 Ken Farmer kicked 23 goals in one match for his team, and the largest number kicked in one season is 188 goals. The longest kicks with an Australian ball are 86 yards with a place kick, 74 yards with a drop kick, and 74 yards with a punt. During the war years the Australian Forces played games in England, but not successfully. They had some amusing experiences in attempting it, however. When they asked to play at Lords, Sir Pelham Warner nearly had a fit, according to Bruce Andrew, who served with the R.A.A.F. Sir Pelham was told that the game was played on cricket grounds in Australia, but smilingly replied: 'Yes, but the grass grows much quicker in Australia!'

On the same ground at Hove there was plenty of enthusiasm shown but it turned to dismay when they found that the cricket square had been roped off and the goal-posts erected at one side of the ground. All appeals were unsuccessful and the game was played on a much smaller area. Wembley, Tottenham, Chelsea and Arsenal grounds were all placed at the disposal of these hardy Aussies, but all were too small. One match was played in Hyde Park, with a barrage balloon over one goal-post.

The game is fast and there are no offside rules, nor are the rules hard to follow. It is certainly a spectacular game, with the ball ever on the move and can be seen by all - a big advantage to the spectator. There is little or no Australian rules rugby in New South Wales or Queensland, but Victoria, South Australia and Western Australia are strongholds.

After many cables between Sydney H.Q. and Manager Gabbatt the party were eventually seconded to the Navy again and passages were arranged on a troop train from Perth to Melbourne, under Navy escort.

Travel on Australian trains is a law unto itself, especially on a troop train. Due to the early inter-State jealousies the gauge of the lines differs in each State. The first length is of 365 miles on a 3 ft. 6 in. gauge to Kalgoorlie, the great gold mining centre. At a very steady speed, with an initial climb out of Perth, we commenced our 2,600 miles trek to our goal of Sydney.

Being under Navy supervision we were given equipment for warmth and meals, but no International touring team has ever travelled as frugally as the 1946 British R.L. team did. Food was provided at wayside halts, and a queue was formed when the hot grub was handed out in real desert manner. And so over this vast continent we travelled across the great Nullabor plain where, at one point, the railway line is 365 miles dead straight. In England the longest such line is 18 miles between Selby and Hull.

Principal diversion on this monotonous journey, apart from the food, of course, and the raiding of any food shop we could see, was a visit to the train by Aborigines. Coming down to the train with their boomerangs and imitation Kookaburra staves, this fast-dying race looked far from being healthy. They were quick to know when a bargain was being made. They had one price and you could argue for an hour but they would not budge. The most depressing sight was to see the millions of flies round their scantily clad bodies. But the flies appeared to worry me more than they worried the Aborigines.

The second leg of the trip from Kalgoorlie to Port Pirie, near Adelaide, was 1,300 miles. This was accomplished on a 4 ft. 8 in. gauge. Sleeping accommodation was limited. Usually eight were fixed in a four-berth sleeping car. The luggage loft had to be used for sleeping purposes, and corridors and floors were a mass of humanity during the night.

Adelaide gave us the first real break, for sufficient time was allowed to have not only a much needed wash and brush up, but also an opportunity to see this beautiful city. Planned by Colonel Light, who had to contend with severe criticism and opposition, it is surrounded by vast parks and is a fine piece of work. He died before seeing his work being publicly recognised. A testimony to his work and his belief that critics would be confounded in later years is indicated on his memorial in the Park overlooking his work. I was glad to have the opportunity of looking round the famous cricket ground, with the Cathedral in the background. The curator, equivalent of an English groundsman, was the father of Ken Farmer, so I was well received and lucky to see it all. The scoring board on this ground, which must be the finest in the world, tells you everything and no score cards are required.

Fresh from Adelaide with its piles of fruit, cheap goods and stately buildings, we went the next 500 miles to Melbourne before being released from the Navy. Here we handed in our blankets and chattels and became civilians again.

At the last calling spot for a meal prior to arriving in Melbourne, Harry Murphy had left his dining equipment in a very hot washing-up tub. Knowing he would not want them again, Harry had left them soaking. When he told this to the Navy authorities he was politely given a bill of 4/2d. for the cost of them.

Melbourne, with its grandeur - I suppose it should be called 'The York of Australia' - was rushed, but sufficient time was given for me, at any rate, with the assistance of friends in a car, to see its great ground, its famous Collins Street, and to have a peep at the Australian rules game. The crowds for this game are larger here than at any other centre, and the enthusiasm is particularly evident.

We had hoped to travel to Sydney on the famous train *Spirit of Progress*, but the tardy arrival of our *Wolves Express*, as one journalist dubbed it in the Melbourne paper, meant our taking a later train. I had the opportunity of seeing this *Spirit of Progress*, and its modern, comfortable, almost luxurious travel arrangements were in direct contrast to our troop train. It shows what will be done with the rail system of Australia when the modernisation project is completed. But what a huge task it is, with thousands of miles to be put on a universal gauge of 4 ft. $8^{1/2}$ ins.!

With a last look at Melbourne our destination was in sight. Only 512 more miles, one more night without a sleeper, and to coin a football phrase 'We're in Meredith.' That last night was a sleepless one. No sleepers, and never shall I forget what it is like to share a compartment with six hefty footballers and try to sleep! Some smart photographer took a shot of the sleeping beauties. He did not get me in the picture, for I was underneath the mass of humanity. We had one luggage change at Aubury where, to crown our travel accomplishments we lost half the luggage. As we steamed out of the station we were amazed to see many of our trunks reposing on the platform with nobody worrying except us. One of the boys tried to make a late dive but was pulled back. But it did turn up a few days later.

It took us from the 6th to the 13th of the month to travel

from Fremantle to Sydney. Although the grumbles had been many and the inconveniences terrific, we had had many good things to atone for the annoyances. We had been the first International R.L. team to travel across this Continent. We had seen every big city and all the States (with the exception of Queensland, which we saw later) and we learned a lot about Australia which we would never have known had we gone on with our original plan and taken the Bight.

The desert and its spiked trees and its very small communities, mostly railway workers, its small schools and its flying doctors, were all aspects of life which made one realise what a vast country this Australia is. I don't propose to say we learned one half of it all, but later I will give a few statistics I learned from various people.

At last Sydney! Much has been written of this City with its $1^{1}/_{2}$ million population. The bridge and its harbour we had heard about, and let me say now all that has been written or spoken of the famous Sydney Bridge and harbour is not one whit exaggerated. It is undoubtedly a wonderful achievement. Naturally, some of the players got tired of being asked: 'Have you seen our Bridge?' It is the favourite question of 'Sydneyites.' So much so, one Yorkshire lad replied to this question: 'Aye, laad, 'ave seen it and dost tha' knaw, it was a Yorkshire firm 'at built it?' The Sydney native was too astounded to reply to this.

CHAPTER IV.

SUPER CLUB. OUR 'OPEN SESAME'. RISKING
LIFE ON THE TRAMS - AND IN THE TAXIS. THE
FIRST MATCH. WE HIT A SNAG.

Sydney is the home of Rugby League in Australia. It is the national game in this State, as in Queensland, and it will never have any serious opposition from any other winter sport. The controlling body of the game is the high-powered Australian Board of Control This committee consists of both New South Wales and Queensland members, and its decisions are the final ones. Mr H. (Jersey) Flegg is the Chairman of this Government, which was formed in 1934. He is an outspoken Chairman, who has had so many battles in his legislative days that his appearance gives an impression of dogged rugby determination. He is a former player, and his nickname of 'Jersey' came from an incident in his playing career.

Many famous names, men who had toured England with representative teams and as Managers, were still closely associated in the legislative capacity. Bill Cann - he toured in 1911 - George Ball and Johnny Quinlan were amongst the more experienced officials. I attended one meeting of the N.S.W. committee and hearing wordy battles between some of the older officials and new enthusiastic members like Lou Moses, showed what a democratic game Rugby League is. In Australia a Press representative is allowed into the meeting. In England this is not so.

Like English R.L., the Australians have had very few secretaries and Horrie Miller was for many, many years the Secretary of both the New South Wales and Australian Board of Control. Mr. Miller held the position until just before our arrival, when Mr. Keith Sharpe, a young, keen and helpful official, was appointed from down country.

The centre of both these organisations is in a vast new building in Phillips Street. For years they held their meetings, and members gathered, at a Club elsewhere. Just before the war they moved into their present quarters. During the war it was taken over by the Americans.

When the question of accommodating the 1946 tourists became acute the possibility of our being housed in the new Club was considered. This gives an idea of its size. Club offices down stairs, with a very big bar, and then lifts to all floors, games rooms, lounges and a concert room were all part of this football club super headquarters.

We were housed at Paddington, not a salubrious district by any means, and the accommodation was so cramped that at one time there was talk of moving, as the 1936 Tourists did. It was, however, very handy to the Sydney cricket ground. From the bedroom windows we could see the ground, and it was well served by trams and many taxis. The Olympic, our hotel, was accustomed to footballers, for the Queensland team and the New South Wales country players were frequent visitors. But 32 all at once was rather a lot. So thought Gus Risman who was sleeping on the balcony - particularly when it rained one night.

The enthusiasm and the fanatical rugby following was evident from the day we stepped off the train, to be greeted by a big crowd and many former English players and visitors. the second day on a tram one old lady summed up the position of Sydney by saying to me (she recognised my blazer): 'Don't judge Sydney as it is now, we are suffering from war effects,' and she was right, I do believe.

We had no fear for the warmth of welcome, and after a severe criticism in the Sydney papers of the bad travel arrangements, they quickly saw to it that we did not lack hospitality whilst there.

The British Rugby League blazer was an open sesame wherever we went, at least when the blazer badge was completed. Owing to the rush only the emblem was fixed on the blue coat in England, the yellow daffodil for Wales, thistle for Scotland, shamrock for Ireland, and the Lion and Crown for England. Thanks to a good friend of the tourists, Alf Mallalue, a native of Oldham and owner of the large departmental store of Murdochs, the words 'British R.L. 1946 Australian Tour' were added. Actually, it should have been 'Australasian Tour' not just the word 'Australian'. However, the added words did the trick, and once we had this inscription we found it was better than any other means of 'moving in' anywhere. Later I will tell how one 'Sydneyite' made good use of the blazer for his own purpose.

We soon got accustomed to the slang words, and when the players were asked if they were going 'crook' it did not mean were they going twisted, but were they not feeling well. 'It's a fair cow' is a favourite expression, while the use of the word 'bastard' must be a means of affection, as it is used so often among good friends. When asked what the tone of the average Aussie sounded like to English ears, the answer of 'just like a cockney' was not exactly satisfying to them. Of course, everyone was called a 'pommy', which appears to have originated from the fact that in the old days the red skin of the pomegranate resembled the fresh complexion of the British sailors. These slang words were all part and parcel of the Australian outlook, and taking exception to them would have surprised the residents.

Australia is such a young country that its phrases and its slang have simply grown with it as a child, and no affront. The quiet demeanour of an Englishman is sometimes regarded with awe by the Australian. Time and time again the excitement on the field of play, and off, left the expression on the player's face unmoved, whatever he felt inside, and the Australian spectator could never understand this apparent lack of enthusiasm.

The Aussie tackles everything with boundless energy. Discretion is often thrown to the winds, but there is no doubting what he means.

They can gamble and they can drink; they can talk and they can tell a tale. The vie with each other for the title of 'ear basher'. After listening to an Australian telling his tale, some companion will lean over and say: 'I'll bet he is giving you an ear bashing.'

To see a Sydney mob crowding on to their 'Toast Rack' trams on race day at Randwick or football day at the Sydney cricket ground, is amazing. In fact, it makes one wonder that there are not daily deaths, although accidents were almost daily. The trams are single deckers with open sides. I called them pneumonia trams, for the wind can hustle round and apart from a concertina blind pulled across there is no way of keeping it out.

The conductor walks on the outside step of the tram collecting fares, and as soon as you shut this supposed draught-keeping-out contraption, he walks along and opens it just to see no one has entered from the other side. Passengers bob on and bob off on either side, and when the seats are taken up and the middle is full of standing passengers, dozens literally crowd on to the running-board. Passengers are often knocked off in the mad rush of a race crowd or football crowd, but then the main thing is to get to where you are going, and if you can see a spare inch it does not matter who gets hurt.

To get on a Bondi tram or a Bronte tram on a Saturday lunch time is a work of art, and certainly a case of the survival of the fittest. Trams run in competition with taxis, whose drivers are just about as mad as any I have seen. Mainly the taxis are Ford eights. I must admit, the speed and the drivers' great skill is terrifying.

City planning is not a feature of Sydney, and where one admires the beauty of Melbourne of Adelaide and, in a lesser degree, Brisbane, Sydney just scorns how it should be done. Narrow streets like Castleraugh Street are turned into one-way streets. The first time I drove a car in Sydney I went down the street the wrong way. Fortunately, the consequences were not severe. But there are no real wide streets and George Street and Elizabeth Street, which are used both ways, are soon crowded.

Sydney is just Sydney, and you either like it or you don't. I like it, and despite its indifference and its toughness it has a personality which you can feel happy in. Throw punches back at it and you are laughing. Cry and you will go under.

My first article for the *Sydney Telegraph* was entitled 'Stop you kidding, Australia!' It brought in a lot of criticism, but it made me many friends, and we threw punches through the letter column like nobody's business. But that is how they like it in Sydney.

One day of our stay was devoted to being photographed, when the new outfits were worn for the first time. I think the English party slipped badly on the question of photographs. One particular firm was allowed to take the long all-standing photo which adorns many Clubrooms both in England and Australia. It is a grand photograph and one to cherish. So much for that picture.

But the sitting group which was taken should have become the copyright of the British League. Some enterprising person got hold of the photograph, made paper print, pasted them on cardboard with the names underneath, and sold thousands. How many he did actually sell I don't know, but wherever the team went they were always sold out. Near the end of the tour the players and Managers began to tumble to this racket, but it was, of course, too late then, and the money had gone elsewhere.

Whether it be an Australian team in England or vice versa, this revenue should go into the pockets of the players and not of a private individual unless, of course, the respective Managers are willing to sell the copyright and not have the trouble of organising sales. The Indomitables certainly made nothing out of their photographs. This is, of course, a different matter from Press photographs.

The first match of the Indomitables was at Junee, a pleasant country town where fog signals, train whistles and hooters welcomed the party in. It was, as in all country towns, a great day for the residents, and bus loads came from miles around to see the Englishmen. The inevitable dance, after an easy win for the Tourists, meant that a good time was had by all.

Little happened in this first match except one item that was noticeable to the visitors. There were certain rule differences, which, I am sorry to say, were never settled throughout the tour. The principal difference was in the forward pass. Home referees ruled that a pass from one player to another was offside if the player taking the ball was in front of the passer. In England, of course, such an infringement made a scrum down. In Australia, it resulted in a penalty to the opposition. In the Junee match, our players - and, remember, they were all Internationals timed to get every fraction out of their moves - were repeatedly mystified to find a penalty given for what they regarded as a forward pass. Unfortunately, the matter was never thrashed out as it should have been.

I am open on the subject. At a Sydney referee's meeting I argued with Tom McMahon, the best referee in Australia - who had two Tests with us - that a forward pass is such and is not offside. But I saw his point of view, that a player in front of another must be offside and the only decision can be, and is, a penalty. This difference arose at the first match, yet it had not been settled when the party left Australia.

Before the first Test, in the dressing room, Manager Gabbatt, the business manager of the party, asked Tom McMahon and Team Manager Walter Popplewell what rules the match was being played under, and the answer was: 'Australian Rules,' and so it was.

I repeat, I am open on the matter, but it should be settled once and for all by a joint body which is the correct decision, or at least what interpretation is to be placed on such a move. It is farcical to think that two countries can play the game of Rugby League and yet there be differences in the rules. This is a matter of interpretation, and as the Sydney panel of referees said the night I spoke to them, it wants settling for the good of the game. Australian tourist who have visited England tell me they have had similar troubles on rules interpretation. We agree it is all wrong, and I hope this is soon altered.

CHAPTER V.

CANBERRA. HARRY MURPHY'S BAD LUCK. AN
AMBITION ACHIEVED, TEN YEARS LATE. THE
FIRST BIG CLASH ... AND THE FIRST BIG
SURPRISE. DIRTIEST GAME. WELSHMEN
NEARLY FLOORED.

The Junee match was followed by another country game which was not in the original itinerary - Canberra. This gave us the opportunity of seeing the capital, which was built only because Sydney and Melbourne both wanted the honour. So a mid-way city was built. It is still only a very small city, but with a vast acreage. What might be in years to come does not require much imagination, but as yet it is just a dream. Of course, Parliament meets there, and we were shown round the Houses - replicas of our own Houses of Commons and Lords. While we were there there was an installation being completed for regular broadcasting of its sittings. Prime Minister, Mr. Joseph Chiffley, gave us a warm welcome and readily submitted to autograph chasing, which was a change from the tourists being chased themselves!

The Governor-General, H.R.H. Duke of Gloucester, came down to the match and the players were introduced to him on the field. This match had two noticeable incidents. Harry Murphy, the loose forward, playing his first game, had the misfortune to break his collar bone after twenty minutes. He did not play again on tour, and so went 12,000 miles to play twenty minutes' football. He took his misfortune philosophically despite the fact that he had his arm in a cage for a long while.

The second incident was of a lighter nature which, although having a laughable ending, might have had serious repercussions. Twenty minutes, with the English team playing twelve men, I saw a man walk towards the touch line side dressed in football kit, with an overcoat over his shoulders. He signalled to a player on the South Tablelands side who immediately developed a very obvious pulled muscle, so bad, in fact, that the referee said he had better go off.

He hobbled to the touch-line side, whereupon this stripped figure immediately threw off his overcoat and dashed on to the field to take his place. Substitution not being allowed, of course, everyone stood in amazement until the cheers of the home crowd were stilled by the approach of George Curran, a tough Lancashire lad from Wigan, who was the team's hooker. George, in a determined and deliberate manner, strode up to this newcomer and in loud Lancastrian dialect said: 'Aye, thee, tha' can't laik on here ... ger off!' Immediately the crowd heard this voice and the demanding attitude of the English hooker, they began to boo and make a regular hullabaloo at this objection. They said England were leading easily, why couldn't he be allowed to play?

The referee then came to and asked Ted Ward, the captain of the day, if he would allow him to play. The referee erred, for it was not right to put the onus on the English captain. Ward, in turn, enforced to say it was all in order, said he could play. This infuriated Curran, who turned to his captain and said: 'All right then, thee cum and shove i' t'pack.'

Above: The author on Tour. Eddie Waring, *extreme right back row*, with the 1958 British Rugby League touring party to Australia. Eddie Waring is the only man to have been on every post-war tour of Australia. Others in the picture are, *Back row (left to right)*: Brian Edgar, 'Vinty' Karalius, Dick Huddart, Alan Prescott, Mick Sullivan, Brian McTigue, Phil Jackson, Eric Fraser, Eddie Waring.
Front row: Eric Ashton, John Whiteley, Tom Harris, David Bolton, Alex Murphy.

Left: The famous Rismans; Bev and his dad, Gus

Above: 1962 Ashes success for Great Britain on the Sydney Cricket Ground. Players have exchanged jerseys with defeated Australians. Only Eric Ashton and Brian McTigue still wearing Great Britain jerseys.
From left to right: A. Murphy, W. Sayer, R. Huddart, Eric Ashton, N. Herbert, G. Round, N. Fox, B. McTigue, H. Poynton and W. Boston.

N.B. All photo captions are as per original book

Left: The most
controversial
scrum-half of
them all,
Alex Murphy
(*extreme left*)

Right: Lewis Jones,
The Golden Boy of
Rugby Union and League

Left: Eric Ashton,
the Wembley supremo
(with ball)

Above: Neil Fox (*centre*) - over four thousand points to his credit

Left: Jim Sullivan,
the points daddy
of them all

Right: Brian Bevan, world record holder of tries

Above: Tom van Vollenhoven, the South African who really made it

Above: Michael Sullivan. No one can touch him for Test match appearances - and tries. Jumping over colleague Alex Murphy

Left: Billy Boston, the man they called the Wigan peer

Above: Alan Prescott (*right*) with Alvin Ackerley (Halifax) after the 1956 Challenge Cup Final at Wembley

Left: Vince Karalius, the man the Aussies christened the 'Wild Bull of the Pampas'

Above: The first post war Test, Sydney, Australia. British players in white, *from left to right*: Gus Risman, Frank Whitcombe, Joe Egan, Ken Gee (behind him Australian Arthur Clues) and Britain's Doug Philips

Left: 'Rocky' Turner - the Aussies did not have to find a name for him

Above: Wembley Test match Britain *v.* France. British captain Ernest Ward, who introduced Lord Tedder to Ken Gee

Below: Jim Sullivan's Tour Trial Team 1932. *Back row (left to right):* 1. JackWoods (Barrow); 2. Arthur Atkinson (Castleford); 3. Bill Morgan (Wigan); 4. Frank Dawson (Hunslet); 5. Les White (Hunslet); 6. Harold Bowman (Hull); 7. Fred Butters (Swinton). *Front row (left to right):* 8. Alf Ellaby (St Helens); 9. Gwyn Davies (Wigan); 10. Jim Sullivan (Wigan); 11. Jack Oster (Oldham); 12. Bryn Evans (Swinton); 13. Alec Fildes (St Helens)

Curran just could not see the sense of continuing with the hard work, having in mind he had been packing with only four other forwards for practically the whole of the game. However, the player stayed on and the game quietly went to its death. But I admired Curran that day for not only grasping the position but having the courage to show what he thought.

I wrote to this effect in the *Sydney Telegraph*, and did I get some strong 'anti' letters! However, the Australian Board of Control quickly stopped any possible repetition by announcing that no more substitution must take place. The sequel I found out later. The substitute had been selected to play against the 1936 Tourists but a last-minute injury had prevented him from turning out. For ten years he had held on to the idea of one day playing against the English team. In 1946 he was past selection, but this did not deter this bright lad who, with the aid of a pal, achieved his long-awaited ambition. Everyone laughed at it in the end, but it might have been serious.

Two country games gave the Sydney scribes the chance to assess the team's value, and the general opinion was that it was not so good or as big as the 1936 side. They wrote 'This team can be beaten and there is not a lot to fear.' How these views became unstuck! For the Indomitables turned out to be the only team that ever came back from Australia without losing at least one Test Match.

The play of the tourists, however, was good enough to show they would be popular, and the stage was set for the first city clash, against New South Wales on the Sydney cricket ground. This would be the testing strength of both sides, for the power of the Australian team was, as yet, unknown, and it was obvious the majority of the Test team would come from New South Wales.

Prior to the city clash there had been a drastic cut on

entertainment. To all touring teams entertainment is lavish, and although well meant, the Managers had to be firm and put on a curfew. This was not quite a success, but the entertainment steadied up, at any rate. In addition, there were so many stories appearing about personal trouble and team troubles that a Press interview embargo was put on the players. The muzzle did not stop the interview stories, however, and in a blaze of publicity the team went up for its clash with New South Wales.

It was not a good game, and although England won by 14 pts. to 10 pts., neither side could feel that it had shown much. England had a goal by Risman which never went through the posts. This was my own opinion, which was later confirmed by the newsreel shots. England scored a try which many said had been knocked-on by Owens. This opinion was also proved conclusively by newsreel pictures of the incidents. These newsreel shots - they must have taken thousands of feet of all the big games - became very useful in settling arguments.

What was satisfactory from the English viewpoint was that the Australian side could not be much better than this New South Wales team, and I knew that England could play a lot better than they had done in this match. But as often happens, a blow quickly fell when, the day following, in a country game at Wollongong, the local side won. A storming game by a forward - Tiny Russell - a hard ground with dust galore, and a couple of injuries put paid to the tourists. The local enthusiasm was wonderful and carrying their hero off shoulder high they had a right royal day.

The trip to to Wollongong was the best of the day for the tourists. We went through lovely country, coming to the top of Sublime Point which, at 2,000 feet up, overlooks Wollongong, Port Kembla and the glorious Pacific with its panorama set below it was an unforgettable scene. Probably some of the players were thinking of this when they played! To make matters worse, this team was invited to play on the Sydney cricket ground on the day of the first Test in view of their splendid win. They played a City side which simply swamped them and knocked out all the good things we had told Sydney folk about them.

Still, they had their hour of glory this day which, incidentally, was a Sunday and resulted in local opposition from religious bodies. A record gate and, to Wollongong, a game they will talk about for ever, gave them unheard of recognition. One of the stars of this match was Bob Bartlett, a youngster who signed for Bramley and should now be enjoying England. There was much dust on this ground - it was like a Rodeo at times - and when the local forwards set up an attack they blinded the English side not with science, but with dust.

After their win they put a salve on the wound by presenting us with a food parcel and box of apples each. We called back at Sublime Point, this time in darkness, and the lights below and out to the Pacific looked like a superior Blackpool illuminations at its best. These country defeats sometimes are quite good for a touring team. This one knocked out any conceit we might have acquired.

No doubt, certain games on every tour stand out in various aspects. The second New South Wales game, which England won by 21 pts. to 7 pts., is memorable to me as the dirtiest game I had ever seen. The best indication I can give of this is to re-write what I published in the *Sydney Telegraph*. I said: 'Referee Bishop must have had the victory celebrations in mind and so, being charitable, allowed a number of players to stay on the field. In this game I saw more punches thrown than Tommy Burns threw against Clarrie Gordon at the Sydney Stadium.' Tommy Burns being the Australian welterweight boxing champion.

It was a real tough fight and with everything thrown into it. Actually, it was hard to understand why, but probably it got out of hand too early and was allowed to develop. This game was Ike Owens' masterpiece. He gave an outstanding exhibition, which resulted in such a big Press hand that it set him right for the remainder of the tour.

The popular phrase of the English visitors is 'Chooms', meaning, of course, the Northern pronunciation of 'Chums'. The *Truth* said in this game of the Chooms: 'Scrums and ruck were hectic. Punches were thrown and collected, dumps were harder than Hades hobs, and cautions were so frequent that they were ignored.'

It was a lusty, roaring crowd who paid £5,429, and they certainly got their money's worth in this game.

We were glad to get the dust of serious football off our boots and a trip to play the West Division at Orange was, I think, the high spot of the many high spots of country reception. This place is as lovely as it sounds, and Orange was at its best. Even the hotel staff welcomed us by putting small English flags in the bedroom with a few nice invitations, which time did not permit being accepted.

The *Central West Express*, with its whistle blowing 'cock-a-doodle-do's,' swept into Orange station, where hundreds of people were gathered to welcome the visitors. Immediately the boys got out of the train the whole town seemed to join hands and start singing 'For they are jolly good fellows.' Cameras and young autograph hunters besieged the players to get a glimpse of the 'sporting Ambassadors,' as the local paper described them. This paper said of the welcome: 'It was a welcome that was warm and spontaneous. The footballers had wide smiles for everyone, and they were as flashing as the warm sunshine which bathed the scene of animation and excitement.' It was described by Harry Sunderland as 'The perfect country outing.' Alan Ridley, the former Australian winger, was from this town, and had the job of broadcasting, which he did well. For the official Banquet the women of Orange shelled 40 lbs. of peas for the party, and I never heard as many speeches as I did that night. I lost count after 17, but they were so enthusiastic that it was impossible to break away.

The Welsh folk of this area gave the party a particularly wonderful late Banquet. There were so many turkeys and hams that some were left, and this, from a touring team, speaks volumes.

A local girl dressed in Welsh costume sang and Risman, the Captain, was presented with a leek, but we nearly came undone when the Chairman spoke in Welsh and a reply was called for in Welsh. Although there were 11 Welshmen in the party, only two could speak Welsh - and one of those was missing! Doug. Phillips, the tallest member of the side, drew on his stock of native words and gave a satisfactory reply. Daffodils were given to the Welsh boys to take to the local dance, and roses were given to us Englishmen, although this Banquet was definitely a Welsh victory.

The game itself was only a small part of the magnificent whole affair. One name in this match was Oriel Kennerson, a big long-kicking full back, whose performance was so good that Walter Popplewell, tour manager, tried to sign him for his club at Bramley. England won easily, but if ever there was a case of the result not counting this was it, for the social side and the ambassadorial effect was far more important than the result.

This is a rich part of Australia, as they showed in there war effort, but it is also rich in its love and affection for England, and particularly the Rugby League touring party.

With such a grand atmosphere it was a pity we were soon to be brought back to earth, but the following Sunday we were not merely brought back, but forcibly jerked back. And the place was easy to remember ... Newcastle.

CHAPTER VI.

WE LOSE A 'NEEDLE' GAME. THE NAVY IN
ACTION AGAIN. AUSSIES KNEW THE WELSH
CODE! FIRST TEST. THAT BITING INCIDENT.

Now Newcastle were keen to be pleasant, but they also meant business so far as the football side of it was concerned. Before giving the incidents of this match I should mention that in 1932 the Newcastle team nearly beat England. In 1936 they did win, and in 1946 this match was arranged two days before the first Test.

It seemed too much of a coincidence that this fixture had just happened like that, and I was surprised that the managers did not insist on an alteration. Even the hardened cute Johnny Quinlan admitted it was wrong, but there it was, and so on this Sunday, England felt the full might of Newcastle in no uncertain manner. The fixture compilation was not all bad in most respects but this was an arrangement which must never be repeated.

Immediately we got on the ground the atmosphere and tenseness were obvious. Only the thirteen players actually playing were allowed in the dressing room. The doorman was very difficult, and although he was later reprimanded for his attitude the players were obviously ruffled. The press box was crammed and jammed with anyone and everybody, and no official would undertake to give the International press visitors proper accommodation, so I took my typewriter and sat on the touch-line with it on my knees.

The game had not been in progress long before England hit trouble. Martin Ryan strained his groin and had to retire. Although we did not know it then, Martin had played his last game on the tour, and an urgent operation was required the following day.

The game itself was hard and rough, and Doug. Phillips received marching orders, to make England's number down to eleven. Newcastle took a second-half lead, and although Curran scored a try in the last minute near the posts, it was not allowed, and Newcastle got the verdict by 18 pts. to 13 pts.

Let me make myself clear. Newcastle played well and deservedly won, but it was far from pleasant or happy football. But two incidents were good. During the morning of the match a certain British ship had arrived in Newcastle, and the Commander, Captain and other high ranking Officers had come to the match. In addition, of course, the matelots had made their presence felt in no uncertain manner. They had scored tries with their caps and kicked goals, and had a happy hour before the game.

During the match, sitting near me was a very loud-mouthed Aussie -and they can be very loud-mouthed if they want to - who had doubted the legitimacy of almost every member of the English team. Now one British sailor did not like this so he quietly told this Aussie supporter to keep quiet. It had no effect, nor had a second censure.

At the third attempt this laddie thought it was time for action, so without further ado he administered a beautiful uppercut that placed the spectator on his back, out to the wide. This sailor intended to do the job properly, so he picked up his erstwhile opponent and proceeded to carry him off the ground. Now it was unfortunate that his course off the ground was past the Navy officers. Probably he should have just given 'eyes right' to his superior officers, but being an unusual undertaking he dropped his cargo, gave a salute, picked up the body, and proceeded to his original destination. Few people saw it done, it was so neat and effective, but the English team had no further trouble from this particular individual.

The second incident concerned the two English half-backs, or really I should say the two Welsh half-backs who, that day, played for the team. In desperation they tried a certain move and spoke of it in Welsh. The move failed. They again passed word in their native tongue, but again the move failed. A third time was a do-or-die effort. But before they could attempt it a voice from behind the opposition forwards said: 'Don't bother boys, I come from Swansea, too!' and the sing-song voice was that of Madge, the Newcastle captain, who came from Garnant, the same place as Ted Ward, the English player.

There was trouble after the game and police protection was needed to get all the players back into the dressing room. The local committee held a meeting after the match and, as is the usual custom, 'sending off sufficient' was the verdict on Phillips.

This was a real set-off for the first Test, which came on the King's birthday, the day following our pleasant Sunday afternoon outing to Newcastle.

Test football in Sydney is unlike any in any other part of the world. It has an atmosphere that is electric, to say the least. With the aid of a wonderful Press, so far as publicity is concerned, the whole situation is one full of dynamite. Sydney papers had diagrams of almost every English move and they produced every possible reason for every possible result.

Anyone who has played on the Sydney cricket ground will tell what a thrill he got when walking on to the ground. Probably the fact that crowds had started queueing the night before, or that every hour on the radio the commentator was reporting how the ground was filling up imparts that sense of importance. Maybe it is exaggerated, but to all the players, and to me - for I was on the field taking movie shots - the feeling as the teams walk out and the roars of the Sydney crowd makes one tremble with sheer excitement.

After laying a wreath on the Sydney War Memorial, the Englishmen were set for the first big Test encounter. Only two of the side - Gus Risman and Tom McCue - had had experience of this Sydney ground in Test football, so it was a speculation as to how the team would react.

It was pretty obvious from the start that Tom McMahon, the referee, was not having a repetition of the New South Wales game, when many should have gone off and none did. So obvious was this that I think Tom slipped up when he sent Jack Kitching off soon after the start for alleged striking.

This incident caused a tremendous discussion, and this is my view of the whole affair. Kitching tackled Jorgenson, and whilst both players lay on the ground, Kitching felt a sharp pain in his side. He pushed Jorgenson off, got up, and immediately put his hand to his side. Referee McMahon thought he had hit Jorgenson, and to the amazement of the English centre he had to walk. At half-time Kitching showed me, and others, what certainly looked like teeth marks on his body. A photograph was taken of them, and newsreel shots later produced, in slow motion, proved conclusively that at any rate Jorgenson was in a position to cause the injury.

I know that Kitching was not the first player to be bitten,

either in Australia or England, nor will he be the last, but both Jorgenson and Tom McMahon slipped badly by stating that this could not possibly have been the case as the players were never in a position to do what was alleged. It caused a terrific stir, for it followed another alleged biting incident where a player had been in hospital for many weeks after losing part of his ear in a tackle.

Like many other things, the Kitching biting incident blew over, but I still feel that Tom McMahon was so worried about the N.S.W. rough game that he sent Kitching off rather prematurely. Had he cautioned him it is doubtful if we should have ever heard of this biting trouble. However, this gave England an uphill battle with twelve men in the first Test.

The result - eight all - was only affected by Australia when Lionel Cooper, now at Huddersfield, scored a great try after drawing Gus Risman beautifully away from the touch-line. As Ron Bailey had kidded Gus with a perfect 'dummy' for the first try, Huddersfield players played a big part in this match. Ron Bailey, of course, was the former Huddersfield player, and to the surprise of English folk gained a place in the Australian team as a centre, whereas in England he had played loose forward.

McCue and Owens were good in this game, and although I was somewhat disappointed at a draw, under the circumstances, it was a good performance and the English players were certainly satisfied.

CHAPTER VII.

ON THE AIR. THE WELSH CHOIR. MARTIN RYAN BRINGS DOWN THE HOUSE. VALUES OF SPONSORED RADIO.

I have previously said that Rugby League in Sydney is of fanatical interest. Let me enlarge. There are a matter of half-a-dozen commercial radio stations and the Australian Broadcasting Commission. On a big match day the side-line is full of commentators, some of these being ex-players like Ray Stehr, the Test forward, who has toured England and is now a coach with Manly; Frank O'Rourke, who played with Leeds as a centre, was with the A.B.C., while Cyril Angles was probably the outstanding commentator. So far as racecourse commentaries were concerned, Cyril Angles had no equals. He had persistently refused big money to go to America and he had a natural manner that made him the most popular broadcaster in Australia. Cyril was also a practical joker and he tried to pull a fast one over Gus Risman and myself at Orange, but our inside information fortunately proved too good.

I was signed up with the 2 U.W. Station which, each Friday night, covered the *Sydney Telegraph Sports Parade*. This consisted of an hour with sports as its main topic. Rugby League had a prominent spot, and we had various personalities in it. On one occasion the Welsh Choir sang a couple of songs, which were well received, and Frank Packer, the popular owner of the *Telegraph*, very generously gave the boys £50 for their 'kitty'. This Welsh Choir was formed because it was felt that all Welsh Choirs are popular, but as often as not, the Welsh Choir consisted of Yorkshiremen, Lancastrians, and a couple of Cumbrians. Still it sounded good to be called a Welsh Choir, and when they got down to business and sang *Cym Rhondda*, *Sos pan fach* or *Calan Lan* (Clean Heart) which were the main items from their repertoire, they were really good.

On another occasion I conceived the idea that a singing footballer would be of great interest to this big radio audience of the *Sports Parade*. While coming back from that beautiful spot, Palm Beach, Martin Ryan with his nice tenor voice singing 'Kathleen' and 'Irish Lullaby', gave me an idea. With the assistance of Hugh Dash, the clever Sports Editor of the *Telegraph*, Martin Ryan was engaged to sing. For a week an organist rehearsed Martin, whose talent did not include musical knowledge. He could sing well by ear, so the big night, with the players remaining in the hotel to listen-in and I taking the budding Crosby down to the studio.

For some reason Martin developed stage fright, and I thought he was going to run out. I got him to the studio in good time, which was my first error, and I had to follow him around for fear of him taking a dive. I had to go on the stage first to give a message of welcome to all the Boys' Clubs of Australia, from the Y.M.C.A. and Boys' Clubs of England, and to tell them that Martin Ryan was a product of such a Boys' Club.

Martin came on to the stage when he heard his name -

much too soon, but we managed to get over that. The first cue for the song was given and the organist went on to the first note. Unfortunately, just at the moment, Ron Berge, the *Telegraph* sports photographer, came up to the front of the stage and 'shot' Martin in the act of commencing his song.

This not only threw him off, but he started about seven notes too high, stopped, looked at me, and eventually went on his way in the wrong key. With a marvellous piece of judgement the organist eventually got on to the same key and away they went, with my knees literally knocking. I was fully aware that near the end there was a very high note, which I was certain Martin could not possibly get, and I wondered what was going to happen. The note came, and by a very brilliant effort the singer got it. He did not crack and finished in superb style. He received a terrific reception, and later was so pleased with himself that he said he would have another go. I was such a nervous wreck that I told Martin I could not possibly stand the strain. I brought back with me the broadcast record of that effort, and my lecture audiences have laughed and enjoyed hearing the reproduction. On a number of occasions and at various places, such as hospitals and dances, the players were called upon to render items.

There is a lot to be said for commercial radio, providing it is not overdone. At least it was entertaining and provided sport presentation far in excess of what we hear in England. Rugby League, which is given such small consideration by the B.B.C., is one of the main sporting subjects in New South Wales and Queensland.

The usual quiz programmes were held and a sporting quiz at half-a-crown doubled, was presented in the *Telegraph Sports Parade*. The racing special of 'Mandrake Rides Again' was an interesting speculation on the racing side, a silhouette of the commentator, complete with topper and glasses, is shown on the studio screen, and to the background of race crowd chatter he gives an imaginary commentary of the big race to be held the following day.

The studio accommodates about 400, and the tickets are always snapped up before the day; in fact, there is always a crowd waiting for any opportunity to get in to see this show. With cheer leaders, who indicate when to applaud and when to subside, and the band leader, who, incidentally, looked remarkably like Brian Aherne, the presentation is full of colour and interest for the whole hour.

It was remarkable, by the way, that out of our full party of 32 there were no outstanding pianists. On previous tours there was usually some individual good with the piano, but we had no pianist at all.

CHAPTER VIII.

CHOOSING THE RIGHT MANAGERS. PLAYERS'
TEMPERAMENTS. PICNIC IN THE COUNTRY.
BEAUTIES OF THE BLUE MOUNTAINS. RAIN
AND SUNSHINE. REUNION IN QUEENSLAND.

On all tours there are winners and losers. When I was told of past tours, when certain players had failed I could not visualise how or why ... but I know now.

Players become homesick and never settle down to the idea of the tour, or get matters into the right perspective. On this tour there were fellows who, from the first few days, became homesick. They never settled down to the job they really went out to do. It was, of course, all the more difficult with the early days on the *Indomitable*, or there was not the usual life of a passenger ship with its mixed company.

The Managers are probably the most important part of a tour selection, and it is most imperative to get two men who not only know their job - one as business manager and one as team manager - but two men who can align their tastes for the benefit of the party. Tours have been known to fail through bad appointments in this department, and I think serious attention should be given to this problem. The Rugby League exclude professional managers from taking a post, but probably the day is not far distant when a professional man might be considered. Fortunately, England have not had the same trouble as some touring teams coming to these shores, but there have been troubles which have never been divulged to the public, and a little more consideration to men's temperament might have avoided such troubles.

Some players make ideal tourists, but others are absolutely unsuited to a trip of six months away from home. I shall never forget the remark a certain International said when he stepped off the boat on the return journey. When asked what he liked best of the trip he said 'Getting home!' Probably it was, but the implication that he had been round the world yet found nothing that stood out showed the trend of his thoughts.

The 1946 tourists were a temperate lot and really behaved in a splendid manner, which gained them praise wherever they went. I repeat, there were winners and losers - even on this trip. Tamworth was a country match where one of the biggest scores was registered - 61 pts. to 5. Most of the English side were non-Test players, and they gave a remarkable exhibition of football.

Naturally, all cannot be Test team players, and it is hard on a player to realise that he is often second best in selection. Yet there were only isolated incidents where a man showed his feelings at non-selection, but there were dozens where a player assisted the chap actually selected.

At Tamworth there was a visit to the 'Farrar' Memorial Agricultural High School. It is a great dairy district, and when Harry Murphy saw the cattle with covers on he said: 'It's the first time I've seen cows with rugs on!'

Tamworth was like most country grounds on which matches are played in Australia, not solely football grounds but exhibition grounds. 'Round ovals' is the usual name -

oval, with seats round the arena and one stand. It is always a red-letter day when an English team plays on these grounds, for there is keen competition by the clubs to stage the game, and it may be that only one game in twenty years in allotted to a particular ground.

Before we left New South Wales for Queensland we had the usual trips to the many beauty spots of this State. One of the outstanding was the picnic - all trips are called picnics - to the famous Blue Mountains and Jenolan Caves.

Katoomba, Blackheath and Lithgow are the most prominent municipalities of the Blue Mountains area, which is about 80 miles from Sydney. We travelled by road to this spot, and for the first time we saw snow in Australia. They have a very famous train called the *Caves Express*, which travels from Sydney at a speed of 73 miles per hour until the last 30 miles, when it climbs over 3,000 feet. A vast area of mountain, forests and amazing waterfalls are just a few of the attractions of the Blue Mountains. The Bridal Veil Falls are centred in some of the most magnificent scenery in the Blue Mountains. Mount Victoria is perhaps the best known of mountain centres en route to the Jenolan Caves. The blazing of the trail to this area was made in 1813 to an unknown area beyond the Great Dividing Range.

The Jenolan Caves - on the style of Cheddar Gorge, yet where far more walking is required - are in the heart of the Blue Mountains. We were guests of the Government at their Trust House, which has accommodation for 200 people who can only remain for a given period so that everyone can have a stay in this beauty spot. The Caves contain, in their subterranean vaults and corridors in the living rock, an endless variety of limestone formations rivalling in fantasy any dram of Eastern art.

Throughout the ages water has dissolved the limestone, forming the great caverns, and by constant evaporation, drip by drip, has built up masses of brilliant and amazingly coloured rock shapes. At the touch of a switch, electric lights in powerful parabolic reflectors, reveal exquisitely decorated floors, ceilings and walls. There are mighty pillars of dripstone and alabaster columns in various designs. Translucent shawls, like woven fabrics, hang from colossal walls, elfin grottoes, golden cascades of glittering crystals, jewels in profusion are just a minute part of the surpassing beauty to be seen during the two hours' tour through part of the Jenolan Caves. It is a real Nature's masterpiece and is world-famous.

Underneath the caves there is a river which can be seen at many points. Amongst the more famous parts of the Caves are 'The Grand Arch', 'The Devil's Coach House,' and into which, incidentally, the large Sydney General Post Office could be put bodily, 'Carlotta Arch' and the 'Lucas Rocks'. Outside the caves the tame, yet frightened, rock wallabies bound about with Red Parrot as company. It was certainly a fascinating three days spent in what is justly described as Australia's most glamorous playground.

Another famous spot we visited was Palm Beach, where it rained so hard that the bus had to stop, as the driver could not see his way through the rain mist.

The Harbour trip is one of the highspots of any touring sides entertainment schedule. But again the weather beat us, although I had the pleasure of this trip before we left Sydney.

Shaking New South Wales off for a while we entrained for sunny Queensland, with Brisbane as the centre. Queensland rightly claims a wonderful climate, and although it was, of course, mid-winter, the weather was gorgeous. Unfortunately, a coal strike placed the city in darkness for a while, and the inconveniences were rather unfortunate.

England To Australia and New Zealand

Brisbane is a keen Rugby League centre, but not so fanatical or hysterical over its sport at Sydney. Yet it is as keen, and when the Queensland side beat the Tourists by 21 pts. to 20 pts., the success of this part of the tour was assured. A last minute effort by Albert Johnson almost brought a win against Queensland, but the State team were the better side and deserved their victory.

The Brisbane Press does not devote so much space to the sport as its New South Wales contemporaries, but still there is plenty written. L.H. Kearney, a former great referee - Frank Gallagher told me he was the best Australia has had - was a writer for one of the Brisbane papers, and his interest in this grand game of ours was only shaded by passing years. Queensland, probably the Cinderella State, has had its periods of success over New South Wales, but in the main it has been second best so far as results are concerned. But some great players and officials have come from this land of sunshine to do credit to Australia. One of Queensland's earlier names to go down to fame was M. Bolewski, who played full-back in London in 1908. Heidke, a name that repeated itself more than once, is well known. Chris McKivatt - Harry Sunderland tells me he was probably the greatest of all half-backs - played with Queensland, as did Tommy Gorman and Cecil Synsley, J. Craig and Norman Potter, Duncan Thompson and Vic Ambruster, Herb. Steinohrt and Dan Dempsey, W. Spencer and Mick Madsen, Hector Gee and Joe Wilson, up to Freddie Gilbert and Jack Reardon. On, yes, I have missed names out, players who, even unlike all these names, did not figure in Test football, such as Eric Harris, Jeff Moores, and others whose names are as well known in England as in Australia.

When we played Ipswich I had a visit from a lady 90 years of age, who asked me if I could talk of Hector Gee. Sure I could, for I had signed little Hector for Leeds when I was manager there. And this grand old lady was none other than Hector Gee's grandmother. How she liked to talk of this lad, who has been a name in Australia and English football! Tom Gorman, an influential member of Brisbane's community, was there to write his version of the big game, while I was able to persuade probably the greatest of all wingers - Harold Horder - to see a Rugby League game after an absence of ten years. How I remember him when I was only a kid, playing for the Aussies against Dewsbury at Crown Flatt, and Dewsbury licking them, too! I reminded Harold of this day, and his memory was so clear and his brain so bright that he told me inside stories and incidents of this particular match. This gives you an idea of how well this dapper winger has worn. His scoring pal of that 1921 side - Cecil Blinkhorn - was there with him at this reunion.

Granted, Queensland have not provided as many players for the International field as New South Wales, but they have produced personalities that have graced the game wherever it is talked about. Eric Simmonds, the present Queensland secretary, a solicitor and a smart little chap who will probably be one of the next managers from Australia, welcomed us in a way that was as warm as the Queensland sun. With veteran Vic Jenson, as President of the Queensland league, they are well served by the men in command.

The name of Vic Jenson followed us throughout our Queensland tour, for in almost every town we visited we saw a Vic Jenson shoe shop. He was a big business man in the sale of footwear. We also saw a lot of the name 'Nigger Brown Transport' and Nigger Brown was a famous Queensland player. These Queensland boys certainly stick to the game even after their playing days are over.

CHAPTER IX.

BRISBANE, CITY OF PARKS. SHARK FISHING.
LONDON GIRLS GIVE US TEA. ON BY GOODS
TRAIN. WE WALK OUT, AND A FRIEND COMES
TO THE RESCUE. MAGNETIC ISLAND.

What of Brisbane? Near the Grey Street bridged, on the City side, there stands an obelisk which reads: 'Here John Oxley landed to look for water, discovered the site of this City 28th September, 1842.' The Governor approved of the site and the settlement was named 'Edinglassie' which, however, was later changed to Brisbane Town.

Such was the beginning of Brisbane. It is the fifth largest city in the world in area, covering 375 square miles. The population is about 370,000, while the total population of Queensland is 1,036,500. The city contains more than 5,500 acres of park lands and the main area, the Botanical gardens, is a wonderful park of tropical and sub-tropical flora. The Domain, Albert Park, and other parks, are well known. New Farm Park, with its 22,000 rose trees, is truly magnificent.

Brisbane River is the main water life and is spanned by five bridges. The City Hall, where we went to many invitation dances, is the finest in Australia. The building occupying an island site of more than two acres. Over the main entrance in King George Square, is the tympanum, the

213

central figure being nine feet high. A feature of this building is the tall clock tower, which is 312 feet high. The observation tower, at 250 feet from the ground, provides a wonderful view of Brisbane. The handsome concert hall in this building seats 2,500 persons, and the city organ is regarded as the finest in the Southern hemisphere.

Like all cities in Australia, Brisbane lacks live theatres of any size. Australia is behind in live entertainment. The shows I saw were certainly nothing near the British standard. Such artists as Tommy Trinder and George Formby obviously have the field to themselves when they get to Australia. Will Geraghty, the famous American, entertained us at his Cremorne Theatre, but the size of his audiences was cut by the coal strike.

There are many natural attractions in the Brisbane area. The Lone Pine and Koala Sanctuary being among the most popular. Many of our players would have like to bring home the Koala, so attractive is this little teddy bear. The Tamborine Mountain trip and the 'Green Mountains' and National Park, reaching a height of 4,000 feet, were other memorable visiting places.

On the car trips place names like Scarborough, Margate and Southport reminded one of England very often.

The two big grounds in Brisbane - the Woolloongabba and the Exhibition - are both good grounds, and the team played on them both. Cricket is also played on these grounds.

We were very fortunate in making the acquaintance of the Gow family. Norman and Stewart Gow, who are wholesale grocers in Brisbane, proved good friends to the British members. Food parcels and cigarettes were very welcome gifts, and later a crowd of us went shark fishing with Norman Gow in the Pacific. Gus Risman, Harry Murphy, Jack Kitching, Ernest Ward, Wilf. Gabbatt, and myself had a day in an effort to chalk up a shark. We were unlucky, but that did not spoil the day aboard the Bonaventure, and to this day Gus Risman will remember the asparagus he had aboard . A keen sportsman, Norman Gow had many shark catches to this credit and his cine film, taken in colour, proved it when he showed the film to the boys in the hotel. The friendship of the Gows is one of the things that stands out in the many happy Brisbane contacts.

Radio is bright in Queensland, and in Brisbane, George Hardman is the shining light. A jovial commentator and announcer, he was quick to exploit the activities of the boys at his Fireman's Ball and his other social interests. George was ever-ready to give the game a boost, and men like him are assets to the code.

I was signed up with a commercial radio to broadcast at each stopping place in Queensland, but after 'doing' a couple of towns the coal situation became so bad that the wireless programmes were cut to a couple of hours a day, with sporting broadcasts cut completely.

From our Queensland defeat we went North. In England that would mean 'We went cold.' In Australia it meant 'We went hot,' and into the tropical region. The first of the country games was at Bundaberg. This was the British team's worst display. They won all right, but very unsatisfactorily. A bad referee, who was too theatrical, and a number of players, tired through travel, asserted themselves. Bundaberg was best remembered for the exploits of Bert Hinkler, the famous flyer.

Mid-winter's day we spent in open-necked cricket shirts, visiting a rum distillery in Bundaberg. The sampling department was the most popular, although the story I liked best was that of the big vat which burst and poured gallons into the local river. Thousands of fish gave themselves up hopelessly drunk, and for some time after this fish could be picked up with no opposition. This distillery is the largest in

Australia but, as in England, the Customs and Excise take their full quota of revenue. Out of every 82/- worth sold, 4/- go to the firm and 78/- to the Customs and Excise.

We also visited a large sugar cane farm. For miles we sat on seats on an open wagon and went through lanes in the fields with tall sugar canes reaching as high as the wagon. This was in a place called Bigara, and late in the afternoon when we were presented with a scrumptious tea with plenty of cream cakes by six London girls working on the farm, they sang 'There'll always be an England.' It was really a little shack, and how the girls had arrived at this remote part of the world I never asked, but it was a grand thing for them to meet people from home, and the hospitality was of the best we struck. But we could not forget Yorkshire, for the machinery in the factory was made by a Huddersfield firm, and the name-plate was there for all to see.

From Bundaberg our travel problems really started. The coal strike had resulted in most passenger trains being taken off, and at one period Manager Gabbatt talked of calling the Northern Queensland tour off. Eventually, accommodation was fixed for our journey on a goods train, or I should say at the rear of a goods train. The first stage of 178 miles took us over 12 hours.

At least it gave us the opportunity of seeing some famous bush country, with its kangaroos diving here and there. We had heard so much of the Australian kangaroo but had not seen it and we began to doubt its existence. However, while on this goods train we saw plenty. The goods train was really good. It made a triumphal entry into Rockhampton with a wagon load of beer, 200 squealing pigs, six prize bulls, a couple of horses, and the British Rugby League touring party. Passing through a place called Gladstone, Frank Whitcombe, at 17 stone, trotted alongside the train 'to do a bit of training,' as he called it.

This bad bit of travel began the urge for air travel, which eventually engulfed us.

The arrival at Rockhampton brought with it more problems of hotel accommodation. The party was split into three and the stay at the hotel, where I went with ten of the players, had an unfortunate ending. It was obvious from our arrival that the place was unsuited for any touring team. It was in the style of a lodging house and the players refused to remain in it. Only because it was well after midnight did they stay the first night. Most of the time was spent in catching the insects which appeared to like this place, and when Frank Whitcombe laid on his bed and it went in, that was the crowning blow.

The following morning this party walked out of their 'hotel'. The incident recalls a similar one when the 1936 Touring Team walked out of their Sydney hotel. We were then taken to a really nice hotel, which should have been booked in the first place. Stewart Gow, of Brisbane, came to our assistance, for his branch manager at each of the towns visited, reported and placed himself at my disposal. The local knowledge in this case was invaluable.

This 'night' episode did not affect the players in their match against Rockhampton, which was won comfortably, and the local Officials were all keen to amend for the slight disturbance.

Although it was probably a genuine error, mistakes over hotel accommodation should not happen, particularly in these country towns, where there are usually sound hotels. The Australian hotels generally fail badly compared with the English ones, so far as things like sanitation, etc., are concerned. The food was always wonderful, but many aspects of hotel life could be improved.

Another lap, this time taking us 20 hours up to Townsville. This was the last straw that broke the back -

almost physically, too. We tried to get some sleep and unfortunately for me, as I was shorter than Ernest Ward, my carriage mate, I had to sleep on the rack with six-foot Ernest coiled up on the seat. Players like Willie Davies, Dai Jenkins and Willie Horne were other unlucky ones. Because of their short stature they were elevated to the rack. To complete a bad night we arrived at Townsville early - 5 a.m. - to find the local hotel keeper did not expect us until 9 a.m., and the beds were not ready. 'Oh, to be a traveller!' said Eric Batten.

The Townsville match was against North Queensland and the Rockhampton game being against Central Queensland. Actually, Townsville was not the most northerly point that Rugby was played, for previous touring sides had visited Cairns, still further up the Coast, say, another 180 miles. Considering the rail problems we were satisfied to halt at Townsville and pay our respects.

This match was the second to be played on a Sunday, but this did not deter a big crowd from seeing the game, which the Tourists won by 55 pts. to 16 pts. Dai Jenkins had his best game in this match, and his combination with Horne was particularly brilliant. Eric Batten scored four tries before he pulled a leg muscle, which was to keep him out of the second Test game. Captain of Townsville was an air pilot - Bob Jackson - who was their best player and a grand fellow.

It is possible in Townsville to climb - I went by road - to the top of a large mountain, from which you have an amazing long view of the surrounding area. In the distance could be seen the county jail - quite a big one - while seawards the famous Magnetic Island was plainly visible. We went out to Magnetic Island, which was discovered by Captain Cook in 1770.

The story goes that the compass on the *Endeavour* would not operate properly when passing this Island, so it was named Magnetic, being supposedly full of iron. It is a very pretty and attractive spot, with a number of landing bays. There a a large number of coconut groves and most of us secured our own coconuts, some of which were brought back to England. There are many coral reefs surrounding this area and, of course, the renowned Barrier Reef is not so far away. There is plenty of tropical fruit. Landings are made at Nellie Bay, Picnic Bay and Arcadia.

Townsville is known as the Queen City of the North. It was founded by Captain Robert Towns in 1864. It has a population of 31,000, and is the second largest city in Queensland. Its wharves are quite good and can accommodate vessels up to 15,000 tons. Principal exports are sugar 120,729 tons, metals 101,838 tons, frozen, chilled and canned beef 23,337 tons, wool 15,591 tons (99,846 bales). Townsville is the leading Queensland export port and a year's total export tonnage is 294,349 tons valued at £7,500,000, so its importance can readily be seen.

There is a very good natural zoo just out of Townsville which Manager Wilf. Gabbatt, Ernest Ward and Eric Batten, and myself, went to see. I have seen Eric Batten do surprising things on a football field, but he got his biggest shock in this zoo. He was giving nuts to a rather vicious monkey, holding the bag in his left hand. The monkey held out its hand for the nuts and, with Eric off his guard, darted down with it other paw and collared the bag, making Eric jump with amazement.

CHAPTER X.

WE START TO FLY, AND GET OUR BIGGEST
VICTORY. REFEREE PROBLEM. 'NO ENTRY' FOR
THE TEST MATCH. UNOFFICIAL GATEMEN
FROM YORKSHIRE. HOW THE PROFITS WENT.
CROWD STOPS A MATCH.

Townsville will go down in the records as the place from where the first British team flew. After all the travel worries air service came into reckoning, and the whole party flew in various drafts down to Mackay or, in the case of one or two Test players, straight to Brisbane.

Air transport in Australia is now a very big affair. The distances are so vast that flying is essential, and Australia holds the record for the cheapest flying in the world. You can fly for 3d. a mile, and while there has been a tendency in other countries to increase travel costs, Australia have actually cut theirs. They are remarkably free from accidents, too! Statistics say that from July, 1941, to January, 1947, nearly 13,000,000 miles were flown per passenger fatality.

Farmers, townsfolk and ordinary workpeople use the planes as means of transport. Of course, Australia has a very great advantage over other countries in her flying - the good weather and an absence of many mountains. The air hostesses are amongst the most attractive girls I have seen, many of whom could make a name on the stage. Intelligence and good looks went together. Cattle are moved by air and Bob Jackson, the Townsville skipper, told me he had moved all manner of goods up North in hours where it would have taken days by any other means of transport. A Shetland pony travelled 900 miles by air and was a very good passenger. By the time the next English team visits Australia the major part of the Queensland tour might easily be done by air.

Townsville to Mackay is a matter of 205 miles, so that the first stage of the trip was done easily and comfortably. Mackay was to provide the team's biggest victory. It was a personal triumph for Jim Lewthwaite, who scored seven tries, and Ernest Ward, who kicked 17 goals, in a total of 94 pts. to nil. This was the biggest score ever recorded by a touring side in a recognised match. When I said this at a recent lecture in Halifax, Frank Williams, who toured with the English team in 1914, said that his team won a Melbourne by over 100 pts. in a friendly.

In this Mackay match the team, composed mainly of what is known in football parlance as 'ham and eggers,' gave a remarkable team performance. With the score at 89 pts. to nil the bell went. In Australia when time is up a bell goes, and at the next dead ball the whistle brings the conclusion of the match. Tom McCue, the captain in this match, heard the bell at 89 pts. to nil and realised that there was still a chance to break the Brisbane record of 91 pts. to 2 pts. by Australia at Bramley in 1921. So he called out to his colleagues to keep the ball in play. It flashed across to Lewthwaite, who raced away from the half-way line to ground behind the posts, for Ernie Ward to complete his day's record of 17 goals. Willie Davies was brilliant at stand-off.

The crowd appreciated the big win, although they advised the Australian side to close the innings at threequarter time. It is to the credit of this local side that they continued to play open football, which, of course, assisted the English team in this mammoth effort.

Towards the second Test a refereeing problem cropped up. It is the custom of the State officials to put forward a panel of three referees from which the English managers make their choice. Three referees Messrs. Chambers, McMahon - Tom McMahon of Sydney - and H. Reithmuller, were named. Only J.W. Chambers had been seen by the English managers, so they asked that Referee Shuttleton, who was in charge of the Rockhampton game, be appointed.

The Australian Board of Control did not like this request and took a strong line by emphatically refusing to consider any officials outside the panel indicated. In the end J.W. Chambers was appointed, but it was felt that the request of the English managers should have been considered. I might add that a similar principal is adopted in England. In 1936 the team manager of the English side made a request for another name to be added to the panel, but it was also turned down in this occasion.

While on the subject of referees there is a remarkable difference in ability. Tom McMahon, the Test referee, is as good as any in England, and some of the City referees, given a chance, would do well. But the country referees were very poor. In two cases the local team were given about 20 penalties, with none for the English side. Now I will never believe that a local team never breaks the rules during a game! I felt that these local referees were refereeing the Englishmen rather than the match. It was not so in city games, where the standard was high.

The stage was set for the second Test - a vital one to England. A win meant the retention of the mythical Ashes. To come 12,000 miles and not take home the Ashes is a sad position, and a win at the Exhibition ground meant that the honour could not pass to Australia. The eventual win by 14 pts. to 5 pts. provided the usual champagne after the battle. The newspapers had gathered the idea that this match might result in a repetition of the famous 'Battle of Brisbane'. It did not, although it nearly developed into no match at all. So great were the crowds that a couple of hours before the game all gates were closed, even the official one. Prominent League officials, press, players, and men with tickets were just not allowed in. The field itself was swarmed with fans and word was sent to the Hotel Daniell, where the English players were staying, to delay the team's departure. Eventually, with the aid of police cars, Mounties and cycles, the procession of taxis with the players in, was made to the ground, and the men who mattered were put safely into their dressing rooms.

It was a record gate for Brisbane. Nobody knows just how many were there, for the gates were rushed, but I should reckon 65,000. Every vantage point inside and outside was used, and the more reckless climbed high up on to an electric standard, which looked very dangerous. Wireless commentators had their tables brushed aside and they finished up by standing on them, looking over the spectators' heads. I never thought the match would be started, and even with the teams on the field, play was held up twice while the white-helmeted police very tactfully drove the spectators back over the touch-line, only just over, but enough for the referee to say 'We'll start.' After the first scrum Referee Chambers stopped the game for another touch-line clearance. Again the match started, and this time it continued. Tom McCue, that grand strategic scrum-half, took England to victory down the blind side, where policeman Arthur Bassett was the hero, finishing off with three tries. It was a great day for Bassett, who had come into the side for Batten. Albert Johnson also played a courageous game, receiving a lot of buffeting but scoring a grand try.

How the Aussies kept falling for McCue's 'dummies' and blind side moves surprised me. Either Ricketty Johnson, the Australian coach, had not emphasised this move enough or the players had forgotten his instructions. Lionel Cooper got a great try for Australia, in which he took three English defenders with him, but it was not sufficient. The famed goal kicking of Joe Jorgenson never came up to reputation. Near the end tempers developed, and after Ernest Ward had received a beautiful uppercut, which put him completely out, Joe Egan was caught retaliating and Joe had to march. But victory was then assured.

The first spectator had arrived at the ground at 3 a.m., and at 4.30 a party of ladies with baskets of food, pillows, scarves, papers and magazines took their stand. By 10 a.m. 30,000 programmes were sold.

The English party were happy and they began now to look at the tour profits, which were so important to them. the players stood to draw one-third of the profits, and with each gate being a record it was expected that their earnings would develop into a record distribution. In 1932 England's share from all matches was £18,539 in Australian currency, which decreased to £15,077 when it was cleared from the bank. It showed a profit of £6,161 after all expenses had been paid, giving the players £100 bonus.

As figures later turned out, on this 1946 tour the expenses were larger than ever, mainly due to flying charges and increased payments to players' dependents, but each player received a bonus of £135. Wives received £2 10s. dependents allowance, and each child 7/6d. The players themselves were allowed 30/- whilst at sea and £2 on land. The managers were each allowed £400.

The players themselves were disappointed at the loss in their bonus, and they made application to the English Rugby League Council to be granted an additional bonus for discomforts and loss of clothes, etc., whilst travelling under difficulties. This was turned down, and the original contract was adhered to.

Whilst on finance, The Australian players were given £32 each for a Test Match appearance, which included loss of work for one week while they trained together.

Another game was played in Brisbane, against the City side, where the spectators threw oranges at the referee. It was a waste of lovely fruit, but they took exception to a try awarded to Jack Kitching near the end, which clinched a 21 pts. to 15 pts. victory for the tourists. Bob Nicholson had played in this game following a long absence through illness. I believe Nicholson would have been one of the successes of the tour had he kept well. Whilst in hospital Ted Ward gave a smart answer when asked how Bob was, replying, 'Oh, he has taken a turn for the nurse!'

Whilst the Australian selectors were tuning up to try and get one win and make the series equal in the third Test, the Tourists played matches at Ipswich and Toowoomba, winning both comfortably. The biggest sensation at Toowoomba was when part of a big crowd climbed on to the roof of a building inside the ground and hundreds fell inside amongst the horse stalls. Police were unable to stop this invasion and, surprisingly, nobody was killed. Damage was estimated at about £500. This was the Royal Agricultural Show ground.

Fred Hughes got his first try of the tour in this game and made himself a candidate for the third Test by a storming display. Ipswich was one of the matches where England never received a penalty award against 17 to the locals. The game finished in a remarkable manner. When England scored in the last minute the crowd burst on to the field and stopped the goal kicker taking the conversion shot. The game finished without it having been taken.

CHAPTER XI.

ERIC BATTEN'S WONDERFUL RUN. WHY THE
AUSTRALIANS FAILED. A PROPHECY COMES
TRUE.

One more country game at Grafton - a lovely little spot with a comfortable win - left us with only the final (third) Test to create history, we hoped. No team had visited Australia without losing one of the Tests and this was an opportunity to bring out another record to add to the many that had already been registered, good, bad and otherwise.

There was more speculation over the composition of the team for the third Sydney Test, for certain players, like Bryn Knowlden, who had been showing brilliant attacking form, and George Curran and Fred Hughes were all candidates for selection. Curran did get his chance replacing Frank Whitcombe who, despite a lot of extra work due to injuries, had played really sterling football in the front row with those two stars, Egan and Gee. What a pair the Wigan boys were! I got a bit tired of saying how good they were, for even when they put Joe Egan in the second row he played blinding football. England have sent many great forwards out to Australia, but none could have done better than Egan and Gee did in their respective positions for the Indomitables.

Ricketty Johnson, the Australian coach, who captained the successful Australian team in 1920, when Australia won by 8 pts. to 4 pts. at Brisbane, was doing all he could to instil a winning-track mind into his boys. And it looked as if he had done, when at half-time, Australia were leading 7 pts. to 2 pts. Jorgenson two goals and Kennedy a try for the home side against a dropped goal by Risman. The crowd, not so big as at the first Test, were really on their toes. The famous Sydney Hill was at its best, and never did the 'Green and Yellows' look so good. But they had reckoned without the recovering power of the 'Red, White and Blues'. A quick goal by Risman and then a great try by Bassett put the scores equal. Then the newcomer George Curran made the most of his Test debut - thanks to Les White - to put England in front, and they never looked back. Arthur Clues, to make matters in the sending off department a bit more equal, took his marching orders from Tom McMahon, and then we had the try of all tries.

Eric Batten's effort in this match must go down in history. He took a defensive ball on his 25-line. Off at full speed, he scattered three would-be tacklers with his shoulder and, still in full flight, hurtled over two more defenders. Then another shattering shoulder charge paved the way for Ike Owens to cross with ease.

What an effort, what a try, and what a shout went up from this Sydney crowd! Although it was against them, it was so great they rose in their admiration for Eric Batten. Arthur Bassett added another near the end, which counted for the statistics, Risman goaled, as he did with Owen's try.

It was all over. Gus Risman went off to receive the splendid 'Courtney' Trophy, and the Englishmen were undefeated in Test football.

Parkinson, the Australian full-back, broke his leg near the end, but it made little difference to the result, and as Joe

Jorgenson, the Australian captain, said at the end: 'We held them in the first half but there is only one answer to the result ... Gus Risman and his clan are too good.' And so they were, for Risman had shown himself a remarkable leader and captain on the field, and his coolness and steadiness was a wonderful example to his younger colleagues.

Referee Tom McMahon, in a Press interview in the *Sydney Telegraph* made some interesting comments. He paid a great tribute to Gus Risman and said; 'You had to be in the middle to realise the inspiration he was to the players, and how he drove them to victory.' McMahon said he heard Risman tell the team when they were down 7 pts. to 2 pts.: 'Now, boys, you have to save this game for England. Let them have it.' It reminded me of the story told by Ray Stehr, the grand Australian forward, who delighted in repeating what he heard passing the English dressing room when they were down at half-time in one match. The captain, Ray said, was just saying: 'Don't forget, boys, this is for England.' 'And the way they came out of that room fair frightened us,' added Stehr.

Tom McMahon continued his comments by saying: 'The English team are not so good as the 1936 combination, whose forwards were tougher, and the present team have no backs to compare with Stanley Brogden and Emlyn Jenkins. But the present team are far too good for Australia.'

I liked McMahon's reference to the much-criticised 'squealing' cry when he wrote: 'The Englishmen never squealed when penalised for infringements,' and later 'The Englishmen were far better than the Australians because they knew more about the game.' That last sentence was the key to the whole thing, so far as this Test series was concerned.

At the conclusion of the Test Match I wrote the following article for the *Telegraph*, and this more or less sums up the position of Australian football.

It was headed 'Australians are not good enough,' and went on: -

'Australia's Rugby League defeat - and it was a decisive defeat - is causing a lot of heartburning as well as a search for scapegoats. Many have picked on Coach Johnson as the victim. But it seems to me that one thing stands out clearly - the players are not good enough. Therefore, the solution is in rebuilding the framework of good, sound Rugby. Surely by now it must be obvious that something is radically wrong with Australian Rugby League when, for 25 years, the same country has won the Ashes. The other day I saw the New South Wales schoolboys soundly defeat Queensland at Ipswich. I turned to Gus Risman and said: 'I wonder how many of these boys will be playing for Australia in 10 years' time?' And I do wonder! I have seen many brilliant young footballers whilst in Australia, and the next five years are going to be vital in their development.

'The New South Wales schoolboys' coach directed his team from the touch-line. He apparently was not willing to allow the boys to learn the hard way by failures, but wanted to move them round like chessmen. Although Rugby is a team game, it is also an individual one, and that is where Australians are lacking. Show me any player on Saturday who could have won the game off his own bat. Australian footballers have lost their individuality, and automatically their confidence too.

'Australians have concentrated too much on planning to stop the Englishmen instead of playing their own advantages to the full. They have been frightened to try moves because of the mistakes they might make, with the result that their football is colourless, uninteresting, and orthodox.

'The simplest of England's moves have left the opposition standing. It is amazing to see blind side moves and 'dummy' passes causing the downfall of Australian teams on this tour. The English team worked out, on the boat, moves which they have not yet put into practice, for the old ones have been sufficient. The English team is by no means outstanding, and by the next tour there will be a big improvement.

'It seems to me that Australian players have allowed criticism, not always constructive, to interfere with their play. There is sufficient talent among the Australian Rugby League rulers to get down to solid rugby. This must first be done with the forwards, who must cut a lot of the fancy stuff, or trying to be backs. The backs need team work, but not at the expense of killing individuality.

'You never see Risman, Batten, or McCue running themselves into the ground, into passing rushes at training. Similarly, Stanley Brogden was a magnificent individualist but, at the same time, was always part of the system. I think Australia would be wise to cut out tours for a couple of seasons and concentrate on building up their game, which is too fine a sport to be allowed to slip.

'Believe me, there are Englishmen who would like the Australians to win the Ashes when they next come to England. It would do both countries good. But to do that Australia will have to get down to solid work. It will have to put aside State jealousies in the campaign to build up a champion team.'

How true these words were to prove, for one season later only one player - Pat Devery - retained his place in the State side, although I grant Cooper and Clues would no doubt have been in.

CHAPTER XII.

STORY OF ALL THE TESTS. LET'S DROP THESE CUPS!

Australian Rugby League football will always remember the name of James J. Giltinan, who blazed the Test trail in 1908. Mr. Giltinan spoke at the farewell dinner given by the Australian Board of Control just before our party left Sydney.

Taking a team from Australia to England was a very different proposition to what it is to-day. Australian tours are now assured of financial success, but the hardships of their early tourists may be best judged from the Test gate receipts in 1908-1909. The best gate of the tour for the Kangaroos was £283 at the second Test Match in Newcastle. The visitors' share of the takings at the first Test at St. James' Park, London, amounted to £22, and at the third, at Birmingham, £107.

The first Test captain of this Australian team was 'Dally' Messenger, who kicked five goals. Billy Batten, father of Eric, of the last touring side, played in all three Tests. He scored two fine tries in the first Test.

Afterwards followed James Lomas' pioneering team of Australia in 1910. They won both Tests to retain the Ashes, but the English managers - J.H. Houghton and J. Clifford - claimed that only one official Test, that at the Show Ground, Sydney, on June 18th, was played. However, Australian records credit the Brisbane game on July 10th, 1910, as being an official Test. England won both games - 27 pts. to 20 pts. and 22 pts. to 17 pts.

Then followed the memorable Kangaroos to England in 1911 - 1912, when the famous team, captained by Chris McKivatt, went through the Test series unbeaten. Johnny Quinlan, present member of the Australian Board of Control, who was one of the joint managers, said, on return, that no team in the world, of any period, could have excelled the Kangaroos in the final Test. After being eight points behind, Australia rallied so completely that they trounced England to the tune of 33 pts. to 8 pts. Mr. Quinlan still claims that no team before, or since, could have beaten the Kangaroos as they played that day.

1914 brought Harold Wagstaff with his never-to-be-forgotten Third Test at the Sydney cricket ground on July 14th, 1914. This became known as 'Rorke's Drift' Test, following a wonderful fight by England. The story of this Test is as thrilling as any of sporting thrills. England had to play three Tests in eight days, much to the disgust of the visiting Managers. Let the late Harold Wagstaff tell part of his story of the scene before the match.

'Mr Clifford, the manager of the team, called the 13 players into a room at the hotel before the match and outlined the whole story of the revision of the fixture. Then he said that he expected every one of us to play as we had never played before.

'You are playing in a game of football this afternoon,' he told us, 'but more than that, you are playing for England and more, even, than that, you are playing for Right versus Wrong. You will win because you have to win. Don't forget that message from home - 'England expects every one of you to do his duty." the Men in my team were moved. You could see our fellows clenching their fists, and when we left the room no one spoke.'

What followed is history. Injuries crippled an already disturbed English side. Frank Williams twisted his leg on the wing very early, yet England led at half-time by 9 pts. to 3 pts. Douglas Clark smashed his collar bone after half time. He had it strapped and twice tried to come back but found it impossible, and there were tears in his eyes as he left the field.

Frank Williams was further injured, and then Billy Hall, of Oldham, had to be carried off. Ten men, with 30 minutes to go. Let Wagstaff continue: 'Never had I nine such men with me on a football field as I had that day. We were in our own half all the time and, for most of the time, we seemed to be on our own line, but we stuck it. Our forwards gave their all.'

England, with three forwards, won the scrums and Holland, Ramsdale and Chilcott were heroes. Chick Johnson, on the wing, scored a wonderful try when he dribbled half length of the field, beating man after man, before he finally tapped the ball over the line and dropped on it. Alf Wood kicked the goal and England were in front - 14 pts. to 3 pts. Australia did score one try before the end, but this was one of the greatest, if not the greatest, of England wins. Australian folk talk of it to this day. The thump of deadly diving tackles, bodies hurled to the ground with stunning force, tearing rushes, checked with smashing violence, fiercely courageous football played in an atmosphere of tense excitement. A game which followed victory through the greatest display of football courage ever seen on the historic Sydney ground, so said a writer of that match.

Wagstaff took a team out in 1920, but this time Australia won the 'rubber', which was their last success in a 'rubber' series. Australia won - 8 pts. to 4 pts. - at the Exhibition Oval, Brisbane, when led by the present Australian coach, Rick Johnson. A combined movement by Harold Horder, greatest of all wingers, and giant Frank Burge, climaxed Australia's 8 pts. to 4 pts. victory that day. A cross kick by Horder sent Burge flying in to score the winning try. Australia won the second game and England the third.

Australia did not hold the Ashes for long, as England regained the honours in England in 1921. Australia put up a grand fight, losing the first by 6 pts. to 5 pts., winning the second by 16 pts. to 2 pts., and losing the third by 6 pts. to nil. The story I like best is of Frank Gallagher, probably the greatest of all loose forwards, who rattled Duncan Thompson so much that Duncan forgot himself to take a slap at Frank. The burly English forward smiled and at the next scrum just pushed Duncan out of the way to score. Frank Gallagher paid great respect to the Australian scrum-half when we called at Toowoomba.

Back in Australia in 1924, 'Jonty' Parkin's grand side retained the Ashes, and no captain did a greater job than 'Jonty' did on those series. His name is still sky high in the minds of Australian sports. Parkin led his second team in 1928 and again retained the Ashes.

Tom Gorman, great Australian centre, led the 1929-30 side to England, which was thought to have the best chance of regaining those mythical Ashes. This was the series with the famous 'Chimpy' Busch try incident. A flying corner flag, Butters' tackle of Busch, and a 'no try' ruling cost Australia the Ashes. Because of the general dissatisfaction a fourth game was given the visitors at Rochdale, and I well remember seeing the flying Stanley Smith going in at the corner to score the try which gave England victory by 3 pts.

to nil. Jim Sullivan then led the 1932 team to carry off the honours with the usual Sullivan efficiency, particularly where goal kicks counted.

This was the series where the famous 'Battle of Brisbane' came into the records. This was the match where most of the injuries were on the Australian side, but they emerged the victors by 15 pts. to 6 pts. Eric Weissel, who coached the Junee side in our last trip, fractured his ankle, but in doing so, paved the way for a try to Hector Gee. Brogden and Feetham made a great effort, for which the Salford player claimed a try. Had Sullivan converted England would have been in front but no try was given and Australia, breathing once again, increased her lead. It was the victory of victories in the annals of Australian records and its title 'Battle of Brisbane' was apparently a correct designation.

The 1933 Kangaroos to England did not win a Test, while Jim Brough maintained the high standard with his 1936 touring team which won the series after losing the first Test by 24 pts. to 8 pts.

The last visit of the Australians to England was in 1937, when Wally Prigg led the side. It was a near thing when England only just survived at Leeds in the first Test by 5 pts. to 4 pts. This was a vital win, for Australia won the third Test after losing the second. This 1937 side were not blessed with good luck, particularly with injuries, and they lost J. Pearce with a fractured leg before they arrived in England.

And then these great series were interrupted with the declaration of war in 1939. The 1946 had all the colour and the glamour of the previous contests, and the future holds just as much possibility as did any of the series I have written about.

Can Australia regain the Ashes in 1948? Her attacking record always promises possibilities, but if she can only stiffen her defence next year might bring the change of successes, and if she does take the Ashes, who will grumble, for Australia knows that if she wins them it will be on her merits. That is typical English Rugby League.

A Test day in Australia is regarded as THE DAY of all days. From early morning the fun starts, and I append the programme of the day of the Second Test at Brisbane.

The first match began at 9 a.m.: State Schools. 6 stone teams. Queensland *v* Brisbane.

9.45 a.m. Brisbane Industrial High School *v* Gympie High School.

10.45 a.m. Under 20 years. Norths *v* Valley Tooraks.

11.45 a.m. State Schools. 7 stone 7 lbs. First Test. Queensland *v* New South Wales.

12.55 p.m. Brisbane Reserve Grade *v* Combined 'Geraghty' Cup Team.

2- 0 p.m. **AUSTRALIA *v* ENGLAND**

4- 5 p.m. Northern Suburbs *v* Fortitude Valley (a match similar to an English club game).

So for the 2/6 admission fee a spectator had seven matches, and all good ones. Some of the teams had travelled miles to play in these matches, and the same thing happened before our matches against clubs. When the Tourists played Toowoomba, one side travelled 250 miles, paid their own expenses to play forty minutes' football, and they were proud to do so.

The ball boys are an important part of the day's play. Each side has a ball boy, who leads the team on to the field - and what a proud moment it is when the boy leads either England or Australia on for a Test game! Other boys are dotted around the touch-line ready to throw the ball in. They are dressed in white shorts and white jerseys, and look very smart. Of course, it is not necessary on the smaller English ground, but it looks good in Australia or New Zealand.

Here I should get off my chest the hardy annual, which

seems to have become a prominent part of Test games. I refer to the presentation of individual trophies. Australia slips up badly with this trophy presentation business. First the Ashes cup, given by Tattersalls Club, is presented in private at the Tattersall Club by the Chairman. I was present at the ceremony, which was attended by a matter of a couple of hundred club members. The Cup itself is only small, but is what it stands for that counts. But why should the Ashes be presented in private?

The most thrilling moment in all big games in England is when the winning captain receives the trophy from some distinguished personage. As soon as the final Test finished Gus Risman went up to take a look at the 'Courtney' Trophy, which was too big to hand to him, and then ran off to join his team mates, who were already in the dressing room. Even if the Tattersall 'Ashes' Cup is retained it should be presented publicly, so that the thousands at the match can see the presentation ceremony. No private club should have the sole rights of cup presentation, and the sooner the Australian Board of Control tackle this job, the more progressive they will show themselves to be. The present method is far too amateurish and not becoming to such an important occasion.

This brings me to the important, but less conspicuous topic of private trophy presentation. This caused a lot of trouble and complaint among the Tourists and should be wiped out. Originally, I believe, a trophy was given on behalf of Claude Corbett, a well-known and well-liked sports writer in Australia, who did a lot for R.L. and toured England with Australian teams. This trophy was given in his memory to the captain of the team winning the Ashes. This idea is all right and quite good, but the many individual trophies that were given privately were just nobody's business - and ridiculous. At each Test a trophy was given by private donors to the best player in the team. Rugby League is a team game, and if the donors had heard the remarks made after each of these presentations they would not have proceeded with them.

One day a Manager will see what harm it does and he will put a stop to it at once. Players who thought themselves worthy of a trophy and did not get it were not pleased, and those players receiving the trophy obviously felt the reactions of team mates, and they were not happy. At another private presentation for something or other - I believe in this case it was for the cleanest player - one quick-spoken English player was so incensed he set up a barracking against the donor at the next public dinner.

I know this will not please some well-meaning folk, particularly in Australia, but they are too big to take umbrage. In any case, stoppage is necessary.

It is a practice that is rapidly getting out of hand.

CHAPTER XIII.

BATTEN AND WARD - CHIPS OFF THE OLD
BLOCK. SPORTSMEN SPIN A YARN. BOYS'
TOWN SPORTS MEETING. REAL SUPPORTERS -
AND A GATE-CRASHER. TWELVE THOUSAND
MILES TO MEET A FRIEND.

Whenever sporting folk meet, tales are told and anecdotes recounted. I met many famous Australian sportsmen who were all able to tell stories of their sporting life.

When we had the 'Tattersall' Cup presented Herbert Collins, one of the best if not the best, of Australian cricket captains, told the tale of the 1926 Australian team playing a match on the private pitch of a millionaire. The appointed umpires did not arrive, so the gardener and his assistant were roped in. All went well until lunch, when the head gardener dined and wined well, but not too wisely.

The millionaire came in to bat and Arthur Mailey gave him a lovely full toss on the leg side, which was duly dispatched. The batsmen ran and Mailey, by way of a sheer joke, said: 'How's that?' 'Out,' said the umpire. 'What for?' queried the batsman. 'The whole ------ afternoon,' was the hiccoughed reply.

The great 'Dally' Messenger said at the official welcome, and his words are worth recording: 'Cobbers of footballers, you had a rough time here. We had a rough spin, too, in 1908. We got ten bob a week in the old days. We played against you boys then. Yes, Batten and Ward and (pointing to them) their daddies. Well, all I can say, gentlemen, I'm still alive.' 'Dally' Messenger was cheered by all, including the English visitors.

The great stumper, Bert Oldfield, proved a good pal when he presented the boys with new football boots, while the usual flannels presentation came along. Alan Kippax, with his sports shop, was also often assisting the Tourists.

Baggage man to the team was Coogee Turner. Coogee being the district from where Harry Turner came. He had been with the 1932 and 1936 teams, and now with us as trainer, baggage man and masseur-cum-handy-man.

Coogee's best tale was how he got Brogden fit for a Test Match after he had gone down with a bout of 'flu'. He knew his country well, for whether it be in Sydney - his home ground - to up-country, Turner could usually find someone when contacts were required.

Hot showers in the dressing room were new to the English players, and Arthur Justice told the story of how in England, in 1929, it was advantageous to get a 'ticket'. Coming off at Hunslet, Justice said the touch judge told him as he left the field: 'Tha'll be alreight, lad, ye'll get clean waater t'day!' Tom Langridge, masseur, with a fine gymnasium in George Street, came with the party as medical man, and later did the same for the cricket tourists.

Whilst we were in Sydney the Premier gave us a grand welcome. He was Billie McKell, now Governor-General of Australia. He had not been appointed when we were out, but he took us to his offices in Sydney and attended many receptions as a token of goodwill to the British visitors. The story he liked to tell best was how, as a youngster, he tried to get into the Sydney cricket ground over or under the fence.

The Police repeatedly turned him back. Now he is a trustee of the famous ground and his climb in the political world has been of great importance. He is a real Rugby League man, and in him the Australian Rugby League folk have a great friend.

Laurie Kearney, the Brisbane writer, told his tale when the Kitching biting incident was under discussion. He said: 'I refereed a match at the Sydney show ground in 1911 between New Zealand and New South Wales. The packs included 'Botsy' Williams and Jim Rukatai, a Maori. Rukatai mixed matters with Williams and later came from a scrum with blood pouring from his ear. Rukatai claimed that Williams had bitten him.

'Williams, however, had the complete alibi that he did not have a tooth in his head!'

One of the biggest things in the sporting world in Sydney is Boys' Town. Modelled on the lines of the American idea this boys' town holds a sports meeting every Sunday afternoon on the Sydney Sports Ground, which adjoins the cricket field. It is a well-organised show and all the best athletes attend at various times. Proceeds are on behalf of the Boys' Town Club. One meeting was given in our honour. Here is the programme put on. First, a R.L. match between two newspaper teams. Then came:

1. Leo Sterling, described as England's greatest trumpeter.
2. Trevor Foster Two Laps Cycle Race.
3. Frank Whitcombe Trotting Display. Four trotting riders showing their paces.
4. Albert Johnson Three Lap Cycle Race.
5. George Curran Trotting Display.
6. Bob Nicholson 110 Yards Handicap.
7. Final - Jack Kitching Two Lap Race.
8. Eric Batten Mile Attempt Record by cyclist W. Guyatt.

9. Jim Lewthwaite Trotting Display.

10. Harry Murphy wood chop.

11. Ike Owens Ladies' Race, Two Laps, Cycle.

12. Dai Jenkins Four Laps Cycle Race.

12a Arthur Bassett Trotting Exhibition.

> (*Note.* - They don't have No. 13).

14. Ernest Ward American Team Pursuit Race.

15. Willie Davies wood chop.

16. Bryn Knowlden Trotting Display.

17. Final - Eddie Waring Four Laps Race.

18. Joe Jones Ladies' Trotting Display.

19. Tom McCue Five Laps Massed Start Handicap.

20. Les White wood chop.

21. Final - Ike Owens Ladies' Race.

22. Ken Gee 'All-Servicemen' Foot Race.

23. Fred Hughes Six Laps Scratch Race.

24. Martin Ryan Schoolgirls' Race.

25. Ted Ward's Gent's Riding Display.

26. Walter Popplewell Reserve Aces Scratch Race.

27. Final - Doug. Phillips Athletic League.

28. Final - Willie Horne's wood chop.

29. Gus Risman's Twelve Laps Cycle Race.

30. Wilfrid Gabbett Grand Finale Trotting Display.

So you will see what a great meeting was presented, and it was done in a slick manner with no time wasted.

The bit I liked best was the Wood-chopping Competition. Eight competitors are put in a row and stand on a wood block. They are handicapped, in seconds, and at the word 'go' they commence to chop at their wood block, trying to chop through, first from one side and then the other. In one of the chops the champion of Sydney had to give an opponent 28 seconds start, and he only just lost. The way his axe flew through the air, kicking huge chunks out at one strike was remarkable. The sports meeting lasts over four hours and is well patronised. The principal Boys' Club are the Police Boys' Clubs and the Y.M.C.A. The Police Clubs appear to get a great deal of support in every way, and the Police organise them.

One of the big supporters is Lady Braddon, who was also keenly interested in the English team. She had been associated with the 1936 team and spent a lot of time taking the players to the Police Clubs and other events. Sir Henry Braddon, a former International sportsman who is now 83 years of age, was a very interesting fellow to speak to. He knew the full life of Sydney, and his reminiscences, particularly of the building of the famous Bridge, were most enthralling. He represented for many years the famous wool firm of Dalghetty.

He was a keen visitor, with Lady Braddon, to the Sydney Stadium, where I saw Tommy Burns, the handsome welterweight who is now set on a film career, fight Cliff Gordon. This Stadium, the self and same where the other Tommy Burns fought Jack Johnson when the police stopped the fight in 1910, was due for alterations but still packs the keen Aussies in when there is anything to cheer about. The present Tommy Burns is a keen Rugby fan and in Brisbane, his home town, he followed the team.

None of the players felt lost through lack of friends and visitors. English teams have a tremendous advantage over those that tour this country, for many of the people, in both Australia and New Zealand, originated here.

Eric Batten had two particularly good friends in Cecil Blinkhorn, 1921 Tourist, and Jim Kenny. This pair followed us wherever we went, and more than once Batten arrived back with fish or fruit for the whole party, thanks to his friends. The people who had been out in 1936 had, of course, a big advantage with contacts. Tom McCue had his namesake, Paddy McCue, a 1910 Tourist, down to see him, and also to present him with some snake skins. I was lucky to get one and brought Frank Gallagher one from McCue senior.

When Nicholson and Ryan were in hospital they were looked after in amazing style. Hourly, visitors brought them goods, food, fruit, and many choice things, and the other occupants of the hospital were sorry when they left.

Players like Eric Harris, Frank O'Rourke, 'Sprag' Hunt, Dinny Campbell and Dickie Fifield, all players who had been with English clubs, were often down, and they were as keen to talk about England as we were to talk about Australia. We had the full support of these boys at the big games, and once we had the support of an unknown guest - a gate-crasher. An hour before the team left the hotel for the ground to play the first Test, a stout, jovial man arrived at the hotel. He bought drinks, wished the Englishmen luck, and talked about the gay times he had spent on Ilkley Moor. He recognised Frank Whitcombe. 'Knew thee lad when tha played wi' Broughton befoor tha signed for Bradford,' he said. He and Frank got on champion. So much so, that Frank invited him up to his room to chat while he packed his bag. While Frank packed, his friend rattled off talk of days at Salford and Wigan. Then suddenly he said to Frank: 'Excuse me, I have a 'phone call to make.'

By the time Frank had packed his bag and reached for his English team blazer, the stout jovial man was wearing the blazer in the members' enclosure at the Sydney cricket ground. While thousands were outside looking in, the fat man was on the inside looking out - for Frank.

At half-time the blazer was returned to the English dressing room. I was offered £2 for the loan of my blazer to get one keen fan in after the gates had been closed, and I could have got more if I would have talked. I saw hundreds who had already paid come out of the ground because they could not see.

England To Australia and New Zealand

We had so many great receptions it would be hard to pick out the best - they were all so good. One that must be mentioned was a trip to Surfers' Paradise. Ten of us went further ahead to Tweeds Head where an Englishman, Les Pearce, the host of the Hotel Currumbin, was so keen to do the English boys well that he put on a 20-course meal. In a speech after the wonderful repast, George Curran made one of the best cracks of the tour. He said: 'When I arrived from England I met a chap who has been my best friend in Australia and his name was ENTREE.' Yet rarely did a meal of this sort pass without someone say: 'If only the folks at home could have this with us.' It was at Tweed Heads where we saw a team of Aborigines, some without boots on, playing another side called The Endeavours.

At Surfers' Paradise the life-saving team gave us an exhibition. Some weeks previously a bather had been snapped at by a shark and lost his life. Someone suggested Frank Whitcombe should play the part of a bather in distress. Frank thought his 17 stone might prove too much for the carriers, so that was off.

Mail was an all-important part of the team's activities, and none were so popular as the man who brought the results. Willie Horne reached his double century with mail and, naturally, had his leg pulled for it.

When the Welsh Choir was formed, one of the early engagements was in a Play given by the local Repertory Company - 'The Corn is Green'. They were able to supply some of the Welsh necessary on this occasion.

While attending a dance at one of the football clubs I was called upon to introduce the members of the team present to the dancers. After doing this and walking off the platform a young chap tapped me on the shoulder and asked: 'Do you remember me?' I looked surprised but could not recognise him, when he said: 'I'm Jeff Simmonds.' 'So you're Jeff

Simmonds?' I ejaculated, 'now we'll take up where we left off'. This boy had been to England with the R.A.A.F. I had been in constant touch with him, trying to get him to Leeds to play for the club. I did everything but actually get him, for one thing and another stopped his appearance. I never met him, but corresponded with him regularly in various parts of England. I had to go 12,000 miles to catch up with him.

I have to thank Sydney and Alf. Mallalue for my initiation into oysters, and the famous Hawksbury River's oysters can never be forgotten. Gus Risman, an expert on these things, put them in the same class as those from Grafton way, but I suppose the New Zealand folk will say we never had their best or we would not say such things.

The fact that cricket and Rugby League football is played on the same ground in Sydney creates a bond of friendship between the two codes. Most of the famous men in cricket were keen followers of the handling code, and they were always to be seen making their way to the grounds or having a word with the boys in the dressing rooms.

A few of the places we visited without preparation, and yet have remembered: Taronga Zoological Park, which is on the harbour foreshore; Centennial Park, not far from the Olympic Hotel where we stayed; Bondi Beach, half-an-hour from the city, with its wonderful beach where 5,000,000 bathers surf annually; Manly, the residential part (the Aussies call it Menly) seven miles on a grand ferry trip; Cronulla, south of Botany Bay (Captain Cook's landing spot), and the Koala Park.

The Botanic Gardens, the War Memorial in Hyde Park, National Art Gallery and University of Sydney, all within easy access, were other worthwhile visits. Yet it was a great spot to be in, even with all its problems.

CHAPTER XIV.

WELCOMED TO NEW ZEALAND. LEAGUE AND
UNION RIVALRY. CINEMA WITH A SKY ROOF.
PILLOWS ON THE RAIL TRIP. A BIT OF
YORKSHIRE IN THE STUDIO.

With shipping transport still being a doubtful quantity and
time being precious, the air service from Australia to New
Zealand was brought into force, and for the first time the
party did the three-day ship journey across the Tasman by
air in eight hours. This trip had to be done in three batches,
and as I had newspaper and broadcasting commitments in
New Zealand I went with the advance party of six players
on the Sunday morning following the Third Test. Our heavy
luggage was to come on by sea.

The journey from the seaplane base in Sydney, starting at
6 p.m., was easy and comfortable, and our first sight of
Auckland on a pleasant Sunday afternoon was as warm as
our welcome. The bright green of the New Zealand
farmlands from the air was a refreshing change of scenery
from the dry, parched land we had left.

Arriving at Auckland on schedule, I was pleased to renew
acquaintance with Jack Redwood, the Chairman of the New
Zealand Rugby League who, in 1939, was manager of the
team visiting England when war broke out. I had been able

to arrange a match - incidentally, the only Rugby game played in the British Isles that day - between the Dewsbury and the New Zealand touring side, following the lifting of the sport ban on the previous Friday night. Jack Redwood had had a short glimpse of England, and I am pleased he is with the 1947 Kiwis as manager. When I had introduced him to the players I met 'Scotty' McClymont, a name I was to hear and think a lot about during our all-too short stay in New Zealand. With other officials of the New Zealand R.L. and a few onlookers, including our first Maori acquaintances, we were taken to our Auckland hotel. Immediately we realised this was one part, at any rate, where this country scored over the Australian folk, for the accommodation was the best available and particularly comfortable.

The marked difference in the hold of Rugby League football on the country compared to what we had just felt was very evident. The Auckland papers gave the team a good show but in its right place, and it did not monopolise even the sporting pages. Auckland is a Rugby League stronghold, against Rugby Union competition, and this is the only city in New Zealand where it can claim such a superiority. The Rugby League people are keen to make progress, but they had to endure severe opposition in their rivalry with the amateur handling code. We soon saw this cutting-in business when a match was played at Christchurch.

League and Union opposition is more obvious than in England. Whereas the two games worry little about each other, and over here at least the League certainly never worry about the Union; in New Zealand it is more or less open warfare. The League officials were very charitable in their outlook, but the Amateur sponsors seemed to show definite opposition. It is strange to me that following a world war, when Rugby Union and Rugby League players fought and, in some cases, lost their lives together, there should be such violent antagonism in the handling code. Should the soccer game ever get a hold in New Zealand the Rugby people will find their efforts need to be aligned together, not opposed. However, I am satisfied that the League authorities are making the most of their efforts and did not resort to the type of attitude as shown in the Christchurch incident.

After an announcement had been made that the British touring side were to play the South Island at Christchurch, the Kiwi R.U. side which had just returned from England were fixed to play a match against South Island on the same day at Lancaster Park. This ground was the main one in the town and, of course, the Kiwis were a big attraction. In addition, the match was arranged to start at 1.30 p.m., an hour-and-a-half before the Rugby League game on the other side of the town. Naturally, the R.U. folk got the larger gate, and the whole business did not reflect well.

Going down from the North Island by boat we travelled in company with the Kiwis team. Speaking to their manager, I ascertained it was not his idea, and he felt the matter could, and should, have been arranged amicably.

There was a lot of indignation in the town of Christchurch over the treatment afforded the visiting English team. Many of the Kiwi boys had played with some of the League players in two Service games in England, and the Kiwis had had the benefit of the use of R.L. grounds.

On the evening of the game I broadcast from Christchurch, and I put out a challenge to the Rugby Union folk for a match to be played between the English touring side and the Kiwis team - *at Rugby Union*. The object of the game to provide Food for Britain. Nothing was heard from the R.U. on the matter. What a pity, and what a chance to show that we were all sport brothers!

The advance party had a chance, in their early stay in Auckland, to train at Carlaw Park, which is the home of Rugby

League in New Zealand. It compares favourably with many of our better grounds, although there is room for improvement. There was one long covered stand and a good open terracing stand opposite. The present secretary of the New Zealand R.L. is Mr. W.O. Carlaw, and the ground was named after an uncle of his. The weather was at its worst during our stay, with the result that we never saw Carlaw Park in good condition.

It was mainly due to the late Auckland Chairman, Mr. James Carlaw, uncle of the present secretary, Mr. Owie Carlaw, that an area of land used by Mr. Ah Chee, a Chinese gardener, was bought and the ground prepared for football. Officially speaking it is the headquarters of Auckland football and the Test ground for the North Island.

Auckland, called the Queen City of the North, was born a little over a hundred years ago - in 1840 - when an official party landed on the foreshore of the Waitemata Harbour and conducted the ceremony of formally taking possession and hoisting the British flag. To-day it has a population of approximately a quarter-of-a-million inhabitants, and is New Zealand's largest city. It has an equable climate and enjoys many natural advantages, including geographical positions. It is the gateway from New Zealand to the Pacific.

The City is on an isthmus, formed by the Estuary of the Waitemata on the Eastern side, and by the Manujua on the Western side. At the narrowest part of the isthmus the harbours are separated by less than a mile. A great part of the busy Auckland shopping centre is reclaimed land which, only 80 years ago, was swamp or mud flats. Like many similar cities in Australia and New Zealand, Auckland has its domain or park, which covers an area of 200 acres. 'Scotty' McClymont, the New Zealand coach and selector, took me through this domain, and many of its oldest relics are maintained for show purposes. Situated round the town are a number of hills with Maori names. Mount Eden, with

250

its volcanic crater, is 643 feet high, and from this you can get a grand view of both harbours. From Mount Hobson can be seen the lofty slopes of Mount Rangitoto (850 feet). One Tree Hill in Cornwall Park rises to 500 feet, and on it is an obelisk erected for the Maori people. This is Auckland's most prominent landmark.

The city is not very well equipped for live theatres, and the outstanding amusement hall is a cinema which appears to have the open sky above. Actually, it has a sky roof, where stars appear on a blue background and occasionally the moon comes over and disappears, while puffs of clouds are constantly passing over. It is all done by electrical contrivances, and I was informed is one of the only two cinemas - the other being in Honolulu - with such a roof. It looks for all the world as if you are in the open air, and whilst the effect might detract from the screen, it is certainly very restful. Some marvellous carvings, particularly of elephants, can be seen in this huge theatre, which was a financial drag for many years and changed hands before it became a paying proposition. It is the most elaborate and fascinating cinema I have ever seen.

The British party received a warm welcome from the Auckland Ladies' Social Committee at a large store called Farmers. This is New Zealand's largest department store and was started by a few farmers and has grown into a vast organisation. A free trolley bus or a free tram takes passengers from town to the store, and it is a most remarkable business place. Each member of the party received a presentation pen and Farmers did the necessary engraving for them.

Auckland is a clean city and our hotel accommodation was the best of the whole tour.

The name of A.T. ('Scotty') McClymont became, as I have said, well known to us whilst in Auckland. Success as a player - for he captained New Zealand in 1924 when they defeated England in two out of three Test Matches - was a beginning to a splendid record for New Zealand Rugby League football. He became a most successful coach of Richmond club, and then coached the New Zealand side which defeated England in the only Test game. A fine example to young players, he is a martinet on fitness and a really fine sportsman. For many years he was selector of the New Zealand sides, and for the 1947 touring side to England he was selector and coach.

Financially, he has done a lot for the game in New Zealand, and only his success as a business man has enabled him to give considerably to the New Zealand finances. With him and Jack Redwood, Auckland have two outstanding sportsmen to represent them. Mr. Watson, of the Auckland Rugby League, was another prominent official, whose sportsmanship was typical example of the many fine folk we met in New Zealand. The men at the helm of New Zealand Rugby League are all men of standing and personality, and could not be bettered.

What of New Zealand as a country? Divided into to two Islands - North and South - there is a total population of 1,676,286 (1945) which includes the Maoris.

New Zealand was first sighted by James Abe Tasman in 1642, and in 1769 Captain Cook took possession and hoisted the British flag. It was not until 1840, however, that there was any real settlement of British folk. The seasons are, of course, in reverse to those in England, yet there are no real extremes of either heat or cold, and severe droughts in summer are never experienced. Snow is chiefly confined to the Southern Alps or to the isolated peaks of the North Island. The season periods are Spring (September, October and November); Summer (December, January and February); Autumn (March, April and May); Winter (June, July and August).

We soon obtained first-hand knowledge of the New

Zealand rail system when we travelled the four hundred miles from Auckland to Wellington. The main lines and branches of the State railways have a total length of 3,320 miles and serve both the North and South Islands.

Most of the long-journey trains have sleeping cars, but owing to our late arrival we were unable to get these and had to make our first journey in a vestibule type saloon car with bucket lean-back seats and pillows obtainable at the stations.

Statistics show that New Zealand is the healthiest country in the world, for the death rate of 8.75 (1936) is the worlds lowest, and that of infants under one year of age (30.96 per 1,000 births) has also the same enviable distinction.

We were rather apt to query this health business, for we constantly hit bad weather. I was told it was a most unusual period of bad weather they were having, and on our arrival in Wellington we could do very little because of the atrocious weather conditions. Again the hotels were good and I had the pleasure of making contact with the New Zealand Broadcasting company, for whom I was scheduled to undertake a number of broadcasts. Government-controlled, it was well organised and run with Professor Shelley, from the old country, in charge. He had a capable lot of folk round him, and, introducing various members of the staff, he told me one of them came from Ilkley, so for ten minutes we had a really hot bit of Yorkshire floating around. There are commercial radio stations in New Zealand, but they also come under the jurisdiction of the Government.

Our first match was due at Christchurch, which necessitated an all-night boat journey from Wellington to Lyttleton, which is the harbour port of Christchurch.

It was not exactly an easy crossing, and to pass time before getting into bed the players sang songs on the deck through the rough period. One by one they had to fall out, for the rough sea was taking its toll.

CHAPTER XV.

Christchurch is a most beautiful city and is regarded as the Tourist centre for the South Island. One acre in every eight is public reserves and recreation grounds, and the city is endowed with many glorious gardens. There is a memorial statue to Captain Scott, the Antarctic explorer, in one of the gardens almost in the city centre.

A very modern city, there are miles of golden sands along the coast and names like New Brighton were not unfamiliar to us. It has a big sporting reputation, leaning on the side of Rugby Union as their winter sport, and Lancaster Park is a particularly good ground, with fine grandstands. Within easy distance of the city, there are two of the finest racecourses in the Southern hemisphere. The best horses in the Dominion compete at Riccarton in flat racing and hurdle events, while trotters and pacers hold their meetings at Addington.

Who has not heard of Canterbury lamb? The Canterbury Plains extend from North of Christchurch to Timaru, and the quality of grazing areas is world-renowned.

The match at Christchurch was a win for the Tourists by 24 pts. to 12 pts. For a long time the South Island team held their own. At one period, with the score 15 pts. to 12 pts., the home team got very near to scoring again, which might have brought about a different result.

Jim Lewthwaite was one of the outstanding men in this match, and it was most unfortunate that he should be one of the few men not be called upon for Test Match representation. With 25 tries he was the leading try-getter. As I have previously said, the counter-attraction not only affected the gate, but did not help the sporting atmosphere of the day. It seems remarkable that the English Rugby Union saw fit to inform the Ilkley Rugby Union Club that they must not allow the New Zealand 1947 Kiwis to train on their ground, after they had said they were willing to allow it to be used. I had said in a broadcast that despite the difference between amateurism and professionalism the unsportsmanlike attitude shown in Christchurch would never appertain in England. How wrong I was, has been proved by the decision of our Rugby Union authorities!

From Christchurch we went across by train to the West Coast, where we got a wetting both off the field and on. I had been invited by Jack Cutbush, whom London and Rochdale folk will remember as a good centre, to travel by road. I was unable to accept, but I am told it is a remarkable trip from East to West by car. Three hours after leaving Christchurch, Arthur's Pass presents itself, and here there is a great deal of winter sport. Mount Rolleston is of majestic splendour. The route goes through the Southern Alps to Greymouth.

One of the first visitors - all touring teams receive visitors - was a party of miners from Kinsley district in Yorkshire, where Eric Batten comes from. They worked in this area - not coal mining, but gold dredging. We were taken to see a gold dredge at work, but when the players asked for samples, none was forthcoming!

The Greymouth ground was really a race track, and the only stand was too far away to be of any use. The ground was wet and had many pools of water. I managed to get one of the few seats and sat with my feet on an upturned bucket with my typewriter on my knee - and some kind reserve player holding an umbrella over me. That is how I saw the West Coast beat England.

Their win was no fluke, for England had almost a Test team out but just could not settle. No player wanted to dive into the pools, and while they were waiting for the ball to float out the locals would dive in and chase away. The final score was 17 pts. to 8 pts., and England had no excuses. It was a great day for the West Coast fans, and when we went to collect our cases prior to leaving they were full of labels with such inscriptions as 'What about the West Coast?'; 'England dubbed and bogged,' and so on. There was a great deal of difference in interpreting the 'play the ball' rule, and this business again asserted itself in the smaller games in New Zealand, as it had done in Australia.

The West Coast adopted one good idea which might well be copied by English clubs. One representative was appointed to stay with the English party whilst in the town, and he was a liaison officer for anyone in the party requiring anything. Local knowledge is an important thing on tour, as it was in this visit. At the celebration dance one Yorkshire member was trying to explain, in broad Yorkshire, what 'Back 'at posts' meant, but the longer he talked the more involved his explanation became. Subsequently, the same player received a telegram from the fair supporter before the Test Match, telling him to put one 'Back 'at post.'

On the West Coast there are many remarkable mountains. The Franz Josef Glacier is one of the beauty sports which must be seen to be believed. I had an interesting experience in Greymouth when broadcasting from the local station. I received a telegram from a place called Invercargill, which is on the Southern tip. It was some time before I could trace the sender, a young lady, who was asking for cheerio greetings to be sent to her. She turned out to be a young bride from Yorkshire, who had just arrived to marry a New Zealand sailor and wanted another breath of 'home'.

This home question is even more evident in New Zealand than Australia. Everyone calls England 'home'. It is immaterial whether they have ever known anyone from the old country. It appears to be everyone's ambition to go 'home', and to hear youngsters with no English connections at all talking about 'home' meaning - England - was truly remarkable.

Alpinists and snow sport enthusiasts can get their fill in the South Island and such places as Mount Cook, with its 12,349 feet, provide plenty of scope for the ski-ing and rock or straight climbing enthusiasts. Previous touring teams have visited Dunedin, which has almost an all-Scots population, but owing to our short stay only two matches were played on this Island. The West Coast is a very strong Rugby League community, and teams like Blackball have produced some fine players. Cecil Mountford, the Wigan player, with his two brothers - Ken and Bill - come from these quarters, and the supporters are naturally proud of the Mountford achievements. Mr. L. Hunter, one of the officials, was rewarded by appointment as manager with the 1947 Kiwis.

We made a return journey to Christchurch to sail from Port Lyttleton, seven miles away, for Wellington, where we had to play the Maoris.

The Maori race is one which mystery and romance appears to surround, yet not a great deal is known about its members outside New Zealand. Some have thought them a wild tribe, uneducated, and just coloured folk lacking in physical strength. Actually, that is the absolute opposite to the grand folk of the Maori race. They are coloured, agreed, but they are intelligent, charming, and well educated folk. There are differences, as always with whites and coloured folk, but the Maori race has played a big part in the development of New Zealand in a sporting and physical sense.

The stories told of the early Maori tribal wars abound with mystery and excitement, and the Maori war cry, as heard before their matches and at all games in England; creates an atmosphere even now. It also creates amusement. The Maori folk are a strong, sturdy race, and their physique is greatly to be admired. English folk who saw such players as George Nepia and George Harrison, will appreciate this.

There are over 100,000 Maoris, mostly in the North Island. In 1945 there were 97,000 resident in the North and 3,500 in the South.

The Maori race peopled the Island of New Zealand from Hawaiki (considered to be the Island of Tahiti) in the fourteenth century. When they arrived they found a more primitive race had preceded them, and the exact place from which these people - the Morioris - came remains a mystery. They were quickly conquered and enslaved. For more than five centuries the Maoris held undisputed ownership, and although a war-like and virile people they possessed natural dignity. Organised colonisation commenced about 1840, and in 1907 New Zealand was raised to the status of Dominion. Now a separate State in the British Commonwealth, New Zealand has great ties of kinship and tradition with the Homeland of the British Isles.

Wellington, the second largest city in New Zealand, with a population of 150,000, provided the venue of the game with the Maoris. Unfortunately, this side was not as strong as in previous years, and the English team won with ease. This game, I reckoned, was the best performance of brilliant all-round football given on the whole trip by the Tourists. They all struck form, and their combination was really amazing. In the 32 pts. to 8 pts. win all were stars, with probably Bryn Knowlden standing out just that bit extra to give him the match award for sheer brilliancy.

The Governor-General, Sir Bernard Freyburg, attended the game and the players were introduced to him. Before the party left Wellington they were guests at Parliament House, where the Prime Minister, Mr. P. Fraser, and other members, made us very welcome.

The long trip back to Auckland by train, through the night was lightened somewhat by musical entertainment, mostly by the Maori boys. An impromptu concert was held in the train saloon and the highlight came when the Maoris taught Hughes, Foster, Batten, Ward, and a few others the Maori war dance, which they did to the accompaniment of actions and facial expressions. In return, we tried to teach the Maoris how to sing 'Ilkla Moor bah't 'at.' Not very successfully, I am afraid, but still it passed the time.

The highlight of the New Zealand tour was the visit to Rotorua, the show place of the North Island. This three-day trip not only provided a rest, but showed us the amazing thermal regions in action. En route we passed through really lovely scenery on the banks of the Waikato River for 40 miles. This is the longest river in New Zealand. Half-way, we stayed for lunch at Hamilton, a very busy dairy centre.

Rotorua is the greatest thermal spa in the Southern hemisphere. Its waters possess remarkable curative properties, so the guide told us, and if the odour and the sulphur action were any criterion, I can well believe it. With a population of about 6,500, Rotorua is a great tourist centre and all world travellers make a point of visiting this place.

There is excellent trout fishing, and we were taken round the Rainbow Trout Gardens, where hatching trout can be seen up to all ages. The most fascinating thing about this trout business is the fact that the fish can be caught in one stream and placed in a boiling hot water stream to cook. This is only one of the many fascinating mysteries of Rotorua, which has a large Maori population. In fact, the visit to the Maori settlement, to be taken round by the native guides, is the highlight of the trip. Boiling mud formations - Hell's Kitchens geysers at work - which shoot to a great height, are all part of the entertainment provided for the visitors.

A world-famous guide named Rangi, who has shown many personalities, including Royalty, round the district, was attached to our party, and all the guides are equipped to answer the smart cracks made at them. At the Maori village of Ohinemutu we were taken to a Maori concert. Demonstrations are given of war dances (the 'Haka') and poi dances. The small round balls which the girls manipulate to make music are most interesting. The Maori songs, with their haunting music, are indicative of the high musical talent possessed by this race. A special who was put on for us, but the fierceness of the warriors with their painted faces and weird weapons was somewhat neutralised by their having to put coats on during the interval because of the cold.

Rotorua is, of course, a volcanic area, and the Maori guides are required to make sure no one takes the wrong path. The story is told of the local inhabitant who failed to keep to the right path one dark night and was seen no more, the mud lakes taking their toll. It was rather surprising to see sulphur springs shooting from all parts of the ground, even from the outside of some of the old burial places. But it is recognised that no outlet must be stopped, for it is sure to reassert itself in some other spot, probably with serious consequences.

At the village of Whakarewarewa the thermal spring, with its boiling hot water, is so predominant that the Maoris here take full advantage of the activity to use it for cooking their food and washing clothes. Hot water constantly runs into their square bathing tanks and the Maori girls dive about to their heart's content. I never knew that so many of our British footballers were as interested in plumbing as they appeared to be in these native baths!

Although the majority of Maoris now live in a proper housing quarter, their native Pa (village) can still be seen and is of special interest with the elaborate carvings and exact reproductions of those built by the Maoris before Europeans came to New Zealand. In the Treasure House in Rotorua there are many Maori relics like Kauri-gum, greenstone ambergergris, and rare New Zealand birds such as the Huia and Kiwi, while there is the survival of the prehistoric ages in the weird tuatara lizard.

A bus ride, a long walk over the site of a once important village, and a boat trip took us through the scene of the eruption of the Tarawera Mountain.

The pupils of the Whakarewarewa school will long remember the visit of the English footballers, but this is reciprocated for the complete school of Maori girls, with about three white girls, gave a demonstration of traditional Maori songs. The most popular with the tourists was always 'Now is the hour,' the song which Gracie Fields sang in her 1947 summer broadcasts. But though Gracie Fields sings this number well, it could not have been more effective than when Maori youngsters sang it at this school just as we were leaving them.

Manager Gabbatt presented a rose bowl for the best girl athlete at their annual sports, and a cup for the best boy. These were to be known as the 'Rugby League 1946 Touring Team Trophies.'

CHAPTER XVI.

MORE MAORIS. DAI JENKINS BREAKS HIS
DUCK. GULLS, NOT GOALS! WE LOSE A TEST
MATCH. FURTHER TROUBLE WITH THE RULES.
WE MEET SOME OLD FRIENDS. FLASHBACK:
THE ALL-GOLDS, AND HOW THEY LEARNED
THE GAME.

The Travel Service Bureau of the New Zealand Government was responsible for our Rotorua trip, and they certainly did us well. On the way back to Auckland we made a stop at another Maori settlement, where we met Princess Te Puah. A very noted lady, now getting feeble and infirm, she greeted us in true style and the local Maoris gave us all the trimmings of age-old receptions. This was at Ngaruawahia, where Steve Wateni, a former International footballer, acted as interpreter for both sides. Risman spoke to the natives and our Welsh choir gave items. All this was followed by a great repast cooked in true Maori fashion, but I am afraid I, for one, just could not get over the smell of the cooking to work up an appetite.

A few members of the party visited the famous Waitomo Caves, with the marvellous glow worm grotto. These are truly remarkable.

After our great reception at Ngaruawahia we left for a game at Huntley. An easy win of 42 pts. to 12 pts. was memorable for giving Dai Jenkins his first points of the tour.

He and Tom McCue - curiously, both scrum-halves - were the only two players without any points to their credit, and what a big moment it was for Dai when he dummied the full-back to score behind the post! He gleefully held the ball up to show his touch-line mates, who cheered him loudly. It was well on in the game, and the South Auckland spectators could not understand the particularly vociferous applause for Jenkins. Tom McCue could not emulate Dai's performance in the last two games and he had to leave his name out of the scoring statistics, not that it affected his fine form on the tour in any way.

Huntley was the place where the usual local dance was given in honour of the visitors, and the organisers announced on the bills that they hoped the local boys would leave their girls free for the English guests to dance with. I did not stop to see the result, but previous experience had taught me that the English dancers were never short of partners.

The New Zealand weather had really got into me, and both Wilf Gabbatt and myself had to be brought back from Huntley with severe chills. Owie Carlaw brought me back in his car and the only signs of life I showed was when we visited the house and birthplace of the late Lance B. Todd, the former New Zealand player and later, a managerial colleague of mine. The Rotorua atmosphere had not done me much good, and the cold I picked up took a long time to leave me.

Three matches were played at Carlaw Park - two against Auckland (both wins) and one Test Match (a defeat).

The first Auckland game was spoilt by the weather and the 9 pts to 7 pts win for the Tourists was not a satisfactory achievement, for the 15,000 crowd, who braved terrible conditions, had a little good football shown to them. It was not possible on a ground inches deep in mud. It was the first time I had seen sea-gulls at a football match, but there they were, with the teams in one half of the field and the 'gulls in the other. I huddled in the back of the stand with Jim Lewthwaite as cameraman for this match, and some of his shots were the best of the lot. England scored three tries to a doubtful one for Auckland, who also scored two goals, but it was a misfortune that the weather was so unkind.

Winning the only Test gave the New Zealand team and officials an impetus, which did them more good than it did the English side harm. One or two players, like Knowlden and Jones, were given their Test places, but on the day's play the New Zealand side deserved their 13 pts. to 8 pts. win.

At one period, near the end of the game, I thought England would win, for with the score eight-all they were showing their full power. A touch-line shot from a penalty by Clark, however, hit the crossbar, and whilst the English defender were day-dreaming a burly forward named Graham came up full on the burst, took the ball, and hurled under the posts for a try, which was converted, giving the Kiwis their win.

It was mainly due to penalties that New Zealand collected points, for in Clark's five goals he had four penalty successes. England scored two tries to one by the home team, but the failure to please the referee with playing-the-ball efforts proved their undoing. It was a grim encounter on a terrible day, with not a lot of brilliant football. New Zealand deserved their win, but I warned such as 'Scotty' McClymont and Jack Redwood not to take this as a guide to their showing in England. With England's best side in and reasonable conditions it would have been a win for the Tourists nine times out of ten.

The referee rule interpretation business again asserted itself, and Tom McCue, after the Test Match, spoke very strongly about the play-the-ball requirements of New

Zealand referees. It is only through lack of foresight and enterprise by the powers of the countries concerned that universal rulings are not designed.

Time permitted another match against Auckland, which was won after a half-time argument. The English players were really hot under the collar about rulings in the first half of this match, and apparently they were justified, for there was a big improvement in the second half, undoubtedly due to a half-time chat with certain New Zealand officials had with the referee in charge. Now that Rugby League is so successful in four countries, an International body should be formed to deal with all rule changes, and none should be changed in any country without notifying the others.

The New Zealand tour was short and sweet with pleasant interludes, despite the atrocious weather conditions experienced. New Zealand sports folk were particularly hospitable with their gifts, and the Jupp family with Maori souvenirs, and Harold Tetley with his leather goods, provided the players with plenty of presents for home.

The difficulties that Rugby League folk have to put up with in New Zealand are shown by recent matters which have cropped up in their sporting realm. Exception has been taken to the 1947 team being called the 'Kiwis', whilst difficulties have arisen over the wording on the 'Courtney' Trophy. This trophy, given my Mr. R.H. Courtney for competition between England, Australia and New Zealand in the best of three Test games has a reference to the war services. Now someone wants to have a word or two altered on it. This sort of thing is foreign to the real nature of New Zealand folk, whose loyalty to the homeland is undoubted. Many British Rugby League players have benefited from parcels sent by the grand people of these Islands. The differences are between themselves and quite unnecessary.

The Great Ones & Other Writings

Whitcombe, Foster, Davies, and Kitching, the Bradford Northern players, had a piece of missionary work when they called on Mrs. George Harrison, whom they knew in Bradford. To facilitate their long journey to the district where Mrs. Harrison lived, the Government placed a car and a driver at their disposal, and they were taken to the house to have a very happy reunion. They then came on to Wellington by road to pick up the remaining members of the party.

Mike Gilbert, a former Bradford players, was in to see his Odsal colleagues, while many other former players came down to various grounds. Roy Hardgrave, of York and St. Helens fame, was regular attendant, as was Jack Cutbush, whose wife, a lass from Rochdale, appealed to him to return to England with the Tourists as she wanted to see Rochdale again. Jack, who was in a good Insurance business, was told by his wife, Lucy, that he could sell as much insurance in Lancashire as he would in Greefton, where he came from, but Jack would not say 'yes'.

I had quite a number of interesting meetings with various people who had left England - sporting celebrities and otherwise. Renwick, a former Warrington captain and Dewsbury player, called in to see me, while the relations of the famous Charles Seeling, recognised as the best forward ever to leave New Zealand, were keen to know of his activities in Wigan. Seeling came from Wanganui way and his relations promised him a happy return if he could make it.

I met the parents of Lou Brown, and I gave a promise to help to get Lou back from England to New Zealand. On my arrival back in England I found that Wigan Rugby League club directors had taken care of Lou following his illness and had arranged for his passage back to Auckland. His house was full of his medals, cups and trophies, which he had won as a young star Auckland athlete. Later he was to fall on rough ground, but he was able to get back to the scene of his early triumphs. Unfortunately, he was not to see a great deal of them, for six months after his return, word came through that he had passed away. It was better he was at home.

Jack Campbell and Ivor Sterling, two of the 1939 Kiwis who came back to fight with the N.Z.E.F. and also played a number of war games with Dewsbury, came down to have their say, although I was disappointed not to see either of them in a match. Campbell should have played in the second Auckland game and did actually get stripped, but a last-minute re-arrangement kept him out.

We were disappointed that George Nepia did not get down from his farm in Gisbourne, up North, to see us, but we learned he was quite well, nor did George Harrison get round to us.

The great doings of Opai Asher on the wing for New Zealand in the 1910 period had made one or two members, particularly Eric Batten, keen to hear something of his activities. Opai Asher had a style similar to Billy Batten, Eric's father, in hurdling over his opponents, and the first time these two grand players met, the Englishman received the shock of his life to find Opai not there, having hurdled clear away. The second time they met, Billy Batten did the hurdling and Asher finished in hospital. By all accounts this Opai Asher, who captained the Maori side in 1908, was a great player.

Among other great names in New Zealand football with English connections George Smith stands out. He was a member of this pioneering party of 1907 'All Golds', but as he had previously been to England, both as an amateur champion hurdler at the Empire Games, and also as a member of the 1905 All Blacks Rugby Union side, he knew just the strength of Northern Union in England.

When I was recently introduced to George Smith, still in Oldham, I was reminded of the great pioneering work of

Baskerville's 'All Golds'. They knew very little of the game they were coming to England to play; in fact, all they really knew was that the ball was thrown from shoulder high into the scrum. They had one solitary rule book, which had come by post, and every morning on the voyage the team held a meeting and eagerly discussed the new game. Yet they got as bonus £120, almost the same as the 1946 Indomitables received for their share of the tour in Australia and New Zealand.

It is a point of interest to consider financial figures of 1907, when the 'All Golds' received a total revenue of £9,494. Ocean travel cost the party over £1,000, and the players received £1 per week. They returned home with a divisible profit of £5,641. At this rate the title, 'All Gold', did not appear to be wrong.

The craft of these pioneers shows they were studious young fellows. In the play-the-ball rule they quickly found nothing to prevent them heeling the ball back, while, placing the ball for a goal kick, they realised they could just kick over the line and pick it up to go on to register a try. They soon learned the tricks of the trade and showed they possessed football skill. It was a happy party, in fact, it was quoted as one of the best managed teams that ever went on tour.

This was 40 years ago. How far has Rugby League advanced in those 40 years?

In recent years several players have come to England from New Zealand. Among them are Brown, Innes, Merritt, Spillane, Mountford, and Nordgren to Wigan. Buckingham (Swinton), Walker (Huddersfield), Falwasser, Cutbush (Rochdale), Desmond (Leeds), Wilson-Hall (Castleford), Hutt, Hall and Hardgrave (St. Helens), and I suppose Charlie Seeling (Wigan and Dewsbury), although he came over at the age of two years with his father.

England To Australia and New Zealand

New Zealand received her biggest blow when the 1939 tour was cancelled on account of the war and only two games were played. Money was lost by the League, and individuals who had assisted in financing the tour also suffered. With the 1926 tour also failing, probably through bad management, for team trouble was rife and resulted in certain players being suspended. The New Zealand touring parties in recent years have not followed on the good work set by the 'All Golds' under Baskerville.

This year gives the Kiwis the opportunity to show their capabilities. They are certain to be well led and advised off the field, whatever the results are on the field.

CHAPTER XVII.

FUN ON THE WAY HOME. HOW TO WIN A TUG-
O'-WAR. THE PANAMA CANAL. LAST RUSH
FOR PRESENTS. THE RECORD COMPLETED.

Curiously, the 1946 Indomitables left Wellington on the *Rangitiki*, the ship that carried back the 1939 New Zealand Tourists during the war time. This same ship brings the Kiwis to England for their 1947 tour.

Although the long Pacific route - 21 days without land - can be boring, the British Rugby League party were glad to have the opportunity to do the complete round trip. On board ship, with a mixed company of passengers, there was plenty of activity, which helped the Pacific crossing nicely. The usual deck sports and Thursday night 'horse racing' competition gave bookie Fred Hughes the chance to do his stuff as the ship's bookmaker. Fred ran the Tote on the daily run, where the passengers guess the mileage for the 24 hours, with the Captain taking his pick as an indication. A good cinema show and a pleasant Sunday service filled in parts of the journey. The Captain of the *Rangitiki* was not at all happy with some Press messages I sent regarding the ship's delay, due to engine trouble, and he obviously did not realise how the clubs in England were eager to know just when the Tourists would arrive in London. Emergency accommodation was still the order, and two dormitories were reserved for the football party. Apart from occasional night visits from dormitory number two members dressed as a Klu Klux Klan gang to the more peaceful members of number one dormitory, the journey was fairly quiet.

In the deck sports some of the lighter members of the team created a surprise by challenging the heavyweights to a tug-'o-war match, with one pull only. To everyone's amazement the lighter players - Knowlden, Egan, Horne and company - were the winners. It was not until the match was over did we find that a stanchion had been used for a weight and that there were a couple more assistants round the corner, out of the way, completing their team. Fred Hughes nearly threw a fit when he found out.

G.I. Brides on the ship were numerous, and because of their presence the route was to be via New York.

After a long voyage we sighted land and prepared for the journey through the Panama Canal.

The Panama Canal is as great as its reputation. We entered it at breakfast time, but I felt that seeing this wonderful engineering feat was even more important than having breakfast, but the meal was not wasted, for my table companion saw to that!

There are three locks on the 50-mile course of the Canal, and the locks take the ship three steps to 85 feet and three steps down, of course. An average ship takes six hours to do the trip. Again lunch clashed with the second lock, but I managed to avert another missed meal disaster by doing it in relays.

The air distance for Balboa, on the Pacific side, to Cristobal, on the Atlantic side, is only 36 miles. The Pacific entrance to the Canal is 25 miles East of the Atlantic entrance, which means that this is the only place in the world where the sun rises in the Pacific and sets in the Atlantic.

The Canal cost 380,000,000 dollars to build. Since the construction there has been a large individual project known as the Third Lock project, a 277,000,000 dollar cost. Work was begun on July 1st, 1941. Construction of the third set of locks, wider, deeper and longer than the two existing sets, had been considered a necessity for large ships and heavier commercial traffic. A reserve set of third locks was erected, and despite their huge size they could be swung into position in two minutes should anything go wrong with the existing set.

In Panama there are two kinds of mules - army and electric. The latter are little cars which propel vessels through the locks. By taking the Panama route the distance by water from San Francisco to New York is shortened by 7,873 miles, or three-fifths of the entire distance around Cape Horn.

The story of the fight by the French Canal Company is one of outstanding odds against success. Tropical conditions were not sufficiently provided against, and one report estimates that as many as one-fourth of all workers imported died from fever and other causes. In spite of disease and graft in Paris, many fine men performed valiant service, and when the money ran out in 1888, more than one-third of the excavation estimated to be necessary had been completed.

When Panama became an independent nation one of her first acts was to sign a Canal treaty with the United States and buy the French rights. The Panama area was changed from a 'fever-ridden pest hole' to one of the healthiest places on earth. In 1904 the first Canal diggers were put ashore at Colon, ten years later, August 15th, 1914, the steamship *Ancon*, made the maiden voyage through the brand-new Canal.

Previous R.L. teams that had travelled through the Canal

had recounted incidents of their time ashore at Colon or Panama City. Our own trip was not without incident when the party took a day ashore at Colon.

Once through the Canal a call was made at Curacao for refuelling with oil. Curacao is a Dutch Island in the Caribbean Sea, and the main town is Willemstad. Plenty of fresh fruit was available, and it was quite a common event to see players with huge bunches of bananas, while other goods were for sale at cheap rates on this Island. Big oil tanks stand out on the hill top and oil is much cheaper here, hence the out-of-the-direct-route calls.

When the Captain informed the passengers that a call was to be made at New York instead of Newport News, Virginia, there was a quick discussion about playing a game in New York. The players held a meeting on their own and all were in favour, but there was not the full support of the whole party, which showed rather a small-minded attitude and certainly not one of progress. However, Gus Risman took the matter in his hands, as captain, and the players were even willing to assist in standing the expenses involved. Cables were dispatched by Manager Gabbatt to New York, but whatever plans might have matured - for we were not making the progress hoped - a further announcement came over the ship's radio that New York was off owing to a dockers' strike and we were going up to Canada.

When this news came over there was a crowd of weeping brides rushing round to send cables to notify their husbands-to-be of the change of port. This was the third change, so the brides were not feeling too happy about it all, and a small fortune was being spent on cables. When we did eventually arrive in Halifax, Nova Scotia, some of the brides were met - some had to make their way by special train back to New York, and one or two were stranded.

What could be seen in a day at Halifax was mainly a

dash round the shops making late purchases. One of the outstanding customs that struck the party was the fact that there were no public houses and that you had to buy your beer at a shop and, what is more, take it straight home - and by the quickest and shortest route. Going off the direct track was likely to bring police action. The bottles of beer were wrapped up like a parcel and away one went - in the case of members of our party, to the ship. With this arrangement, naturally, there is little drunkenness to be seen.

A night at an 'All-in' wrestling show gave the Tourists an insight to this tough sport abroad. Half-a-dozen policemen were in attendance, and they were kept busy attending to the wrestlers, who spent more time out of the ring wanting to fight the police than their opponents. When, eventually, one wrestler was counted out he commenced to fight the police, and he was carried away by the men in blue. We were guests of the Stadium, so we sat quietly and enjoyed the interlude, which at least had its laughs.

Leaving Halifax we stared on our last lap across the Atlantic. Rough weather and engine trouble kept us back a little. One interesting pastime was to watch the big fish come up to the ship and race astern and then, cutting in with a side-step in the best Willie Davies manner, rub their bodies against the ship and so clear their barnacles. Gus Risman pointed this business out to me, and to see these fish making a fast sprint to catch up with the ship was most entertaining. None of them was knocked out, their timing was so good.

One girl on board had ideas about catching flying fish which, by the way, are quite small. She asked 'Curley', the ship's handyman and M.C., if she could have some string or rope to make a net. When asked what it was for she reluctantly told 'Curley' that she wanted to catch some flying fish and intended hanging the net outside a port hole with a flash lamp in it, so that, attracted by the light, the fish would fly in. Needless to say, she did not get the materials to make her net.

Most of the ship's sport prizes were won by the players. An exception was deck tennis, despite a brave effort by Eric Batten and a Leeds lady.

And so, six months, all but one week, from the time of leaving Plymouth with little expression of farewell, the party arrived back at Tilbury having done a job of work for English sport, and in an ambassadorial manner of which it could well be proud. There were more officials to see the team arrive than to bid them adieu, but then the players were needed to take part in the Cup games that were on hand. Records of all descriptions - financial, playing, and other kinds of records - had all been shattered, and, to me, reputations had been enhanced.

Repeating what John Wilson had said, 'It had been a trip of a lifetime.' This party of Indomitables had done a great deal no other party had done, and it had pioneered many ways by which future Tourists will benefit.

Nearly 40,000 miles had been covered by ship, train, plane, and foot. Naturally, it was good to be home but the experiences, the contacts, and the friendships made and the sights seen were so fine that were I never to have another Australasian tour, I am glad I had this one with the Rugby League Indomitables.

[THE END]

RECORDS OF TOURS

1910 - *Managers:* J. Clifford (*Huddersfield*), J.H. Houghton (*St Helens*), Jas. Lomas (*Captain*), J. Sharrocks, F. Young, C. Jenkins, F. Farrar, J. Leytham, W. Batten, J. Bartholomew, T.Y. Newbold, T. Helm, G. Ruddick, F. Shugars, R. Ramsdale, E. Curzon, W. Winstanley, F. Boylen, H. Kershaw, W. Jukes, W. Ward, F. Webster, A.E. Avery.

1914 - *Managers:* J. Clifford (*Huddersfield*), J.H. Houghton (*St. Helens*), Harold Wagstaff (*Captain*), A.E. Wood, Gwyn Tomas, A.E.Francis, S. Moorhouse, J. Robinson, F. Williams, W.A.Davies, B. Jenkins, W. Hall, J. O'Gara, W.S.Prosser, J. Rogers, F. Smith, L. Clampitt, D. Clark, F. Longstaff, W. Roman, D. Holland, J. W. Smailes, W. Jarman, J. Chilcott, J. W. Guerin, A. P. Coldrick, A. Johnson, R. Ramsdale.

1920 - *Managers:* S. Foster (*Halifax*), J. Wilson (*Hull Kingston Rovers*), Harold Wagstaff (*Captain*), G. Thomas, A.E. Wood, W. Stone, S. Stockwell, C. Stacey, J. Bacon, D. Hurcombe, E. Davies, J. Doyle, E. Jones, J. Parkin, R. Lloyd, J. Rogers, J. Cartwright, A. Milne, J. Bowers, W. Cunliffe, G. A. Skelhorne, B. Gronow, A. Johnson, W. Reid, G. Rees, H. Hilton, D. Clark, F. Gallagher.

1924 - *Managers:* J. Harry Dannatt (*Hull*), E. Osborne (*Warrington*), Jonathan Parkin (*Captain*), J. Sullivan, E. Knapman, F. Evans, J. Ring, C. Pollard, W. Bentham, S. Rix, T. Howley, C. Carr, J. A. Bacon, W. Mooney, S.Whitty, D. Hurcombe, B. Gronow, H. Bowman, J. Darwell, R. Sloman, W. Cunliffe, J. Bennett, J. Price, D. Rees, J. Thompson, W. Burgess, A. Brough, F. Gallagher.

1928 - *Managers:* G. F. Hutchins (*Oldham*), E. Osborne (*Warrington*), Jonathan Parkin (*Captain*), J. Sullivan, W. Gowers, A. Ellaby, E. Gwynne, A. Frodsham, T. Askin, J. Oliver, J. W. Brough, M. Rosser, J. Evans, L. Fairclough, W. Rees, B. Evans, W. A. Williams, N. Bentham, O. Dolan, H. Bowman, J. Thompson, W. Burgess, A. E. Fildes, W. Horton, R. Sloman, W. Bowen, B. Halfpenny, H. Young.

Exhibition Games. Vancouver and Montreal

1946 TOUR PHOTO ALBUM
Images from the original book

'Reds' at Fremantle (Winners)

Curran calls to Gee

The famous scoreboard at Sydney

'Old and new'. Eric Batten, Cec Blinkhorn,
Gus Risman, Harold Horder, The Author

'Blues' at Fremantle

Cooper 'fends' Batten

Receiving the 'Ashes' Cup

'Welsh' choir return compliment
(Note the Yorks, Lancs, Cumbrian singers)

At Rotorua

Kitching scoring at Huntley

Plenty of mud - White after Clark

Maori girls dance for us

JOURNALISM

London or the North?
Rugby League Review - October 1947

Eddie Waring, Rugby League expert of the Sunday Pictorial, *invites your views on this very important question. Read his carefully prepared review, complete with hitherto unpublished facts and figures, and then answer the three questions put by Mr. Waring.*

Next month we propose to publish an article dealing with existing R.L. Clubs in poorly supported districts.

Certain members of the Rugby League Council consider that our game has a future in London. Others do not think so but are prepared to allow the experiment to be made. In the recent new staff appointment at League headquarters one of the duties will be to further Rugby League in London.

The whole angle of London is so important that all sides should be considered before money, time and worry is expended. Only then if the Council are agreed that it has a fair chance of success should the scheme go forward; if they are are not satisfied then it should be scrapped.

In this article I wish to put forward all sides and then

leave it for *Rugby League Review* readers to decide what they think.

Three questions are asked:

(1) Can Rugby League succeed in London?

(2) Can the Rugby League Council stand the expense it is likely to cost?

(3) Is it right to concentrate on London in preference to say, Doncaster, Blackpool, Sheffield, Barnsley, Bolton and many other Northern towns?

FORMER LONDON CLUBS

Now let us analyse these three questions (1) Can Rugby League succeed in London? In 1937 two teams, Streatham and Mitcham, and Acton and Willesden, were members of the League. They had very good grounds and two fine teams. Look at some of the players on their books - George Nepia, Eddie Holder, Jack Cutbush, Charlie Smith, Fred McDonald, Arthur Veysey, Fred Bibby, Dai Jenkins, Con Murphy, Gil Morgan, Bryan Langford, Shirley Crabtree, George Harrison and many others whose names were ranked high in R.L. football ability. They had financial backing and what happened? In two years they had failed. Their Manager was Ivor Halstead, a colleague and friend of mine. While in London recently I asked him some questions on London football clubs and here are the questions and answers:-

Question: 'How much did it cost to run Rugby League in London?

Answer: The Rugby League venture of Mr Sydney E. Parkes cost him £35,000 and that sum does not, of course, take into account the money he expended on grounds and stands, which were meant ultimately to become greyhound racing tracks.

Question: How much did Mr. Parkes lose?

Answer: I am sure he lost £25,000.

Question: Do you think Rugby League might succeed in London?

Answer: I do think Rugby League could succeed in London. The Sydney Parkes angle was a purely commercial one and had no fusion with the true spirit of the game. Rugby League football in its best class is as swift and spectacular as Soccer, and I am perfectly sure that if those of us who love the game put the best that we know into the business of getting it over in the South, success will come. There should be an enthusiastic start at the bottom among those who truly love the game, and a continuous development of interest until it is established in junior and senior leagues. All this can be done with the right sort of drive.

This is something that has never before been published and I am indebted to Ivor Halstead, the London Author-Journalist, for these facts and figures. They reveal quite plainly the position.

HEAVY COST

Can the Rugby League, which has not the resources that Mr Parkes, the boss of the London clubs had, succeed where he failed?

This brings us to Question No. 2: Can the R.L. stand the cost? It certainly cannot stand the amount it cost Mr Parkes, because they have not got it. The R.L. is not such a a wealthy organisation so far as ready money is concerned, for while their assets are valued at about £40,000, cash to play with amounts to around £15,000, which in these days of finance cannot be called terribly wealthy.

Of course, the League will not expect, hope or intend to pay out anything like the amount to foster football in London as the two professional clubs had to. But it will cost money. Two recent meetings attended by just over 100 persons in London with publicity, etc., cost about £36. Petty cash I agree, but still I know many a junior League who would jump at the £36 if they could get it. Whatever the cost is the probably success of London more important than establishing the game in the towns I mention in my No. 3 question?

DONCASTER'S ENTHUSIASM

I will take Doncaster as an example. I visited this town along with the R.L. Secretary, who spoke well and wisely to this bunch of League minded folk. Since then they have secured 1,000 members, almost obtained a ground, got a junior League on the move without one penny piece or help whatever from the Rugby League. What will happen if and when they get the League backing to go full out with their plans?

Now for Blackpool. Only recently when I attended a match at Batley, a Blackpool visitor asked me to push this resort as a Rugby League newcomer. He said that numerous people had spoken to him about an article I had written in the *Sunday Pictorial* on the possibilities of Blackpool and the handling code. Sheffield, Barnsley, Bolton, Burnley and other towns are all possibilities. Should they have preference to London?

There it is. So far I have not given my personal views - in this case I want yours.

Unlike the Editor of *Rugby League Review*, I believe in the Wembley Cup final. However, even in these days of shortages we still have the right to free speech, and difference of opinion is rightly held by us both. The Wembley Cup final, to my view, was the winning move for National establishment of Rugby League. It could also be the key card of winning the London move.

I know of no better organiser than Harry Sunderland to crack at London. It is his pet ambition and his Utopia. Can he succeed or will he fail? Your guess is as good as mine. All I ask is 1? 2? 3? What do you think? The Editor has promised to publish as many of your letters as possible, so please send them to me, marking the envelope, 'London'. At least we shall get an idea what the men who keep the Rugby League game going think about the whole business. One Two or Three? What do you say?

Victory for the North!
... But Expansion is Favoured
Rugby League Review - December 1947

Eddie Waring reviews the letters received in answer to his three questions in our October number

My article on the subject of 'London or the North?' with its three questions resulted in a good deal of discussion. Naturally the majority of letters favoured concentration in the North, but there was a general viewpoint which indicated the concern of the average follower who desired the game to extend itself.

In places like Doncaster there was, of course, a wish that help and progress should be made with this embryo club. In this particular instance, following approaches from Mr H Holden, the organiser of the Doncaster club, I asked the chairman of the R.L. Council to visit the members and give them encouragement, and I am pleased to state that this was very readily agreed to.

Many of the letters received showed what keen interest is taken in Rugby League football in areas outside those already playing the game. This has also been the case with my recent book, over a hundred applications being received from places like Ryde (Isle of Wight), Newlyn and the London district. This again indicates the outside interest in Rugby League. The seed is obviously there.

ALMOST UNKNOWN

It is, of course, impossible to publish all the letters received, and I must be content to give extracts from as broad a selection as possible. Seeing that we have London under discussion I will take the first letter from Mr K Wormald of London, N.W. 8, who writes: 'The majority of the folk here do not realise that a game called Rugby League exists, but those who know it and have seen it played agree that it is a great game. It seems, therefore, that years of publicity would be required before the game could succeed in London, and the Wembley final is the best publicity ... Teams like Featherstone Rovers would probably be well advised to move to larger towns where they would have better gates and thus avoid having to sell the players they have made.'

From Holmfirth (Yorkshire) Mr N Haigh observes: 'I believe that the R.L. game could be established in either London or in the other Northern towns you mention, providing the matter was tackled in the right way. A long term policy is needed, with enthusiastic workers who will devote their time to teaching youngsters the game. Lectures should also be arranged, but it will take three or four years to get things moving ... We need a lot more initiative from our R.L. Council and publicity used to better advantage than at present.'

COMPLICATED LAWS

Over to Selby, where 'J.R.H.' write: 'Whether there is ever a successful R.L. club in London is immaterial. Until Rugby is played in elementary schools we don't stand much of a chance with our comparatively complicated rules against the simple 'hoil at awther end' ideas of Soccer. For don't make any mistake, to those not brought up in a R.L. atmosphere the rules are very difficult to understand. This is the real problem, whether at Liverpool, Doncaster, Blackpool or the South. The Rugby League should not attempt to subsidise a new senior club anywhere, but should give sympathetic consideration to schoolboy and junior football. South Wales is still the most promising field for expansion, but it will never arrive while we upset Celtic feelings with our pigheaded Saxon ideas such as setting Englishmen to select the Welsh International team. There should be a Welsh fund and every club signing a player from Wales should pay into it a sum equivalent to say five percent of the signing fee, the money to be used for propaganda purposes in Wales'. This latter idea is certainly worth consideration.

From Mr R J. Radcliffe of Manchester, 18, I received the following: 'I think the Midlands should be examined and some big matches played at Coventry, Leicester and Birmingham. The last two cities are real centres of Rugby. I will go further and suggest that when the Wembley agreement expires the R. L. Challenge Cup Final be played on the Aston Villa ground. This would be more central and help the London scheme.'

EXAMPLE OF WORKINGTON TOWN

From the hotbed of Cumberland Rugby in Workington, comes Mr J Wright of Henry Street, with this letter: 'I have read with great interest your article on London, and I think support and encouragement should be given to all the Northern towns who have shown enthusiasm in establishing the code. The great success at Workington should be an inspiration to any new club. The North has kept the game alive and the addition of new, vigorous blood would create more interest for the loyal 'fans' who have supported the great game for which the rest of the country, including the press and the B.B.C. have so little time.'

Very few followers possess the data of R.L. football as Mr J W Holmes of Sandal. He offers sound suggestions, and as one who was responsible for bringing J A Ledgard of Dewsbury, into R.L. football, he believes it would be unwise to be bitten in a second London venture. If space permitted I would have like to have published the whole of Mr Holmes' letter, which gives interesting accounts of early R.L. struggles.

Another non-League centre at Harrogate has its followers, one of whom is Mr A Chippendale of Crab Lane. He believes that if the game was properly organised it would succeed in London, but 'An outstanding organiser must be appointed'. He concludes: 'The best way, however, would be to work South gradually with new clubs.'

My last space goes to Barrow, where Mr W H Shaw of Rakesmoor Lane, is definitely against London. He considers concentration should be made on Blackpool. In addition Mr Shaw believes too many scrummages are killing the game, and that we shall never get converts until this is remedied.

These are just a small selection from readers who are so keen on the game that they are prepared to put forward their views. In neither article have I given my personal views on the subject but left it to the people who go through the turnstiles and by buying members' cards keep this great game of Rugby League going.

Now or Never!
Drop World Expansion for the Job at Home
Rugby League Review - March 1948

Drop world expansion for the job at home... is the sound advice of Sunday Pictorial *columnist, Eddie Waring*

Our contributor wrote this article before reading the Editorial Viewpoint in last month's Rugby League Review. *It now serves to dot the i's and cross the t's of what we wrote. Read in conjunction with the news of the projected R.L. club at Whitehaven contained on another page, home development of the game is clearly the first duty of the Rugby Football League.*

Is the development of Rugby League football in England being shelved for world development? I have been asked this question on numerous occasions of late, which indicates the home supporter has such doubts in his mind. To paint a true picture of the position, let me give you facts of the recent International Board conference which has probably been the cause of these doubts.

I was present at Bordeaux when the International Board of Rugby League football was formed. Previously representatives of England, France and New Zealand had met to discuss International matters, but this was the first time an official title was adopted.

Mr Paul Barriere (France) was the chairman of the meeting. Mr Walter Crockford and Mr Tom Brown (England), Mr Jack Redwood (New Zealand), and M Peilot (France) were other representatives. The secretary of the Rugby Football League was appointed to the position of secretary to the Board. Others present, in the capacity of interpreters, were M Maurice Blein (the first secretary of the French Rugby League, who is now a journalist and broadcaster); M G Fraiche, a prominent sportsman in Bordeaux, and also representative of *Rugby League Review*); and Mr George Hargreaves, Paris representative of Messrs. Thos. Cook and Son. Ltd. (travel agents).

Only two English Press representatives were present: Mr Harry Sunderland, who has done a great deal for French Rugby League in the early days, and myself.

HOW IT WILL WORK

The first day was given over to the constitution of the Board and main principles of working. It was decided to meet annually, and to allow two representatives to be present from each country.

It will be observed that Australia was not represented at the Bordeaux meeting. Here was the first mistake, for Australia should have been invited, and could have sent representatives by air. It was decided that a country unable to be present could appoint delegates to represent them, but that they must be members of an official organisation of the Rugby League, and approved by the country in question. For instance, the New Zealanders are unlikely to be present at the conference early next year. They can, however, appoint any member of the Rugby League Council, but they cannot appoint say Mr John Wilson or any person who is not on an official body. This is an unwise arrangement for there are certain men who know the angles of Rugby League in New Zealand far better than a man who has never been abroad. Probably the idea is to keep certain men out who would be strong advocates for different policies, but I think the door is being closed too tight in this respect.

As previously stated, the Board will meet annually, and the home country holding the conference will take the chair.

A BAN AND A CONCESSION
More detailed work was considered on the second day of the conference, which immediately made news. The possibility of Rugby League football in Canada, Spain and Italy was reported, and it was decided to hold a World Cup Competition in 1951 when New Zealand will be visiting England and France. The Australian team will travel by air, and the tournament will take place either in England or France. Since this meeting, information has been received that California is another likely spot for the game, so there is certainly world development afoot.

The Board discussed many other points and decisions of importance were made. The French chairman reported that the representative of a Yorkshire club had been poaching French players, which was contrary to the gentleman's agreement made by the two countries that no poaching would take place.

To counter any possibility of a French player coming to play in Yorkshire, a ban was immediately put on players of both countries, except men placed on the transfer list. Now any player on the transfer list can be signed by either country.

Rules, management and other matters received attention, and at the end of the two days it was generally agreed that a great amount of good work had been done for the game. A viewpoint which I heartily endorse.

VIA DONCASTER AND MANSFIELD

This brings us back to the first paragraph. Coming from my stay in France I was called upon to visit Mansfield (Notts.) where they are trying to establish Rugby League. The glamour and colour of the French trip faded into the common light of Rugby in the raw.

Travelling from Mansfield to Warrington, I wondered if the same careful attention and expense which had been put into the French conference would be put into development of the game in England. Needless to say the die-hard follower of the game at every lecture I give makes a point of that, and there is no doubt in my mind what view he takes.

Due to the inspiration of a Yorkshireman, Mr W Cameron, and a Welshman, Mr Fred Smart, Rugby League has made a start in Mansfield. Two hundred followers showed keen interest and asked many questions about the game, which proved to me success is possible in this town, which is ideally situated.

To those who advocate London so much, I suggest they move gradually South by concentrating first on Doncaster, then Mansfield, then Leicester, Coventry, and so get a trail of sound clubs. In the light of many failures - Newcastle, London, Ebbw Vale, Pontypridd, and others - can this be done successfully? I believe it can, but the R.L. Council must get a blue printed plan with no holes in it.

PLAN FOR SUCCESS

A development committee should be appointed to work with the local enthusiasts. Take team down to let the people see the beset in the game. Send members down to give lectures on Rugby League; get the local newspapers to give it space; and generally adopt an attacking policy which will ensure success. Workington Town is an example of what can be done in a short time. Doncaster and Mansfield are on the way, but they must not fail for the sake of experienced advice and, if necessary, money.

At Warrington an amazingly enthusiastic audience of 1,200 persons, with hundreds turned away, saw my Rugby League show. At York - and remember, they are at the bottom of the League table - the supporters are still keen for Rugby, if only they had something to cheer about. I know this to be true, for another packed house attended my lecture.

This all indicates that now or never is the time for expansion of Rugby League football in this country. Italy, Spain and Canada can be developed by other countries - England can only be developed by England. Must we remain in the North all the time and never become 'National', or can we get in on this wave of sport enthusiasm?

It is now or never and it is up to the men at the helm. Either they take Rugby League into a bigger circle or it remains static. I know what the average supporter thinks. He is concerned with the development of the game at home and a more direct policy of progress by his leaders.

'Land of my Fathers' Disappoints
Swansea Game is Rugby League Turning Point

Rugby League Review - April 1948

Arrangements have now been made with our distinguished contributor to write a regular monthly article in these columns. Former Secretary - Manager of Dewsbury and Leeds Rugby Football League Clubs; R.L. columnist of the Sunday Pictorial; *author, lecturer and radio commentator - Eddie Waring knows the game and men as no other writer does. Always scrupulously fair in what he writes, his forth-right pronouncements have earned him a high reputation as a sports writer.*

Rugby League football received its hardest blow in Wales on March 20th, 1948. Not because the Welsh team lost to France and thereby also lost all hope of the International Championship, but because the match, the gate, and the whole atmosphere was a dismal failure.

Many lessons were learned from this visit to Swansea and the Rugby League powers that be are going to be faced with making some important decisions in the very near future regarding our game in Wales.

The first lesson was the failure of the interchange of

referees idea. M Pascal, of Toulouse, was in charge of the match, and gave a very poor showing indeed. All the good impressions created by M Rene Guidicelli at Huddersfield, last October, were wiped out.

M Pascal showed little knowledge of the requirements of the 'play the ball' rule, and he gave Wales one penalty to France eighteen. It was shades of the country games in Australia to me. However, it was not just the penalties that drew the boos of the Welshmen - it was the first time I had heard a Welsh crowd so disturbed with the decisions of a referee - but M Pascal's whistling repeatedly pulled up movements which could have been kept going.

As a result of this exhibition it is obvious that the R.L. Council must cut out interchanging of referees. The risk is too great and this game did more harm to R.L. football in Wales than any thing else has done for a long time. Everyone I spoke to in Swansea after the match told me that Rugby League in Swansea was finished after what they had seen. And they really believed it!

IS IT WORTH THE COST?
But, and a very big but, M Pascal could not be blamed for the poor crowd that watched the match. No official 'gate' figures have been given. It was just too bad to give. I will guess 6,500 and not be far off the mark.

What I do know is that the expenses, with two matches to reckon in, will show that the League has lost a nice packet over this match.

This is the third failure in Swansea this season. What is to be done about it? Can the Rugby League afford to keep losing money as they have done? Would not this money be better spent on some other possible club at Doncaster, Mansfield or Whitehaven, or is it felt that the propaganda work in South Wales is worth all it costs?

It is obvious that a stated policy must be forthcoming of what is expected and hoped for in Swansea. Are matches to be taken there just to keep the game known in South Wales or is there a hope that one day a League will be formed? It is hard to ascertain just what is in the mind of officialdom over the South Wales plan.

What is certain is that we are at rock bottom now with R.L. in this area. We can only rise or fail together; we cannot go any lower. Following the big 'gates immediately after the war, this decline is disheartening.

POOR ADVANCE PUBLICITY

I talked with many people in Swansea and I am satisfied that they want R.L. down there. They complained of the lack of publicity and told me that they cannot read enough about the game. They blame both the press and R.L. publicity for not telling them more about the game. The press are tied and I don't think R.L. publicity can do a great deal more. I know one way of doing it, but as I fancy this would not be acceptable to some folk I will leave it alone.

Preparations for these Welsh games are bad. things are done in a haphazard way. Players are not assembled, they just roll up as if it were a club game, and the whole atmosphere is not of International standard but of a club game and a very ordinary one at that.

Spectators criticised the lack of posters, etc., but as I did not get into the valleys to see just what had been done, it would be unfair to make any comment. In any case, it would be a difficult job to placard all South Wales satisfactorily. There are other means of publicity far more effective.

A GOOD WALES COMMITTEE

I talked to Rugby League officials present at the game and they were really disturbed. They realised - if they didn't they were quickly told- that the game is dying rapidly. They now realise that they will have to do something if they mean to keep the game alive.

What must be done? Appoint an advisory committee and label it 'South Wales'. But don't appoint men who have never been there and do not know the temperament and requirements of these Welsh folk. This committee must plan its attack carefully; it must get the aid of every individual who can assist them; and it (the committee) must blue print the plan so perfectly that there will be no risk of failure. Otherwise forget it all and wipe Wales off as a bad debt and another failure.

The game has many friends in South Wales - men of standing who can help. One question should be asked. Do we want Rugby League football in South Wales? If the answer is 'Yes', then start properly and see that it is a success.

A Roar or a Whisper? Why Our Game is at the End of the News Queue

Rugby League Review - August 1948

It is only a matter of days to the big kick-off of the new football season. As always, Mr Waring is anxious to secure for our code the maximum amount of publicity, and in this article he urges both clubs and officials to co-operate with the Press and the B.B.C. to achieve this very desirable object.

The old, old story of Rugby League publicity - or the lack of it - again asserted itself recently when I visited Cockermouth (Cumberland) with the B.B.C. 'Sports Expert Team' to answer questions of the Cockermouth members of the Workington Town Supporters' Club.

The question of publicity, both with National newspapers and the British Broadcasting Corporation, arose when Alan Clarke, the genial sports chief of the B.B.C. was asked why more space was not given on the air to Rugby League matters. The answers and discussion which followed was as interesting as it was enlightening.

I have in a previous article referred to this sort of thing, but at Cockermouth new facts and figures were given which add more light and at the same time remind those responsible of their obligations at the commencement of a new season.

In the Sports Team at Cockermouth I was the only member representing Rugby League. It was very soon obvious to Mr Clarke and the Soccer advocates, Henry Rose and Kenneth Wolstenholme, that they were in a Rugby stronghold. The audience included George Plummer, a member of the Press and Publicity Committee of the Rugby Football League, but he failed to take the chance offered to him of boosting the game.

ONE PER CENT

When Mr Clarke was asked why more space was not given on the air to Rugby League, he answered that space was allotted in accordance to the listening following. He then gave the remarkable fact that only one per cent of listeners followed Rugby League commentaries. To R.L. folk this seems a surprisingly low figure, and many in the audience afterwards queried it. However, this was the figure given.

It was then Mr Wolstenholme's turn to surprise the audience. He stated the Swinton club had asked their members in the club programme to write the B.B.C. asking for more space, and that they had received only one letter out of a 'gate' of around 15,000. I can believe the one letter, but rather think the attendance figure too high.

Mr Clarke assured the meeting that Rugby League was getting a better showing than it ever had done in the past, and he hoped to continue this allocation of sport space. A statement which was warmly approved by the enthusiastic Cumberland folk.

One prominent member of the party said Rugby League got far more space than the game warranted, due to the persistent efforts of people like Harry Sunderland and Eddie

Waring, who were constantly fighting its battles. Fortunately the game has got good backers in both Phillip Robinson, Director of Outside Broadcasts, and Alan Clarke, and more rather than less programme space will be given to the Rugby League game.

The same thing applies to National newspaper space. Men like Tom Longworth, Alfred Drewry, Jimmy Breen, Harry Sunderland, Tom Reynolds, Ernest Cawthorne, J. Bapty, A Haddock, W.E.Riley and G. M. Thompson, are fighting daily to put the game in their columns. With limited newsprint this is a hard job and it is only for love of the game by these people that as much space is devoted to Rugby League.

But are the club, officials, and followers doing their part? I say No!

LET THEM KNOW WHAT IS WANTED

I have already written of the Workington and Swinton experiences. There are countless others.

The pressmen I have mentioned together with the Editor of the game's own paper (Stanley Chadwick) do their utmost to keep Rugby League football in the news, but I repeat, do others?

What can be done, you ask. Sports Editors of newspapers take a great deal of notice of the letters their writers get. Because these are not printed today the tendency to write in complaints, views, and news, has fallen off. That is one way readers can help. It is no use telling the writers they should put more football news in their papers for they don't allocate the space. The same, of course, applies to the B.B.C.

What can club officials do? Give news out and get the game talked about. I can assure them they will get support from the writers of our game.

A SUGGESTION

Last year the Press and Publicity Committee looked like being a most progressive body. Why they faded out I do not know, but they did. New members have been put on this committee this season. I do hope they realise their importance to the game. Incidentally, I sometimes wonder whether individual qualifications are considered when appointing sub-committees. Probably the most successful Press and Publicity Committee would co-opt a journalist to serve with its members. The opportunity is there and the Publicity members must be Publicity-minded.

All this leads back to the point from which I commenced my article. Rugby League football is still not a National game and the only people who love it are Rugby League folk themselves. Small mindedness, petty jealousies, false pride and envy, has retarded the progress of the game long enough. Despite everything the game has survived and prospered simply because it is such a good game. Every single person who likes the code can do it some good and assist in its future, which I still believe could be a National one. Do we continue to crawl or can we really stride out this season? I wonder.

The Trials of a Television Commentator

John Player Rugby League Yearbook 1973-74
Edited by Jack Winstanley (Queen Anne Press),

One especially appreciated Christmas gift I received last year was Peter Black's most interesting book about the BBC, *The Biggest Aspidistra In The World*. I say especially appreciated because Peter, the eminent TV critic of the *Daily Mail*, was, along with Bernard Hollowood of *Punch*, one of the early writers to say kind things about Rugby League on television, and both have been advocates of the game ever since.

One quote from this book I find particularly relevant. 'It is always easier to abuse than to praise ... Through all its 50 years, broadcasting has been a medium whose faults got the attention. Nor lagged the public critics behind the individual ones.' He wasn't referring to Rugby League in particular; rather to folks in all walks of life.

No subject has caused so many words to be written, comments to be made, and arguments to be created as television has done, and especially so in the world of Rugby League. For example, would those immediate post-war gates totalling 180,000 have been maintained in Rugby League if television had never been invented? Of course not!

In the immediate post-war period everything was on ration, so sport was the only free outlet. Now there are 17 million cars in England, every electrical appliance imaginable, holiday abroad, new houses, changing fashions in clothes, people eating out, and so many other things that have attired the pattern of life.

A serious, sensible Rugby League fanatic said to me recently: 'You know, we're lucky to have a place in the sun. We could easily have been a small, unknown game nationally.' And he is right. But, as Peter Black says, it is easier to abuse than to praise.

So I'll do a bit of praising. Without television of Rugby League football on a national network, I don't believe we would now have 30 professional clubs playing the game. We certainly wouldn't have the strong core of the Southern Amateur Rugby League. There would be no university clubs playing the game and no Methodist Sevens. And before anyone cries 'so what,' let me tell you that in the Methodist Sevens, 150 teams take part and games are followed by a rally of 12,000 people in the Royal Albert Hall.

I could take up a lot of space extolling the virtues of TV, and no one knows better than I do what the critics have to say. I do, however, know that my mail shows a big national audience appreciative of Rugby League and contains far more praise than abuse.

When and how did TV and Rugby League get together? The first Cup final coverage was in 1948 but was shown to southern viewers around the London area only. The 1950 Cup final between Warrington and Widnes was transmitted from the Midlands, but with the aid of freak reception it was seen by some people in South West Lancashire. Warrington fans thought it was great; Widnes fans didn't like either the match or the commentator who, by the way, wasn't me - I was on my way to Australia. Warrington won 19-0.

The first game televised from Holme Moss, the northern TV station high on the Pennine Hills above Holmfirth, was on Saturday, November 10, 1951. The match was the second Test between Great Britain and New Zealand at Swinton which Great Britain won 20-19. Four people - Harry Sunderland, Alan Clarke, Alan Dixon, and myself - took part in the live broadcast. But it was viewed by only thousands as compared with the present-day millions. The producer was Derek Burrell Davis, now head of BBC North Region.

For a period there was no regular schedule of televised matches. Some Cup finals were covered; others were missed out. One final was scheduled to be televised at a fee of £500 - much less than fees paid today. It was, if I remember rightly, cancelled because one of the Rugby League sub-committees voted against the committee which had agreed to the coverage.

When Rugby League grounds were built, no one had any thoughts of television. And when some clubs installed floodlights, they also forgot to think about the possibilities of television, with the result that some grounds produce immense problems for TV coverage.

I think I know by now most of the adverse comments directed at producers, commentators, the lighting man, sound engineer, and scaffold erector. 'Why can't we have it like they do it at Twickenham?' is one of the popular cries. The answer is so simple: none of our grounds was built like Twickenham. Rugby League clubs, with a few exceptions, never anticipated the demands that would be made on their grounds.

Number one problem is the sun, for the producer's biggest worry is having to shoot into it. Just the thought of this produces nightmares, even though I've told many a producer that we rarely get sun on Rugby League grounds. There is another problem. On many grounds, the cameras must operate from the main stand - and you know what that means. Officials, members, and VIPs have their view obscured. Some clubs have not helped themselves by installing floodlights in front of the stands; after all, a camera cannot hook its eye round a big stanchion. That is yet another problem - and you can see how they mount up.

Leeds, Wigan, Castleford, Warrington, and Widnes now have permanent positions for TV cameras and crews. Leeds also have their own power sub-station, which is of great advantage to the TV engineers, particularly if a last-minute switch is required. Another advantage at Headingley is the underground heating of the pitch. You can usually rely on Leeds' home games being played.

Clubs are becoming more TV-minded, despite the critics who would like to do a King Canute act. There are many other problems that require careful sorting-out. In last season's Yorkshire Cup final between Dewsbury and Leeds, the Dewsbury colours of red, amber, and black looked quite different to the blue and gold strip of Leeds. To spectators at the match and viewers watching colour TV, that is. The four millions viewers watching black and white couldn't tell the difference. One official at the game was asked if he could arrange a change of strip. But his answer, which I'm sure he believed, was 'I can easily tell the difference.'

I had to try to save the match for the black and white viewers by talking about light stockings, numbers on shorts, and constant identification of teams and individual players. This prompted one irate viewer to write: 'Why keep telling me which team is which when I've known them both since before you were born?'

Many followers of sport, both men and women, would like to be a commentator of some sort, and a surprising number of people write to me asking how they should go about being a a commentator. One attribute is necessary as far as Rugby League and the North is concerned - you must have a sense of humour of some sort. On the 1950 tour of Australia and New Zealand I became a choirmaster of the British touring party. We had two tremendous pianists in Dickie Williams and Frank Osmond, some fine singers like Fred Higgins and Martin Ryan, and regular choir practice attenders such as Ken Gee. Tough, solid, likable Ken, of Wigan fame, who once described another forward as looking 'like a knocked-up thumb', is said to have created the first TV story while playing for Wigan. He asked a team-mate what time it was. The team-mate replied: 'I don't know - but why do you want to know?' Answered Ken: 'I must belt this bloke before telly come on at four o'clock.'

Another tough, likable prop, Jim Drake of Hull, always told me before a match to remind the cameraman which was his best side - cauliflower ear and all. Talking of Hull: as a youngster, I had been reared on the wild and weird stories of Hull's notorious Threepenny Stand. In one of the first games to be televised from the Boulevard, I was positioned slap-bang in the middle of the Threepenny Stand. I wasn't sure what to expect, but amidst all the colourful adjectives there were some amusing incidents and comments that made me smile. The fan, for instance, who strongly criticised referee Eric Clay for giving penalties and finished with the usual gag: 'Give 'em another ref!' Eric Clay promptly did so and the fan called out: 'Nay, I didn't think you'd take notice of a silly so and so like me.'

In an effort to find a 'Twickers' position for cameras, TV producers go higher and higher and over the top of stands. It's like climbing the steep steps to heaven (to quote the hymn 'midst toil, peril and pain ...'). There are certainly some risky ascents to be made. I've known colleagues refuse to climb up to some positions, and only two years ago a well-known player and a well-known manager refused to climb the Leeds ladder. This has been altered a little now, particularly since I suggested that the club chairman should try it for himself.

With the advent of colour in television, more problems have been created for outside broadcasts. The popular BBC2 Floodlit series is an expensive project for which special scaffolding and special lighting have to be mounted. No club in the Rugby League has lights strong enough to take the amount of power required for colour cameras. That is why some Saturday Rugby League games necessitated a 2.15 p.m. kick-off. This factor brought criticism and comment, but it affected both Rugby Union and Rugby League coverage and was due solely to the light problem. One point struck me about all the fuss over a 2.15 p.m. kick-off. Before the advent of floodlights, games had to start at 2.15 during one part of the season - and that was in the day when most people worked on Saturday mornings. Now, many football followers have Saturday mornings off, and most of them have cars to make travelling time much shorter.

Among the problem grounds for TV coverage is Bradford's Odsal Stadium. Various producers have tried every conceivable camera position but they've all had to return to the low position in front of the main stand. In the wonderful Championship final of 1959 when St Helens beat Hunslet at Odsal Stadium, I had one of my most disappointing moments. Most Rugby League fans will remember the wonderful Tom Van Vollenhoven try when he ran down the main stand side. We were filming this match from a position near the back of the main stand and we covered the whole of Van Vollenhoven's run and the efforts of the Hunslet defenders to stop him going behind the posts. As the Hunslet cover came across, the Saints winger put the ball down for the try - but one of the main stand iron supports was smack in the way. All the camera's eye could see was a pillar of metal.

Fortunately, Vollenhoven's magnificent run itself had tremendous impact, but this was one moment of Rugby League history which was not recorded because of the problems of camera positioning. Slowly but surely, however, these and other such problems will be surmounted as Rugby League, which I still say is the best game in the world, marches on towards its centenary in 1995.

AFTERWORD

by Tony Waring
Eddie's son

When I was asked to write this afterword I had a look at my copy of *The Great Ones*, which my father had given me in November 1969. It made me smile. On the flyleaf he had written: 'To Tony, the best lad in the Northern Union'. It was typical of the man. He was always quick to praise and he frequently drew upon his treasure trove of expressions to illustrate his point. Best was a word that he liked too.

He told me that his school motto *Semper optimus*, always the best, was a good principle to strive for and he certainly did. One of the pictures in *The Great Ones* shows my father with the 1958 Great Britain touring side at Surfers Paradise in Australia. I came across the original photograph recently and on the back it was signed by all the players. There were some great names amongst them, Vince Karalius, Dick Huddart, Eric Ashton, Alex Murphy, Tommy Harris and the captain, Alan Prescott, who had written: 'To the best reporter in the business, and also a very great friend'.

I count myself extremely fortunate to have had Eddie

313

Waring as my father. He was great company, good fun and generous to a fault. He was well respected by players and officials alike, as I saw when he took me to rugby league matches across the north of England. Grounds with names like Knowsley Road, Wilderspool, Naughton Park, Headingley and Central Park had been his territory for so long that he never needed a ticket to get in. He would always have a cheery word for the gateman, who he made feel that he was doing an important job. He knew about the importance of good gatemen from his time as manager at Crown Flatt, Dewsbury, where he was responsible for many aspects of the club as well as running the team.

I saw that my father was always good with people and his ability to interact with them whatever their background or position was a skill that he used to great effect. I also witnessed this ability and his versatility at first hand when I accompanied him on the famous *Jeux sans Frontieres*. He got on very well with the foreign television commentators, presenters and producers and, although it was a very different world from rugby league, he took to it like a duck to water. Whenever the international rounds were staged in the UK, he made sure that his foreign colleagues were well looked after. He believed that as they were on his territory they were his responsibility. For instance, on one occasion in Harrogate, the British summer caught them all out and I was despatched by my dad to buy plastic macs to keep them dry!

When visitors from the South came to see him he would often take them up to see the Cow and Calf rocks on Ilkley Moor. When I asked him why, he told me it was because he had had visitors from London who thought that Yorkshire was all coalmines and industry and he was keen to let them see them how beautiful Yorkshire really was.

Education was always important to my father and it was at Eastborough School in Dewsbury that, as well as honing his writing skills, he became a keen sportsman. On the soccer pitch he was a speedy forward who scored many goals. His footballing skills led him to have professional trials with Nottingham Forest and Barnsley but, apparently, my grandfather told him he should get a proper job.

My dad encouraged me to participate in whatever sports were available. Football was the winter game at my junior school but, when I was 12, they decided to start to play rugby union. In a move that was ahead of its time, but which has since become the norm, they called in a rugby league expert to help develop the players' skills. In this case it was my father. I have a lasting memory of him on the touchline, helping to turn footballers into rugby players. His efforts were rewarded when we won the only match we played that season against an experienced rugby school. We did not tell them who had been our coach.

It was difficult for my father to come and see me play very often because he was working on Saturdays, but I recall one occasion when he was able to watch me play for my senior school. We were playing away near Blackpool and as we were getting changed before the match a buzz went round the home dressing room. 'Eddie Waring's here. Who has he come to watch? It must be Smithy [their star centre]!' Our side managed to resist telling them who he had really come to see until after the game.

I expect that the change in the relationship between rugby league and rugby union would have made my father smile. Playing the Challenge Cup Final at the home of English rugby union at Twickenham and having a former league star, Jason Robinson, scoring the try that helped England to win the rugby union World Cup would have been totally impossible under the old guard. It was that attitude which led to a retired rugby league player who was playing union for a side in the Channel Islands, at a match we watched on holiday, saying to my father: 'Please don't tell them where you last saw me playing or I'll be banned, and I enjoy playing here'.

One of my dad's policies was always to look forward. He was a great respecter of the past and the work of pioneers in building the game of rugby league, as can be seen in his writing. But on a personal level he rarely talked about what he had done, preferring to concentrate on what he was going to do next. It was only when I came across a silver salver, presented to my father when he left Dewsbury RLFC, on which it was written that 'the club had won every possible Rugby League honour' during his time in charge that I discovered he had been a coach and manager.

It was this attitude of 'looking forward' that had taken young Eddie into rugby league management. At the time he joined Dewsbury he was the youngest manager in the game, and his people skills helped him to take his team to the top. He had plenty of drive, a strong personality and when, during the war, he realised that rugby league players from other clubs were available, he was quick to persuade them to come and play for him.

His realisation that journalism and broadcasting could bring more exciting opportunities led to his decision to leave rugby league management and travel to Australia and New Zealand. Having had a grounding in radio, he realised that television was set to be the most powerful communications medium on the planet and was determined to be involved. He had to be persistent as he was not in the traditional BBC mould, but that did not worry him and once he had become the BBC's rugby league man he made himself indispensable. His love for the business of television, and pleasure in the company of television people continued until his retirement.

One of the pleasures that journalism and broadcasting allowed my father to enjoy was travelling. The details in his book *From England to Australia* give a good idea of his delight at being able to see new places and experience new things. That continued throughout his tours to Australia and New Zealand and subsequently to the many places he visited across Europe during the *Jeux sans Frontieres* years.

But despite this love of travelling he always enjoyed coming home to Yorkshire. He used to say that the 'county of broad acres' was where they played the best game in the world and that it was the best place to live in the world.

There's that word best again. As well as being the creator of the 'early bath' and the 'up and under', Eddie Waring was the best dad a lad could wish for.

Past deeds. Present voices.

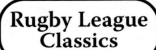